DICTIONARY OF HISTORY

DICTIONARY OF HISTORY

Edited by

Satish Ganjoo
Centre of Central Asian Studies
University of Kashmir
SRINAGAR

ANMOL PUBLICATIONS PVT. LTD.
NEW DELHI - 110 002 (INDIA)

ANMOL PUBLICATIONS PVT. LTD.
H.O.: 4374/4B, Ansari Road, Daryaganj,
New Delhi-110 002 (India)
Ph.: 23278000, 23261597
B.O.: No. 1015, Ist Main Road, BSK IIIrd Stage
IIIrd Phase, IIIrd Block,
Bangalore - 560 085 (India)
Visit us at: www.anmolpublications.com

Dictionary of History

First Edition, 1990
Reprint, 1991, 1992
Second Revised Edition, 1994
Reprint, 1995, 1996, 1997, 2005
Reprint, 2008

PRINTED IN INDIA

…ted at Mehra Offset Press, Delhi.

Preface

This revised edition of this dictionary has been carefully compiled and edited to provide students of History at all levels with a handy and reliable source for the entries taken from pre-history to the present day. This dictionary has been indispensable for anyone who enjoys finding out about those famous characters and events which have contributed to the unfolding of world history.

Every effort has been carefully made to write the entries in a clear and lucid style to provide both straight forward definitions and invaluable background information.

The dictionary will be of immense value to Undergraduate, Postgraduate, history students. This will be also useful to those who have opted history for competitive examinations.

When a dictionary of this kind, is being compiled, it becomes essential to draw upon the work of many authorities and seek the advice of colleagues to whom the editor is deeply indebted.

—Dr. Satish Ganjoo

Acknowledgements

I gratefully acknowledge the encouragement and cooperation received from Dr. Z.L. Jalla, Prof. S. Maqbul Ahmad, Dr. B.K. Deambi, Prof. A.M. Mattoo, Dr. K.N. Pandita, Sh. J.L. Bhan, Sh. Gulshan Majid, Dr. G.M. Mir and Prof. Manzoor Shah. My thanks also go to my parents and younger brothers for their constant help.

Finally, for my wife Kaushilya, no words are enough. She collected and organised a large part of the material for this project, gave unflagging moral support and suffered patiently through episodes of anger—all while managing a wildly fluctuating household of transient dependents.

—Dr. Satish Ganjoo

A

Abdul Ghaffar Khan. He is also called Frontier Gandhi. He had close relations with Gandhiji, Nehru, Maulana Azad and other Indian nationalist leaders; actively participated in the Indian freedom struggle; was a member of the Congress Working Committee and took a leading part in all the Congress movements between 1920 and 1947; spent about fourteen years in jail; was against the partition policy of the Muslim League; after the partition of India he migrated to Pakistan and started agitation for the establishment of Pakhtoonistan and was jailed a number of times; believed in the cult of *Charkha* and favoured the development of village industry; founded an organisation as the *Khudai Khidmatgars* (Servants of God) for carrying on his work. On November 15, 1969, Khan was presented the Nehru Award for International Understanding for 1967. Also known as Badshah Khan; he is one of those legendary figures of the freedom struggle who have not fallen prey to the comforts and glamour of governmental offices, and his struggle against the injustice to humanity and the upliftment of the neglected areas has been continuing. For sometime Badshah Khan has been staying in Afghanistan as a self-exiled person. He sacrificed his all for the sake of what he believed to be right.

Abacus. Apparatus of very ancient origin used by the Egyptians, Chinese, Gks. and Roms. for teaching children the elements of arithmetic and for visual calculation. It consists of a frame containing a number of parallel wires on which are strung rows of beads.

Abbas. Uncle of Mohammed and ancestor of the Abbasids; *d.* 652. His descendant Abul-Abbas was made caliph 750, a position retained by the Abbasids in Baghdad and then Cairo until the 16th cent. when the Ottoman sultans took the title themselves.

Abbas I. (Abbas the Great), 1557-1629, Shah of persia (1587-1628), of the Safavid dynasty. He broke the power of the tribal chiefs, ended the threat of the Uzbeks, and extended his domain at the expense of the Turks and Portuguese.

Abbasid or Abbaside. Arabic family descended from Abbas, *d.* 653, the uncle of Muhammad. They rose to power by massacring the ruling Umayyad family and held the Caliphate from 749 to 1258. Prominent Abbasid caliphs include al-Mansur and Harun ar-Rashid, under whom the caliphate reached its greatest power and splendor. The long Abbasid decline culminated in their overthrow by the Seljuk Turks in the 13th cent.

Abd ar-Rahman. Muslim rulers of Spain. Abd ar-Rahman, *d.* 732, governor of Spain (721-32), fought the Franks and was defeated by Charles Martel. Abd ar-Rahman 1, *d.* 788, first Umayyad emir of Cordoba (756-88), escaped after his family's massacre by the Abbasid and fled to Spain. There he defeated (756) the emir of Cordoba and established himself firmly in power. Abd ar Rahman III (891-961), Umayyad emir in first caliph (929-61) of Cordoba, regained lands lost by his predecessors, maintained a powerful military force, and made Cordoba one of the greatest cities in the West.

Abdication Crisis. Constitutional crisis that arose in 1936 when Edward VIII wished to marry Wallis Simpson, an American divorces, and chose to renounce the throne (abdicate) in favour of his brother, George VI. The British and Dominion Governments considered his intention of marrging the lady incompatible with his position as monarch and head of the Church of England.

Abdullah. 1882-1951, Emir of Transjordan (1921-46) and king of Jordan (1946-51). In the first Arab-Israeli. War he commanded the Arab Legion and annexed those portions of Palestine not assigned to Israel.

Abdullah, Sheikh Mohammed. He was the Chief Minister of Jammu and Kashmir State. He was India's leading statesman and freedom fighter. He was born in 1905 at Saura, a suburb of Srinagar. He was elected President of Muslim Conference founded in 1932; it was converted into National Conference in 1939; in May 1946 sentenced to 9 years imprisonment; elected President of All India State People's Conference in 1946; appointed Prime Minister of State on

March 5, 1948; dismissed and arrested on August 9, 1953 for alleged secret and prejudicial contacts with foreign powers with the object of attaining independence for Kashmir; released on January 10, 1958; re-arrested on April 29, released after about 6 years; to be arrested again in 1965 after his foreign tour; released in 1968; externed from State in 1971; elected Chief Minister after return to State; was a greater supported of Hindu-Muslim unity; a statesman and administrator of high order.

Abraham or Abram (c. 2300 B.C) (C.T.). Founder of the Jewish nation. With his father, his wife Sarah and his nephew Lot, he moved to Canaan. Plains of Abraham. Heights outside Quebec where the British under Wolfe, beat the France under Montcalm (1759).

Accession. Refers to the act by which one nation becomes party to an agreement already in force between other powers.

Accession, Treaty of. Treaty signed in Brussels in 1972 by the 6 members of the EEC, plus Denmark, the Irish Republic, Norway and the U.K. The Treaty concerned the accession of these 4 new members to the EEC and the European Atomic Energy Community. The countries were obliged to hold referendums, as a result of which Norway refused to join.

Accord. A formal act of agreement; a treaty.

Accra. Capital of Ghana, having road and rail communications with the interior. It has an internat. airport.

Achilles. In Greek mythology, foremost hero of the Trojan War; son of Peleus and Thetis. Thetis attempted to make him immortal by bathing him in the river Styx, but the heel she held remained vulnerable. Knowing Achilles was fated to die at Troy, Thetis disguised him as a girl and hid him at Skyros. He was found by Odysseus, who persuaded him to go to war. At Troy he quarreled with Agamemnon and sulked in his tent until his friend Patroclus was killed by Hector. Filled with grief and rage, Achilles slew Hector and dragged his body to the Greek camp. He was later killed by Paris, who wounded his heel.

Aden. The capital of the People's Democratic Republic of Yemen. It was a British possession (1839-1967), but with a decline in importance after WWII became (1963) part of the South Arabian Federation of

Arab Emirates. It was overrun by the National Liberation Front (NLF) in 1967. The NLF was the victor in a civil war with the Front for the Liberation of South Yemen (FLOSY), and took over the counter coincidentally with the departure of the British from Aden.

Adenauer, Konrad (1876-1967). German statesman, first Chancellor of the Federal German Republic (1949-63), Foreign Minister (1951-55), and founder (1945) and leader of the CDU party (see Christian Democrats). He dominated West German politics and was responsible for the integration of his country into strong Atlantic and European alliances, as a partner and not a former enemy. He was also responsible for reconciliation with France, and for recognition of Nazi crimes against the jews.

Aeolian. *n.* A member of a group of Greek peoples of Thessaly and Boeotia that colonized Lesbos and the adjacent coast of Asia Minor.

Afghanistan. Republic of Asia, bounded by Iran, the U.S.S.R., and Pakistan. It is a mountainous, Country, esp., in the N.E. where peaks of the Hindu Kush rise to over 24,000 ft. Two important Mt. passes, the Khyber and the Bolan, provide routes into Pakistan. The chief rivers are the Helmand, Kabul, Amu Darya and Hari Rud. The climate is dry, with great ranges of temp. In the valleys where the soil is fertile, wheat, barley, rice, millet and fruit are grown. Sheep and bred, and wool and skins are exported. Kabul is the cap. During 19th and early 20th cents. Brit. influence over the country was strong. In 1921, Afghanistan's independence was recognised, and in 1973 a republic was declared. In 1979, the U.S.S.R. invaded the country, beginning prolonged warfare with Muslim rebel forces.

African National Congress (ANC). It was founded (1912) in South Africa to unify African opinion and to draw white attention to the problems of blacks by demonstrations, deputations and overseas delegations. The leaders were mainly Christian, middle-class, and Western-educated, and believed constitutional advance could be made by argument and passive resistance rather than violence.

After WWII the movement became more violent is response to the repressive measures adopted by successive governments and in 1960 it was banned. Guerrilla activity associated with the movement has been now common in South Africa.

African Nationalism. A prime force in the political awakening of Africa, and in the rebellion of its peoples against colonial rule. An important element was the development among the native populations of a sense of identity as black Africans rather than as subjects of colonial powers, and this was combined with a determination to achieve independence.

Forty nations in Africa became independent between 1956 and 1975. The adjustment of pre-industrial living conditions to the modern world became a major task—but hindrances incl. tribal factions, political instability and grave socio-economic problems, which led to demands for development aid.

Agadir. Port in SW Morocco which became the centre of an international crisis (1911) with the arrival of the German gunboat *Panther*, ostensibly to protect German nationals and commercial interests, but in fact intended to counteract what Germany thought was French expansionist policy in Morocco in contravention of the Conference of Algeciras. In the end Germany recognized French rights in Morocco in exchange for territory in the Congo, and the *Panther* was withdrawn. The incident alarmed Britain, which feared the establishment of a German base close to Gibralter and vital trade routes, and a strong warning was issued to Germany.

Agrarianism. A social or political movement designed to bring about land reforms or to improve economic states of farmers.

Ahab. (a'hab), d.c. 853 B.C., king of Israel (*c*. 874-*c*. 853 B.C.), son and successor of Omri. One of the greatest kings of the northern kingdom, he was killed in a war against Damascus. The biblical account of Ahab's reign (1 kings 16.28-22.40) is mostly concerned with its religious aspects, especially his marriage to lezebel, a willful woman of Tyre who was attached to foreign cults and behaviour. To the devout she represented evil, and she met her match in Elijah.

Ahasuerus. Name of several kings of Persia mentioned in the O.T., one of whom, the husband of Esther, is usually indefined with Xerxes.

Ahaz (a'haz`), *d.c.* 727 B.C., king of Judah (*c*. 731-727 B.C.). His reign marked the end of the real independence of Judah. In the Bible he is opposed by isaiah for his alliance with Assyria against Israel and Syria, and denounced for having heathen abominations and for using the Temple gold to pay tribute to Assyria. 2 kings 16; 2 Chron. 28; Isa. 7.

Ahimsa. The Hindu and Buddhist doctrine of refraining from harming and living being.

Ahmed, Sir Syed Khan (1817-98). A great Muslim reformer and educationist, founder of Aligarh Muslim University.

Akali Movement. Among Sikh reformist movements most important was the Akali who claim for themselves 'a direct institution' by Guru Govind Singh, the tenth Guru, in present century their great achievement was the passage of Sikh Gurdwara Act in 1925; it enabled Sikhs to take over control of Gurdwaras from the hereditary *Mahants*.

Akbar. 1542-1605, Mogul emperor of India (1556-1605). An outstanding general, Akbar added Afghanistan, Baluchistan, and N India to his domains. This reign was marked by administrative reform, religious toleration, and the flowering of art and literature.

Akhenaten. Egyptian 18th dynasty king who reigned 1656-25 B.C. He set up the worship of Aten as the state religion and built a new cap. on the E. bank of the Nile, 190 m. above Cairo modern Tel-el-Amarna.

Akbar-namah. A ponegyric contemporary history of emperor Akbar. written by Abu'l Fazl; also the title of some other histories of Akbar.

Akkadian. A member of a Semitic people inhabiting central Mesopotamia before 2000 B.C.

Alaric. (*c.* 370-410) King of the Visigoths. Became king in 395. He led his men through Italy to Rome, which he sacked in 410. Alaric II became king in 485. He was defeated by Clovis at Tours in 507.

Ala-ud-din Khilji. He was a great conqueror and administrator. Southern India was conquered for the first time by him. He claim to fame rests on secularisation of administration and various civil, military and economic reforms.

Albania. Republic of SE Europe. Area: 28,748 sq. km. Pop : 2,750,000 (est.). Language: Albanian. Religions: Islam, Eastern Orthodox (prior to 1967), now atheist Cap: Tirana.

Albania became an Islamic independent principality (1912) after more than 4 cents. of Turkish rule. A republic was established (1925) and Ahmed Bey Zogu became President with the anomalous title of King Zog I. The country was economically dependent on Italy, which occupied it in 1939, deposing Zog.

After Italy's defeat in WWII a Communist republican government was established (1946). Albania was a member of the Council for mutual economic assistance and the warsaw pact but was expelled from the former (1961) because it sided with China in the Sinosoviet split and for what the USSR considered to be its deviationist policies. Albania with drew from the Warsaw pact (1968) because it disagreed with the policy of interference in czechoslovakia. It was economically and ideologically linked with China from 1968 to 1978, when the association was terminated by China.

Albigenses. *n. pl.* members of a Catharistics sect of southern France between the 11th and 13th centuries.

Alcibiades. (*c.* 450-404 B.C.). Athenian statesman; educ. by his kinsman Pericles (*q.v.*), *c.* 422 he became leader of the party that favoured war with Sparta. His expedition against Syracuse had just sailed when he was accused of sacrilege. Recalled to Athens for trial, he escaped, but was sentenced to *d.* in his absence. In Sparta, Alcibiades became an implacable enemy of Athens. The Spartans began to distrust him and he fled of Persia. As leader of the Athenian army he won several battles over the Spartans. The failure of a further expedition led to his downfall and once again he was exiled (406). He was murdered order of the Spartan Lysander.

Alberuni. Famous author of *Tarikh-i-Hind*, written in 10th-11th century A.D. giving detailed information about Hindus, their philosophy, customs and manners; original name Abu Rihan Muhammad, born at Khiva in 973; A.D. came to India with Sultan Mahmud (A.D. 997 A.D. 1030) and stayed on in India.

Alexander. (The Great) (356-323 B.C.) King of Macedon. A son of King Philip II and his wife Olympias, he succeeded his murdered father in 336. Alexander decided to attack the huge Persian Empire, marched in 334 into Asia Minor and quickly mastered that country. He then conquered, with comparative ease, Phoenicia and Syria and overcame resistance at Tyre by the use of his fleet. Alexander next attacked. Egypt which submitted without a struggle. Having founded the city of Alexandria, he passed through Syria into Persia and marched up the valley of the Tigris, through the country known as Mesopotamia. He captured Susa. Persepolis, Ecbatana and other wealthy Persian cities and advanced to the Caspian Sea. In 326 he crossed the Indus near Attock and gained a great victory. He returned to Persepolis, then set himself to organise his great empire. In the midst of this work he *d*. His *d*. Prevented the consolidation of his empire, which fell rapidly to pieces.

Alexander. (1888-1934). King of Yugoslavia, son of Peter of Serbia. In 1909 he became Crown Prince and Regent in 1914. He led the Serbian Army in World War I and in 1921 became king of the new state, Yugoslavia. Disorder led him, in 1929, to estab., a royal dictatorship. He was assassinated at Mar seillers.

Al Fatah. The Palestine National Liberation Movement. Fatah (Arabic for 'conquest') was the first Palestinian guerrilla organization set up to liberate Palestine from Israeli occupation. Syria has provided arms, money and training facilities. Its leader is Yasser Arafat. See also Palestine Liberation Organization.

Alfonso XIII. (1886-1941) King of Spain. In face of growing evolutionary feeling, he established a royal dictatorship, but discontent increased, and in 1931 Alfonso went into exile. Sp. became a repub.

Alfred. (*c*. 849-901). King of Eng. called the Great, *b*. Wantage, a son of King Ethelwulf. In 871 Alfred was chosen king. The struggle with the Danes had Intervals of peace which he used to organise the army and create something like a navy. In 878 Alfred was forced to take refuge in Somerset, but he soon collected an army and won a battle at Edington. The resulting Treaty of Wedmore divided the country between him and the Danish leader, Guthrum; Alfred received the S. and W. and was acknowledged by Guthrum as his lord.

Algeria. Republic of NW Africa. Area : 2,381,745 sq km. Population 20,200,000 (1983). Language: Arabic. Religion: Islam. Cap: Algiers.

The country was colonized by the French during the 19tn cent. While settlers enjoyed most of the privileges of citizens of France, the indigenous population had practically none, and it was not until after WWII that promises were made of political and social equality.

These were slow to materialize and provided reason for a rising tide of nationalism among the native population which culminated in a revolution (1954-62) waged by the National Liberation Front (NLF) in the form of guerrilla warfare.

During the independence struggle a factor intervened that ultimately led to the destruction of the Fourth Republic in France (1958). The French officers fighting in Algeria suspected that the French Government would negotiate a settlement with the FLN, and by their insistence on keeping Algeria French they and the settlers brought down the Government. They also went some way to repeating matters with the Fifth Republic when the Secret Army Organization (OAS) under General Salan (1899-1948) on several occasions attempted to assassinate De Gaulle. The OAS ceased to function when its leaders either dispersed or were captured.

Eventually the way was clear for independence, and this was achieved in 1962. The first President was Ben Bella who was deposed in 1965 by Colonel Boumedienne (1925-78), a left-wing socialist whose repressive regime and intransigence towards Algeria's neighbours only ceased with his death. His successor Bendjedid Chadli, restored better relations with neighbouring states and France.

Algonquian, Algonquin, Algonkian, Algonkin. An Amerindian people of the Ottawa river valley.

Alhambra. The palace of the Moorish Kings at Granada, Spain.

Ali. (*d.*661) Fourth caliph of Islam (656-61) and son-in-law of the Prophet Mohammed, whose daughter Fatima he mar. The period of Ali's reign was marked by continuous disharmony and civil war and the great schism between the Sunites and the Shiites. Ali was murdered at Kufa by a band of fanatics. He is regarded by the Shiites as one of the great saints of Islam.

Alliad. Joined in alliance by compact of treaty.

Ally. A sovereign or state associated with another by treaty or league.

Almohads. Berber Muslim dynasty that ruled Morocco and Spain in the 12th and 13th cent. It had its origins in the puritanical sect founded *c.* 1120 by ibn Tumart. By 1174 the Almohads had completely displaced the ruling Almoravids. The Almohads in turn, were defeated in Spain by the Spanish and Portuguese in 1212, and in Morocco by the Merenid dynasty in 1269.

Alsace-Lorraine. The region of NE France. Area : 14,522 sq km. Ceded to Germany by the Treaty of Frankfurt (1871) after the French defeat in the Franco-Prussian War (1970-71), it was restored to France after WWI by the Treaty of Versailles (1919). From 1871 to 1914 it was the major source of embittered Franco-German relations, largely due to the prosperity engendered by rapid industrial expansion, esp. steel manufacture. During WWII it was under German occupation (1940-45).

Alien'. *Adj* belonging or owing allegiance to another country or government; foreign.

Amalekite. A member of an ancient nomadic people living south of Canaan.

Amenhotep III. Egyptian king (Reigned 1656-25 B.C). His chief wife was Tiy, who was ambitious and a woman of strong character. She was the mother of Amenhotep IV (Akhenaten) (*q.v*). The period of Amenhotep III was one of great prosperity. His building operations were enormous, and included the temple of Mut at Karnak, the greater part of the temple at Luxor, the great temple which the Gks. called the 'Memnonium'.

Ambassador. One who represents his country in a foreign land. Ambassadors form the highest rank in the diplomatic service. They are *ordinary* when they reside permanently at a foreign court, or *extraordinary* when they are sent on a special occasion. *Ambassadors extraordinary* given full powers, *e.g.*. of concluding peace, making treaties, etc. are called *plenipotentiaries*.

Ambedkar, Bhimrao Ramji. He was born on April 14, 1891, at Mhow, in the Mahar caste of untouchables. He has gone to USA for higher studies and went next to England to study law where he was called to the bar; on return to India dedicated his life to fighting the cause of Scheduled Castes, Scheduled Tribes and other Backward Classes and worked steadfastly for their progress, amelioration and the achieving of their rightful place among caste Hindus; Encouraged inter-marriage and offered satyagraha for establishing their civic, social and religious rights; became professor in and then principal of the Government Law College, Bombay; entered national and political life in 1930 and desired that separate electorates be established for these groups but not hopeful of success that they would gain social and other types of equality with caste Hindus, became a Buddhist with many of his followers, continued his struggle and was able to secure funds, scholarships for their education and reservation of posts in government services, he himself being appointed member of the Governor-General's executive council. After independence, he was made a member of the Constituent Assembly, Minister for Law (with cabinet rank) in the Nehru Government and Chairman of the Committee for drafting the Indian Constitution and also prepared the Hindu Code Bill; resigned as Law Minister in 1951 and died in 1956; author of many books founder of many (Marathi) journals; etc., and an organization for the and uplift of those socially down-trodden groups. He has been widely recognised as an author, thinker, leader, dynamic force and eminent jurist but most for his breaking new ground as the emancipator of the Sudras.

American Indian. *n.* A member of any of the indigenous peoples of the western hemisphere usu with the exception of the Eskimos constituting one of the divisions of the Mongoloid stock.

Amin, Idi. Ugandan political leader. In 1971, he led a military coup while President Obote was abroad, proclaimed himself head of state, and dissolved parliament. His tyrannical regime led to the extermination of numerous opponents. Most Asians and many British were expelled in 1972 and their business interests confiscated. He was Chairman of the OAU (1975-76). In 1979 President Obote regained power in a military coup supported by Tanzanian forces, and Amin went into exile.

Amir Chand Master-B. 1869 at Delhi. He was son of Hukam Chand Vaishya; school teacher. He took active part in social reform and educational activities, such as widow remarriage, temperance and spread of education. He is prominent worker in the *Swadeshi* Movement. On coming in contact with the famous revolutionary leader, Lala Har Dayal, brought him into the revolutionary movement. He became leader of the Ghadr Party and worked in close collaboration with Ras Behari Bose and directed revolutionary activities in the whole of northern India. He was arrested in February 1914 on the charge of conspiracy to kill Lord Hardinge, the

Viceroy of India, and also accused of complicity in the Lahore Bomb Case. This case is known as the Delhi Conspiracy Case, it started with the throwing of a bomb on Lord Hardinge while he was passing on an elephant through Delhi's Chandni Chowk in a State procession marking the inauguration of Delhi as the capital of India. Sentenced to death on October 5, 1914, along with his three compatriots—Avadh Bihari, Bal Mokand and Basant Kumar Biswas. He died in the gallows on May 8, 1915 in the Delhi Central Jail.

Amir Khusro (1275-1325). Famous Urdu and Hindi poet, associated with the Cout of Balban, famous for *Pahelis*.

Amnesty. The act of pardoning a large group of individuals, especially for offences against the government.

Amphora *n. pl.* **Amphorae, Amphoras.** An ancient Greek or Roman jar with two handles, a large oval body, and a narrow cylindrical neck.

Amritsar. A city of NW Punjab, India, centre of the Sikh religion. In 1919, 379 people were killed and over 1,200 wounded when British troops opened fire on unarmed supporters of Indian self-government. The India nationalist movement was strengthened by the subsequent outrage.

In 1984, Sikh separatist extremists took refuge in the Sikh Golden Temple and were defeated after heavy fighting with government troops. Shortly afterwards, Indira Ghandi was assassinated by 2 of her Sikh bodyguards.

Anarchism. A political doctrine that all forms of authority interfere with individual freedom and that government and the state should be replaced by freely associating communities.

Modern anarchist theories developed in the 19th cent. Anarchists have proposed differing strategies for achieving their ends, varying from violent direct action to passive resistance or civil disobedience. Although Lenin believed the state must ultimately wither away, leaving a voluntary regime without class or government, anarchists have generally opposed all state systems, whether capitalist or Communist.

Anarchist movement were politically significant in Russia, France, Italy and Spain at various times in the late 19th and early 20th cents., and were particularly prominent on the Republican side in the Spanish Civil War. Anarchist ideas were revived by student activists in the 1960s, but have failed to gain widespread support.

Anarchist. One who rebels against any authority, established order or ruling power.

Ancient. Of or relating to a remote period, to a time early in history or to those living in such a period or time.

Andropov, Yuri Vladimirovich. (1914-84) Soviet statesman. Head of the KGB (1967-82), then General Secretary of the Communist Party (1982-84) and president of the USSR (1983-84).

Anglo-French Entente. See Entente Cordiale.

Angary. The right in international law of a belligerent to seize, use, or destroy property of neutrals.

Angle. A member of the Germanic people that invaded England along with the Saxons and Jutes in the 5th century A.D. and merged with them to form the Anglo-Saxon people.

Angola. Republic of SW Africa, formerly the colony of Portuguese West Africa. Area : 1,247,000 sq km. Pop : 7,100,000 (est. 1983). Cap.: Luanda. The country has rich mineral resources.

Civil uprisings in the 1960s were repressed, but the country achieved independence in 1975 following the change of government in Portugal. Civil war followed between the various liberation movements, principally the Marxist-Leninist MPLA and the South-African backed Unita. With Soviet aid and the assistance of Cuban troops the MPLA achieved victory in 1976 though guerrilla warfare continues.

Anglo-Indian. British person who lived long in India.

Anglo-Saxon. A member of the German people that conquered England in the 5th century A.D.

Anjou. One of the provs. of France before the Revolution. It was the district around Angers, its cap. and its chief river was the Maine. The duchy was lost by King John, 1203, and its later counts were members of the royal family of Fr. In 1360 the count was made a duke, and the dukes ruled it until 1584.

Anschluss. A term referring to the political union of Austria and Germany, in effect 1938-85. Hitler's plans for union were checked in 1934 when Mussolini sent troops to the Brenner Pass to safeguard Austria's independence. By 1937 Mussolini was in the Axis camp and Hitler was able to put pressure on Chancellor Schuschnigg to legalize the Austrian Nazi Party. The Party stirred up unrest and in 1938 Hitler demanded that Schuschnigg postpone a planned plebiscite to determine Austria's future. Schuschnigg resigned and the Nazi Seyss Inquart became Chancellor. He invited the Germans to occupy the country and restore order. A plebiscite favoured formal union as the 'Greater Germany'.

Anti-Comintern Pact. An agreement between Germany and Japan (1936) declaring their hostility to international Communism. Italy joined the Pact in 1937; Hungary and Spain in 1939.

Antipope. One elected or claiming to be pope in opposition to the pope canonically chosen.

Antiquity. The ancient times; *esp.* the period before the Middle Ages.

Anti-Semitism. Opposition to the Jewish race. In its modern form the movement became conspicuous in Europe during the 19th cent. and was the cause of many brutal outrages in Russia and Hungary. The Dreyfus case is an illustration of Anti-Semitism in Fr. Under Hitler's rule in Germany the movement culminated in a deliberate policy of race-massacre in the concentration camps and 6,000,000 Jews were put to *d*. See Jews.

Anthony, Frank. Anglo-Indian leader educationist and successful lawyer.

Antonescu, Ion. (1882-1946) Romanian general and dictator, closely associated with the Iron Guard Fascist movement. In 1940, he became leader of a right-wing government and proclaimed himself 'Conductor' allying his country with the Axis powers in WWII. Heavy Romanian losses in the USSR undermined his position and he was executed in 1946.

Antoninus Pius,Titus Aurelius Fulvus. (A.D. 86-161). Rom. Emperor of Gallic family. He was adopted by the Emperor Hadrian and succeeded him in 138. He brought peace to the Empire. The wall built between the Forth and the Clyde bears his name.

Anzac. A solidier from Australia or Newzealand.

Anzus Pact. A tripartite security treaty concluded between Australia, New Zealand and the USA in 1951. It provided for collaboration should any of the countries be a victim of an armed attack in the Pacific area. For Australia and New Zealand the Pact meant a lessening of their dependence upon the UK and a close collaboration with the USA. However, following New Zealand's adoption of a non-nuclear defence strategy in 1984, the USA has refused to cooperate with New Zealand on defence matters.

Apartheid. The official South African government policy of racial segregation and 'separate development'.

In 1960 the introduction of identity cards for non-whites and the suspension of their parliamentary representation was followed by widespread demonstrations, often violently suppressed—as at Sharpeville. Other aspects of the laws which have aroused hostility around the world and at the UN incl. segregated education, a prohibition of mixed marriages, and deportation of blacks from specified districts.

The policy of 'separate development' led to the Bantu Self-Government Act, which provided for the establishment of 7 native African areas with non-white chief ministers, e.g., the Transkei in 1963; these self-governing territories later became autonomous, though not widely recognized as such internationally. South African left the Common-wealth in 1961 rather than modify its apartheid policies.

Apis. A sacred bull worshipped by the ancient Egyptians.

Appeasement. A form of foreign policy seeking to avert war by making concessions to a potential enemy. Such a policy was unsuccessfully adopted by British and French governments towards Germany between 1936 and 1939.

Appian Way. An ancient paved highway extending from Rome to Brundisium.

Apocalypse. Refers to one of the Jewish and Christian writings of 200 B.C. to A.D. 150 marked by pseudonymity, symbolic imagery, and the expectation of an imminent cosmic cataclysm in which God destroys the ruling powers of evil and raises the righteous to life in a messianic kingdom.

Apolitical. 1. Having an aversion to or no interest or involvement in political affairs. 2. Having no political significance.

Arab. 1. A member of a Semitic people orig. of the Arabian peninsula but now widespread throughout the Middle East and N. Africa. 2. A member of an Arabic-speaking people.

Arabian. (Characteristic) of Arabia or Arabians.

Arab-Israeli Wars. A series of conflicts, culminating 4 times (1948, 1956, 1967, 1973) in outright war between Israel and Arab countries over the existence in Palestine of the Independent Jewish state of Israel.

The 1948 War. The proclamation of the state of Israel (1948) led to the immediate invasion by neighbouring Arab states, which was successfully resisted by Israel. The UN inter vented and in 1949 established an armistice treaty: Jerusalem was partitioned, the West Bank became Jordanian, and the Gaza Strip Egyptian.

The 1956 War. As a result of Nasser's anti-Israeli Pan-Arab policy and Egyptian nationalization of the Suez Canal, the Israelis invaded Egypt in 1956, supported by British and French military action, and occupied the Gaza Strip and most of Sinai. The invasion was condemned by the UN, who secured a ceasefire and the withdrawal of the occupying forces. See also Suez Crisis.

The 1967 War. In 1967 the 'Six Day War' resulted from border incidents, increased action by Palestinian guerrillas, and the Egyptian blockade of the Gulf of Aqaba to Israeli shipping. Israel secured a rapid victory over Egypt, Syria and Jordan, and occupied Sinai, the Gaza Strip, the West Bank of the Jordan, and the Golan Heights.

The 1973 War. In 1973 Egypt launched the 'Yom Kippur War', but after early Arab victories, Israeli forces crossed the Suez Canal. In 1974, after Arab states imposed an embargo on oil exports to the West, an agreement of disengagement with Egypt and Syria was reached.

After the Camp David Agreement, in 1979 Egypt and Israel signed a peace treaty, following which Israel withdrew from Sinai; the other territories seized in 1967 remain occupied. Tensions in the area remain high despite international attempts to find a solution.

see also Lebanon.

Arab League. An organization to promote inter-Arab cultural, technical and economic and to minimize conflict between Arab states. A pact was signed in 1945 by 8 states. A council was established in Cairo, but the League remained an essentially loose association of states and never acquired a strong central authority. Until 1967 the League was concerned with organizing opposition to Israel, but since the PLO's increase in strength, the League has become a mouthpiece of moderate Arab opinion and a body favouring economic unity. It now has 19 member states.

Arab Nationalism. A loosely defined sense of cultural and political solidarity expressed by members of Arab states in the face of outside influences and pressures.

The pan-Arab movement was led by Nasser from 1945-70. Plans for unification of the various Arab states did not conceal rivalries among the leadership nor tensions between various factions. Plan-Arab policy only tended to retain its appeal as long as it was directed against Israel (see Arab-Israeli Wars). Attempts at unification by Egypt and Syria as a United Arab Republic (1958-61) were not very effective. Prime issues remain the existence of the Jewish state of Israel and the rights of Arab refugees driven from the West Bank, represented by the Palestine Liberation Organization.

Arafat, Yasir, 1929. Palestine commando leader, *b.* Jerusalem Head of the guerrilla group Al Fatah, he became (1969) leader of the Palestine Liberation Organization (PLO). In 1974 Arab leaders recognized him as the "sole legitimate" spokesman for the Palestinian people. The PLO was considerably weakened when Atafat and his guerrillas were forced to leave their stronghold in West Beirut, Lebanon, after the 1982 Israeli siege of the city (see Arab-Israeli Wars).

Aragon. Former kingdom of Spain, lying S. of the Pyrenees. It arose in the 11th cent. and was extended to include the Balearic Is., Naples, Sicily and Sardinia. In 1467 Aragon united with Castile.

Arbalist. A medieval military weapon with a steel bow used to throw balls, stories and quarrels.

Arawak *pl* **Arawak, Arawaks.** A member of an American Indian people of the Arawaken group now living chiefly along the coast of Guyana.

Arawakan *pl* **Arawakan, Arawakans.** A member of a group of American Indian peoples of South America and the West Indies.

Archaeology. The scientific study of material remains (*e.g.*, fossil relics, artefacts, and dwellings) of past human life and activities-archaeological *adj*. archaeological *n.*

Archaeozoic. Of or being the earliest era of geological history; *also* relating to the system of rocks formed in this era.

Archon. A chief magistrate in ancient Athens.

Argentina. Republic of South America.

The country achieved independence from Spain in 1816. In the 20th cent. elected presidents have been overthrown by military coups on numerous occasions.

In 1946 Juan Peron was elected president. He propounded policies combining nationalism, populism and state socialism, known as Peronism. However his power was largely dependent on the popularity of his wife Eva (known as Evita). She died in 1952 and he was overthrown in 1955, returning from exile 18 years later to again become president with his second wife, Maria Estella, as vice-president. He died 9 months later and was succeeded by his wife, but economic crises and urban guerrilla activities led to her downfall in 1976.

The subsequent military regime carried out a 'dirty war' against its opponents, during which thousands of people disappeared. In 1982 the regime invaded the Falkland Islands. Following the Argentinian defeat, the regime fell and was replaced by a democratically elected government, which has had to contend with high inflation.

Aristides. (*c*. 529-*c*. 468 B.C.) Gk. statesman. He became known as an opponent of Themistocles and the people decided in 483, by vote, to expel or ostracise him. He took part in the war against Persia and commanded the Athenians at Plataea. In 477 he was responsible for the change by which any citizen of Athens could become an archon (magistrate).

Aristotle. (384-322 B.C) Greek philosopher, pupil of Plato and tutor to

Alexander the Great.

Armada, Spanish, 1588. Fleet launched by Philip II of Spain for the invasion of England. Commanded by the duque de Medina Sodonia and consisting of 130 ships and about 30,000 men, the Armada was delayed by storms and finally set sail from Lisbon in May. The English fleet, under Charles Howard, sailed from Plymouth and inflicted long-range damage on the Armada but did not break its formation. Anchoring off Calais, Medina Sodonia intended to pick up Alessandro Farnese's army in Flanders and convey it to England. But on Aug. 7 the English sent fire ships into the anchorage to scatter the Armada and then attacked the fleeing ships at close range off Gravelines. The battered Armada escaped northward, sailed around Scotland and Ireland while buffeted by storms, and returned to Spain after losing about half its ships.

Armistice. Agreement between combatants to cease fighting. It may be either temporary or it may be a preliminary to a general peace, as in 1918 and 1945. The 1st between Germany and the Allied powers was signed on Nov. 11, 1918; the 2nd on May 8, 1945. That between Japan and the Allies was signed on Aug. 10, 1945. A. Day, Day on which the dead of both World Wars are remembered. Now celebrated on the Sun, nearest to Nov. 11.

Armstrong. Neil Alden (1930) American astronaut; first man on the moon.

Arthur. King of the Britons. According to one account he lived in the 6th cent. and was killed in battle. The Arthur legend was a son of King Uther Pendragon. He founded an order of Knights of the Round Table. His capital was Camelot. He mar. Guinevere, but she proved false to him. The order was then broken up and the king mortally wounded in battle. He was carried to the Isle of Avalon where he *d*.

Artillery. 1. Weapons for discharging missiles. 2. A branch of army armed with artillery.

Aryan. (Sanskrit, *noble*) Once used for the race speaking Indo-European and for the language itself, probably originating in the Indian sub-continent but applied later to inhabitants of the Iranian plateau and, esp. during the Hitler regime, to Germans of non-Jewish extraction.

Ashoka Also Asoka. 295-232 B.C. King of the Mauryan Empire in India

(273-232 B.C).

Ashram. *n* the hermitage of a Hindu sage; *broadly* any Hindu religious retreat.

Asiento. A treaty concluded in 1713 between England and Spain for the provision of slaves to the Spanish colonies in America.

Asquith. Henry Herbert 1852, 1928. 1st Earl of Oxford and Asquith, British statesman and prime minister (1908-16), leader of the Liberal Party (1908-26).

Assassin. Refers to one of a secret order of Muslims that at the time of the Crusades terrorized Christians and other enemies by secret murders committed under the influence of hashish.

Association of South Asian Nations (ASEAN). An association established in 1967 in Bangkok by Indonesia, Malaysia, the Philippines, Singapore and Thailand to accelerate economic progress and increase stability in SE Asia.

Asvamedh (Horse Sacrifice). The term used for the elaborate rite (probably Seythian in origin by ancient solar kings about (1200 B.C.) for adding territory to kingdom, atonement of a sin, obtaining progeny or wealth; legend has it that (god) Brahma celebrated one at Prayag (Allahabad) and another at Varanasi; a white horse for sacrifice was made sacred by an offering of fire and other ceremonies and then left to wander at will for a year. This horse would be followed by princes of the realm and their entourages; if meant for extension of territory, all land covered by him was claimed as his king's domain, any claimant having to establish his right by battle; on successful return, horse was sacrificed (killed) by priest with assistance of king and queen (who underwent some sexual rites of beastiality with carcass), some of its flesh being cooked and eaten by priest and other participants, some offered to gods and rest horned; rite described only in *Rigveda* so perhaps was on the decline by then (India).

Asylum. The protection form arrest and extradition given, esp to political refugees, by a nation or by an agency (*e.g.*, an embassy) enjoying diplomatic immunity.

Ataturk, Kemal, 1881-1938. Turkish leader, founder of modern Turkey, first president of Turkey (1923-38). Originally known as Mustafa

Kemal, he was an army officer who took part (1908) in the Young Turk movement, distinguished himself in World War I, and, after the collapse of Ottoman power, founded the Turkish Nationalist Party. With the Allies controlling the government at Constantinople (Istanbul), he set up a rival government at Ankara. He expelled the Greeks who were occupying at Anatolia (1921-22), abolished the sultanate (1922), and forced the European powers to recognize the Turkish republic. He ruled the new republic for 15 years as a virtual dictator, changing Turkey profoundly. He instituted widespread internal reforms in his efforts to Westernize his nation; those change included abolishing the caliphate (1924), which in effect disestablished Islam. In foreign affairs he pursued a moderate policy, maintaining friendly relations with Turkey's neighbours, especially Russia, with whom he established the Balkan Entente.

Atlantic, Battle of the . Socalled by Churchill to describe the struggle for control of the sea routes around the UK during WWII. It lasted for the whole period of the War but was particularly severe 1940-43 when Allied convoys were attacked by U-Boats (frequently operating in packs), armed surface raiders, and long-range aircraft. Allied counter-measures included the escorting of convoys by warships, special escort aircraft carriers, armed merchant cruisers, submarines, land-based air cover, radar, and the underwater detection device, Asdic. Air attacks were also made on enemy naval bases and, in conjunction with the Royal Navy, on enemy warships at sea.

Atlantic Charter. A declaration of common objectives signed by Roosevelt and Churchill in 1941. It contained plans for the postwar world: the right of all peoples to choose their own governments and to alive free from fear and want; no territorial changes without the consent of the peoples involved; the disarmament of aggressive nations; a wider and permanent system of international security; and access to essential raw materials through trade between all nations coupled with freedom of the seas.

Attlee, Clement. (1883-1967). British statesman, PM (1945-51). He became leader of the Labour Party in 1935. He entered the war time coalition with Churchill, and was deputy PM (1942-45). As PM in the postwar Labour Government he oversaw the creation of the welfare state. He ended his career as Leader of the Opposition (1951-55), receiving an earldom in 1955.

Attila. (*c*. 406-453) King of the Huns. In 434 he and his brother succeeded their uncle. Having killed his brother, Attila brought many other barbarians under his rule and was soon at the head of a vast host. In 447 he led them across the Danube and their ravages made a terrible impression on the Byzantine Empire. Attila's hordes swept across Germany and entered Fr. Aetius, the Rom. and Theodoric, the Vandal, fought them on the Catalaunian Fields, near Chalons, in June 451, and the Huns were utterly defeated, but were soon on the march again, invading and devastating Italy.

Attic. Greek dialect of ancient Attica which became the literary language of the Greek speaking world.

Augustus. (63 B.C.—A.D. 14) Roman emperor, son of Gaius Octavius and grandson of the sister of Julius Caesar (*q.v.*). After his father's *d*. he was adopted by his uncle. When Caesar was murdered in 44 B.C. he formed an alliance with Antony, form which sprang the triumvirate—Lepidus making the 3rd member—that restored order in Rome, by a ruthless severity towards its enemies. In 42 they defeated the murderers of Caesar at Philippi. Octavian took the W. portion and Antony the E. Octavian crushed Sextus Pompeius, and removed Lepidus from power before finally quarrelling with Antony in 32 B.C. contributory causes being Antony's intrigue with Cleopatra in Egypt and his repudiation of his wife, a sister of Octavian. Octavian's fleet won the famous sea fight at Actium in 31 B.C. Octavian was now sole ruler. A visit to Egypt was followed by a splendid triumph in 29 B.C. when the title of Augustus was given to him. In 27 B.C. further powers were given to him, including the command of the army with the title of imperator. For the next 41 years Augustus was an emperor with unlimited powers. These years were a period of peace and prosperity and have been named the Augustan Age. Reforms of various kinds made easier the lot of the people. Rome was rebuilt and literature flourished.

Aurangzeb or Aurangzib. (Or' engzeb', -zib), 1618-1707, Mogul emperor of India (1658-1707), son and successor of Shah Jahan. He ascended the throne after defeating his three brothers and imprisoning his father. The Mogul Empire reached its greatest extent under him, but he was fanatically devoted to Islam and persecuted the Hindus (see Hinduism) and Sikhs, thus fatally weakening Mogul control over the Indian population.

Aurelian. (Lucius Domitius Aurelianus), *c*, 212-275, Roman emperor (270-75). He succeeded Claudius II and defended the empire vigorously against the barbarians and ambitious rulers (*e.g.*, Zenobia of Palmyra). One of Rome's greatest emperors, Aurelian regained Britain, Gaul, Spain, Egypt, Syria, and Mesopotamia and revived the glory of Rome. He was murdered, and Marcus Claudius Tacitus succeeded him.

Australia. In 1900 the Australian Commonwealth Act untied 6 former British colonies (now the 6 states) into an independent Commonwealth Dominion with a federated government, which came onto being at the beginning of 1901. The Labour Party was the dominant political grouping in the new country, but was not strong enough to gain clear electoral victory until 1914. During WWI about 20% of the 300,000 volunteers were killed in Europe and the Middle East fighting for the Allies.

Between the Wars there was inter-state and federal friction over taxation in relation to defence expenditure, which nearly led to the break up of the federation. That this did not happen was largely due to the rise in wool prices and the growing realization of Japan's aggressive intentions in the Far East and the Pacific.

Australia entered WWII in 1939, Australian forces being principally active in the Far East. As a result of WWII, strategic links were formed with New Zealand and the USA and resulted in troops being sent to serve in Vietnam in 1965.

Industrial growth was stimulated which incl. the huge Snowy River hydro-electric scheme in New South Wales. Trade with Japan and the USA has developed as it declines with Britain esp. after the latter joined the EEC in 1972. The Liberal Party (more or less equivalent to the British Conservative Party) has been dominant in government since WWII, Labour holding power only twice.

Austria. With the defeat and dissolution of the Austro-Hungarian Empire at the end of WWI, a republic was established in Austria in 1918, with Karl Renner (1870-1951) as Chancellor. The 1920s were marked by much social and political unrest, with frequent clashes between Fascist and socialist elements culminating in serious riots in Vienna in 1927. Dollfuss became Chancellor in 1932 but his home and foreign policies pleased neither left nor right and he was assassinated by a group Nazis. He was succeeded by Schuschnigg, whose authority was undermined by increasing Nazi pressure leading to German annexation of the country (Anschluss) in 1938.

The country regained independence in 1945, again under Renner's leadership, but was occupied by the Allies until 1955, when it achieved full official sovereignty.

Austro-Hungarian Empire. A political unit which dominated C Europe from 1867 to 1918, incorporating what are now Czechoslovakia and parts of Italy, Poland, Romania, Yugoslavia and the Ukraine. There was a common monarch of the Hapsburg Dynasty (founded in 1153), and joint control of the armed forces and financial policies, but each state had its own parliament.

Independence and nationalistic issues, supported by the Allies at the end of WWI, caused the Empire's disintegration, formally recognized by the Treaties of Saint Germain (1919) and Trianon (1920).

Austro Prussian War or Seven Weeks War. June 15-Aug. 23, 1866, between Austria (seconded by the various German states) and Prussia (allied with Italy). It was provoked by Bismarck as a way of expelling Austria from the German Confederation, thereby assuring Prussian hegemony there. The pretext was a dispute between Prussia and Austria over the administration of Schleswig-Holstein. Prussia quickly overran Holstein and the German states allied with Austria, and was victorious in Bohemia and Italy. The Treaty of Prague ended the War. Austria was excluded from German affairs and forced to cede Venetia to Italy. Prussia demanded no territory from Austria but annexed Hanover, Hesse, Nassau, and Frankfort, laying the groundwork for the establishment (1871) of the German empire.

Autarky or Autarchy. A nationalist system or policy of economic self-sufficiency aimed at removing the need for imports by producing all requirements at home. Germany adopted such a policy in the 1930s to make herself blockade-proof.

Authoritarian. (*a*). Favouring or devoting strict obedience to authority, or to government by a small elite with wide powers; (*b*) Despotic, dictatorial or domineering.

Autocracy. (*a*) Government by an individual with unrestricted authority (an autocrat); (*b*) The unrestricted authority of such an individual; (*c*) A country or society ruled by an autocrat.

Autonomy. The right or state of self-government, esp., when limited.

Auxillary. A member of a foreign force serving a nation at war.

Avadh Bihari. B. 1889 at Delhi; son of Govind Lal; teacher. He took active part in nationalist activities against British rule; member of the Revolutionary party and directed revolutionary activities in Utter Pradesh and Punjab. He was the associate of Rash Behari Bose; took part in the plot to throw a bomb on Lord Hardinge, the Viceroy of India. Known as the Delhi Conspiracy, it was carried out on December 23, 1912, when Lord Hardinge was passing through Chandni Chowk, Delhi, in a State procession, marking the inauguration of Delhi as the capital of India. Arrested in February, 1914 and charged with conspiracy to kill Lord Hardinge and also accused for complicity in the explosion of a bomb in the Lawrence Garden, Lahore, on May 17, 1913. He was tried along with his three compatriots—Amir Chand, Bal Mokand and Basant Kumar Biswas; sentenced to death. Died on the gallows in the Ambala Central Jail on May 11, 1915 (India).

Awami League. A political party in Pakistan and Bangladesh. Founded in 1949, it became the vehicle for the political interests of East Pakistan. When East pakistan won independence (1971) as Bangladesh, the league became the new nation's dominant political party. However, in 1981 the National party defeated the league in national elections.

Axis. Name given to anti-allied forces in World War II. The Rome-Berlin Axis was formed in 1936 during the Ital, invasion of Abyssinia. The term was extended to include Japan (Sept. 1940), and then Hungary, Bulgaria and Rumania.

Ayatollah Ruhollah Khomeini. See Khomeini, Ayatollah Ruhollah.

Ayodhya. (Sanskrit, 'invincible'). The term used for the place of great antiquity (called *saket*) and one of the 7 *saptapuris* (sacred cities) of the Hindus. This town is situated on the Ghaghra (or Saryu) about

6.40 km from Faizabad (in Utter Pradesh); founded by Iksvaku, first king of solar dynasty—also called North Khosala dynasty; made it his capital and it continued as the capital of the great line of solar kings among whom was Rama Chandra (here of the *Ramayana*) who was born and cremated here; the Jain *tirthankaras*, Adinath, Rishabha, and Ajita were born here and so it has been sacred to the Jains as well; was a celebrated Buddhist centre and the famous Chinese monk, Fa Hien, who travelled in India from A.D. 400 to 411, visited the city of Sha-chi which historians have identified with Saket, where he saw a *stupa* where grew a tree which has sprouted from the toothbursh stick used and thrown away by the Buddha; when Hiuen Tsang, another famons Chinese pilgrim visited about 640, it had 20 Buddhist *chaityas* (chapels) and 3,000 monks; it is having many temples built on sites associated with Rama and his kin also a big one dedicated to Hanuman.

Aztec. Indian people living in Mexico when the Spaniards invaded the country in the 15th century. They came from the North and usurped the Toltec culture. They founded a powerful kingdom, conquered by Cortes in the 16th cent. The race and its language still survive; the latter is a *Nahua* dialect. The Axtecs were advanced an agric., art, archit. and engineering. They worshipped many gods and the priests were powerful.

Azad, Chandra Shekar. Born July 23, 1906 at Bhaora, Distt. Jhabua, Madhya Pradesh. He took part in the Non-cooperation Movement (1921). He was arrested at the age of 14 years and punished with fifteen cane strokes; in his court statement, he described his own name as " Azad", his father as *Swadhin* and his address as "the jail". After release, he was hailed as a young hero; joined the Indian Revolutionary Party in 1922; he was the member of the "Hindustan Socialist Republican Army", took part in several political dacoities, including the "Kakori Mail Dacoity"; declared an absconder and remained underground for several years; attended the meeting of the Revolutionary Party on September 8, 1928, at Delhi and was appointed "Commander of the Military Division " of the Hindustan Socialist Republican Association. In order to average the death of Lala Lajpat Rai, he organised, along with Sarder Bhagat Singh and Rajgurua, the shooting of British Police Superintendent, J.A. Scott, in Lahore. Scott escaped and the Asstt. Superintendent of Police, J.P. Saunders, was killed; planned the bomb explosion in the

Central Legislative Assembly on April 8, 1929; successfully evaded arrest by the police for about two years. He was betrayed by a companion and surrounded by the police in the Alfred Park at Allahabad on February 27, 1931; fought along against the big police party with a revolver in each hand; killed several policemen and wounded the British Police Superintendent, Nott-Bower and Indian police officer, Bisheshwar Singh. He died fighting the police on February 27, 1931, after his arm and leg had been riddled with bullets.

Azad, Maulana Abu-'l Kalam. (1888-1958 A.D.). Muslim liberal, opponent of Syed Ahmed Khan, and founder of the periodical, the *Al-Hilal* of Calcutta, in 1912, who tried to show that Hindu-Muslim unity was a progressive social ideal. He became Minister of Education in independent India, author of several works in Urdu particularly *Tajmahal Quran, Shubor-i-Khater* etc.

B

Ba'ath Socialist Party. A pan-Arab movement which based upon the union of 1952 of two Syrian political parties, the Ba'ath ('resurrection') Party and the Socialist Party. The basic philosophy of the United Party has been 'Freedom, unity and socialism in one Arab nation with an external mission.

Babar. He was descendant of both Timur and Chinghiz Khan. He has been regarded as the founder of the Mughal dynasty in India, who invaded the Panjab in 1525, dealt a death-blow to the Lodhi Sultanate, and defeated the Rajput power.

Bad Godesberg Meeting. See Godesberg meeting.

Badoglio Pietro (1871-1956). He was Italian field marshal and politician. He was Governor of Libya (1929-33) and completed the conquest of Ethiopia (1936). He opposed Italian entry into WWII when Chief of the General Staff and resigned (1940) after the fiasco of the Greek campaign. He was appointed PM (1943) by King Victor Emmanuel III. After the fall of Mussolini, he concluded an armistice with the Allies and took Italy into WWII against Germany.

Baghdad Pact (1955). A defence and security agreement between Iraq and Turkey which was subsequently joined by Pakistan, Iraq and the UK. The Suez Crisis (1956) and the Iraqi revolution (1958) practically ended the agreement, which survived only in truncated form as a basis for the Central Treaty Organization.

Bagwig. An 18th century wig with the back hair enclosed in a small silk bag.

Baha'i. An adherent of a religious movement originating among Shia Muslims in Iran in the 19th century and emphasizing the spiritual unity of mankind.

Bahadur Shah II. B. 1775 in Delhi. He was son of Emperor Akbar Shah; succeeded in 1837 to the Mughal throne and assumed the title of

'Badshah' (Emperor) and 'Ghazi' (holy warrior). Pensioner of the British East India Company. He inaugurated the annual Hindu Muslim fair—*Phoolwalon-ki-Sair* near the precincts of Sheikh Qutbuddin Bakhtiyar Kaki's tomb at Mehrauli (Delhi). He assumed leadership of the Great Revolt of 1857 as their King Emperor. He set up a national government at Delhi on May 14, 1857, and sent circulars to the jagirdars and amirs calling upon them to join the war against the British. Continued the anti-British struggle till September 14, 1857, when the British succeeded in breaching the defences of Delhi. He fell into the hands of the British and surrendered to the British commander, Major Hodson, on September 21, 1957. Imprisoned in the Red Fort and tried by a military commission. Banished to Rangoon, where he died in December, 1862.

Bahaism. Religion founded by Bahau'llah (1817-92) in Persia. Son, Abdul Baha succeeded his leadership; (*d.* 1921). Shogi Effendi, grandson, followed as 'Guardian of the Cause'. It teaches world brotherhood on a spiritual basis. It has followers Europe, in Asia and the U.S.A.

Balance of Power. Refers to the doctrine of maintaining a European system in which no single power has been dominant. In the past many countries were concerned to support coalitions opposing one power gaining control over Europe, *e.g.*, the German-Austro-Hungarian alliance balanced by the alliance between Britain, France and Russia Prior to WWII.

Balance of Terror. Refers to an equilibrium of military power (*e.g.*, nuclear capability) between potentially opposing nations sufficient to deter one nation from waging war on another.

Bala Sahib Dev Ras (Sar Sangh Chalak R.S.S.). He took over as Sar Sangh Chalak of R.S.S. in 1972 after the death of Shri Madho Rao Sadashiv Rao Golwalkar (Shri Guruji). He streses on the social uplift projects of the society in addition to the various activities of R.S.S. He preaches and practices the adage "untouchability is the greatest sin against humanity".

Balboa, de Vasco Nunez (1475-1519). Spanish explorer who discovered the Pacific Ocean.

Balfour Declaration (1917). Refers to the statement by the British Foreign Secretary A.J. Balfour declaring British support for a

Jewish national home in Palestine provided that safeguards might be reached for the 'right of non-Jewish communities in Palestine' and that Jewish political status in any other country should not be endangered.

The declaration formed the basis of the League of Nations mandate for Palestine which got assigned to the UK in 1922 and lasted until 1948 when Israel was established.

Balkan Pact (1934). The term used for the defensive agreement between Greece, Romania, Turkey and Yugoslavia whereby they agreed to guarantee each other's frontiers. It was especially aimed at Bulgaria which desired to recover territory previously lost to all 4 states. The signatories later formed an Entente, but this foundered (1940) when each state went its separate way in WWII.

Balkans, the. Refers to the peninsula in SE Europe which has been comprising Ablania, Bulgaria, Greece, Romania, Yogoslavia (which has incorporated Serbia, Montenegro and Bosnia-Herzegovina) and European Turkey. Previously it was an area of political and revolutionary upheaval characterized by the Balkan Wars and involvement in WWI and WWII.

Balkan Wars (1912 and 1913). Two short wars between the Balkan States and Turkey, which almost involved the Great Powers. In 1912, Serbia, Greece, Bulgaria, and Montenegro allied to free Macedonia from Turkish rule. Turkey was expelled from all Europe except the Constantinople area. Serbia, cut off from the sea by the creation of an indep. Albania, demanded from Bulgaria a greater share of Macedonia. Bulgaria attacked Serbia, (1913), only to be attacked by Greece, Rumania, and Turkey. The Balkan Wars prepared the way for World War I by enlarging Serbia, alarming Austria and causing discontent in Bulgaria and Turkey.

Ballista *pl* **Ballistae.** An ancient military engine often in the form of a crossbow for huring large missiles.

Baltic States. The term used for the collective name of Estonia, Latvia and Lithuania, territories of E. Europe. Up to 1918 they were part of Russia and were then independent republics (1919-40). In 1940 they got occupied by the Russians, since when they are constituent republics of the USSR.

Bamboo Curtain. A political, military, and ideological barrier between China and the capitalist world.

Bamburgh. Village on the coast of Northumberland, famous for its castle, which, in the 6th cent., was the residence of the Kings of Northumbria.

Banana Republic. A republic that is politically unstable and generally economically underdeveloped.

Banda, Hastings Kamuzu. Malawi statesman. He became leader of the Malawi National Congress (1958), PM of Nyasaland (1963) and led the country to independence as Malawi in 1964. He became President (1966) and subsequently has followed a cautious and moderate policy in relationships with South Africa. Internally he has created a l-party state on dictatorial lines.

Bandaranaike, Sirimavo. Sri Lanka stateswomen who succeeded her husband, Solomon, as leader of the Freedom Party. She became the world's first female PM in 1960, but by following her husband's language and nationalization policies contributed to the Party's defeat in 1965. She regained power in 1970 on a platform of advancement to social democracy and held office until 1977.

Bandaranaike, Solomon W.R.D. (1899-1959) Ceylonese statesman. As leader of the House in Ceylon's first parl. And Min. of Health he helped to make Ceylon the first Asian country free of malaria. In 1951 he resigned from the Government and organised the Sri Lanka Freedom Party. Assassinated 1959. Succeeded by his wife, the Hon. Mrs. Sirimaro Bandaranaike, who in 1960 became the first woman P.M.

Bandung Conference (1955). The first international political conference of African and Asian states. The idea has been to adopt a 'non-aligned and neutral' attitude towards the Cold War confrontations between East and West, and to create a 'united front' against colonial oppression.

The increasing rivalry of India and China within Asia, and the separate objectives of anticolonialism in Africa and Asia, weakened the subsequent effectiveness of the Conference. The Conference was a forerunner of the non-aligned movement.

Banner. 1. A usually square flag bearing heraldic arms and originally used by a monarch, feudal lord, or banneret as a rallying point in battle. 2. A flag displaying a distinctive device or legend; *esp* one for carrying in a procession (*e.g.*, by a church or guild.).

Banerjea, Surendranath (1848-1926 A.D.). He was great Indian educator, journalist and nationalist. He was one of the founders of the indian National Congress in 1885, opponent of Lord Curzon's partition of Bengal, whose autobiography, *A Nation in the Making*, discusses the early stages of Indian nationalism.

Banneret. A knight leadings his vessals into the field under his own banner and therefore ranking above a knight bachelor.

Bangladesh. Densely populated country in S. Asia, consisting of the farmer Indian province of E. Bengal and the eastern part of the Ganges delta. It has a trophical monsoon climate, and is susceptible to flooding and cyclones. Agriculture is the main occupation, with rice and jute the most important products. Bangladesh was formed when East Pakistan seceded from Pakistan after bitter warfare between Pakistan and India in 1971. The resulting peace enabled Bangladesh to be established as in independent state (1972).

In 1975 the PM and leader of the Awami League, Mujibur Rahman, was assassinated in a military coup led by Brigadier Khaled Mosharraf, who himself was assassinated three months later. The country has remained politically unstable, with alternating periods of military rule and parliamentary democracy.

Bantu. Black people of S. Africa. The orig. home of the Bantu seems to have been N. of equatorial Africa, whence they spread S. supplanting the aboriginal inhabitants, of whom the Bushmen and the Hottentots are the remnants. The Bantu tongue is the native speech of all Africa S. of the equator.

Bantustan. Generally *cap* an all-black enclave in the Republic of South Africa with a limited degree of self-government.

Barbarossa. German Supreme Command code name for the invasion of the USSR in 1941.

Barotseland. Tribal territory of S.C. Africa in Upper Zambezi territory, cap. Mongu, formerly a kingdom, it became a Brit. Protectorate in 1953, and the 18th province of Zambia, 1964.

Barriers. A medieval war game in which combatants fight on foot with a fence or railing between them.

Basque. Language with no known affinities, having 1,000,000 speakers in N.E. Spain and S.W. Fr. Basque Provinces. Ancient division of N. Spain, corresponding in area to the modern Biscay, Alava and Guipuzcoa provs. The coastal area is densely populated, and the chief industries are fishing and iron mining; hydro-electric power is being developed. The Basques are a people of uncertain origin, inhabiting the Basque Prov. and Navarra, and the dept. of Basses-Pyreneess in S.W.Fr.

Batista, Fulgencio (1901-73). Cuban dictator. After deposing President Machado (1933) he established a Fascist state, but in 1937 allowed opposition political parties to be formed. Free elections (1939) resulted in his appointment as President. He held office until 1944, when he went voluntarily into exile in the Dominican Republic.

Because of another coup (1952) he returned to power, suspended the constitution and established a 1-party state. He was forced again to flee to the Dominican Republic (1958) following the army's refusal to support his corrupt and repressive regime against Castro's successful guerrilla campaign.

Battle of Buxer (1764). This battle was fought between the Nawab of Rudh and Emperor Shah Alam and East India Company at Buxer (Bihar). The main reason was that they had taken up the cause of Mir Qasim, the deposed Nawab of Bengal. Their combined forces were defeated by Major Munro. This battle completed the work of Plassey (1757) and ensured continued British supremacy in Bengal, Bihar and Orissa.

Battle of Haldighati (1576). This battle was fought between Akbar and Rana Pratap of Mewar. The main reason was that, unlike the other Rajput rulers, Pratap refused to acknowledge Akbar's sovereignty. In this battle, the Rana was defeated and compelled to take refuse in remote fortresses. However, he never gave up hope and succeeded in recovering a greater part of his kingdom in Akbar's lifetime.

Battle of Plassey (1757). In this battle, Siraj-ud-daulah was defeated by Clive. It fully established the authority of East India Company in Bengal, Bihar and Orissa. Henceforth, the East India Company got complete control over the finances and revenue administration of those provinces. It ensured their paramount power in India.

Battleship. A warship of the largest and most heavily armed and armoured class.

Bay of Pigs (1961). The site of an invasion of Cuba by 1,200 anti-Castro Cubans, trained by the CIA in the USA and using US military supplies. Most were killed or captured within a few days. In the same year Castro proclaimed Cuba a socialist nation.

B.B.C. (British Broadcasting Corporation) Administrative body for U.K. radio and television broadcasts. Estab. by royal charter Jan. 1, 1927, it superseded the Brit. Broadcasting Co. (formed 1922). Controlled by a board of governors apptd. by the crown, it is responsible to the Government; executive responsibility is vested in a Director-Gen. The revenue of the B.B.C. is derived from the sale of television receiving licence and from the sale of publications. The overseas services are assisted financially by a grant-in-aid from the Treasury. See Broadcasting.

Beaver. 1. A piece of armour protecting the lower part of the face. 2. A helmet visor. 3. An especially tall hat made of beaver fur or a fabric imitation and worm esp. by men during the 19th century.

Beelzebub. The devil.

Beethoven, L.V. He was the greatest German musician and composer.

Begin, Menachem. Polish-born Israeli politician, PM (1977-83). He reached Palestine during WWII, and became leader of Irgun Zvai Leumi, a member of the Knesset from 1948, and leader of the Likud (Unity) Party (1973-83) which won the 1977 general election.

His administration had to contend with high inflation, Arab disturbances, and the maintenance of Israeli authority on the occupied West Bank, and PLO incursions from Lebanon. Begin was jointly awarded with Sadat the 1978 Nobel Peace Prize for efforts in achieving the Camp David Agreement.

Beja (A Member of). A nomadic pastoral people living between the Nile and the Red sea.

Belgae. A people occupying northern France, Belgium, and England in Caesar's time.

Belligerent. Means engaged in war, *specif* belonging to or recognized as a state at war and protected by and subject to the laws of war.

Bema. 1. Raised platform in ancient Athens from which orators addressed the citizens. 2. A stage for the seating of clergy in early Christian churches. 3. A part of an early Christian church containing the altar.

Ben Bella, Mohammed Ahmed. Algerian national revolutionary leader. After WWII he became head of the extreme nationalist 'Special Organization'. Imprisoned by the French (1950) he escaped (1952) to Egypt where he founded the National Liberation Front (FLN) which played a leading role in the fight for Algerian independence. Again imprisoned by the French (1956) he was released (1962) to participate in the independence talk at Evian which also led to the end of hostilities. He became PM and in 1963, President. He was overthrown (1965) in a military coup led by Colonel Boumedienne.

Benelux. This term refers to the customs union (1948) between Belgium, Luxembourg and the Netherlands which developed (1960) into an arrangement for the free movement of capital, goods and people between each state, and for joint commercial relations with other countries—principles merely restating factors imposed by EEC membership.

Benes, Eduard (1884-1948). Czechoslovak statesman. During WWI he worked hard for his country's independence and became its first Foreign Minister (1918-35) and was PM (1921-22). His foreign policy was based on firm support for the League of Nations, the development of close associations with France and the USSR, and the strengthening of the Little Entente. He remained President (1935-38, 1946-48), and headed a provisional government in France and England during WWII.

Ben Gurion, David (1886-1974). Israeli statesman. In 1930 he became leader of the Mapai Party, the strongest socialist grouping in Israel. He was PM (1948-53, 1955-63). Much of this time he led a country at war with the Arabs but was able to carry out agricultural and industrial reforms.

Berbers. Indigenous white race of ancient origin which occupies the Medit. coast lands from Egypt to the Atlantic. Their language is essentially Berber, which has a close affinity with Hamitic; their relig. mainly that of Islam; their government a system of councils which determine all matters of legislation, taxation and justice. With the exception of the Tuareg they are not nomadic. They have many industries which include mining, weaving, milling, quarrying, pottery and jewel-making.

Beria, Lavrenti Pavlovich (1899-1953). He was Soviet politician and chief of the secret police. In 1938 Stalin appointed him Commissioner of Internal Affairs, and he later became head of the Soviet Security Service (NKVD). During WWII he remained Vice-President of the State Committee for Defence. It was widely assumed he had hastened Stalin's death in order to succeed him, and later the same year he was dismissed, tried and shot as a traitor. A ruthlessly ambitious plotter, he was a skilful organizer of espionage, forced labour and terror.

Berlin. The city of N Germany which remained capital of united Germany 1871-1945. Since 1945 it has been divided into 2 sectors. The E sector is occupied by forces of the USSR, while the W sector is occupied by US, UK and French troops.

During 1948-49 the Russians imposed a rail and road blockade on the W sector, in response to the introduction of currency reform in West Germany, which the Soviet authorities refused to accept in Berlin. The UK and the USA organized an airlift of supplies, the success of which convinced the USSR of the furtility of the blockade.

During this tense period 2 municipal authorities were established and the city administratively divided. In 1961, the East Germans built a wall dividing the sectors to halt the flow of refugees from E to W.

Bhabha, Dr. Homi Jahangir (1909-1966). Formerly Chairman, Atomic Energy Commission and Director, Indian Institute of Fundamental Research. Died in the Mont Blanc Air disaster in the Alps in Europe in 1966.

Bhagavad Gita. A Hindu devotional scripture consisting chiefly of discourses of Krishna in poetic form.

Bhakti. The devotion to a deity constituting a way to salvation in Hinduism.

Bharat Itihas Samshodhak Mandala, Pune. It registers, acquires and preserves historical material; promotes writing of articles monographs, etc.; relating to Indian history and culture; promotes critical study and research in Indian history, culture and allied subjects; publishes books on historical material, journals, periodicals, *Swiya Granthamala, Pariskrita Granthamala*, etc.; 13,500 books, 27,000 mss., 15,00,000 documents 5,200 coins and 1,200 paintings.

Bismark. He was most prominent and capable statesman of Germany of the 19th century. He was mainly responsible for German Unification.

Bhutto, Zulfiquar Ali (1928-79). He was a Pakistani statesman. He joined President Ayub Khan's government (1958), becoming Foreign Minister (1963). He resigned (1966) and established the Socialist Anti-Indian People's Party (1967). It won an Assembly majority in 1970, and in the following year Bhutto became the first non-soldier to achieve the Presidency. He led his country out of the Commonwealth (1972) and initiated a new constitution under which he took office as PM with responsibility for foreign affairs, defence and atomic energy (1973). He was overthrown by a military coup (1977) and charged with conspiracy to murder, for which he was executed in 1979.

Biafran War (1967-70). The term used for the civil war in Nigeria resulting from the secession on Biafra, the predominantly Ibo eastern region of the federated republic. The secession was led by Colonel Odamagwa Ojukwu, and had been preceded by heightened inter-tribal conflict. Federal forces intervened to quell the rebellion, and although the main bases of Enugu and Port Harcourt were soon occupied it was not until 1970 that Biafran resistance was overcome and Ojukwu fled to the Ivory Coast.

Bible. The books of holy scripture. They comprise 39 Heb. works in the O.T. and 27 Gk. works in the N.T. besides 14 books of the Apocrypha. The O.T. contains the law, the prophets and others collectively entitled Hagiographa. The N.T. contains 4 gospels, apostolic acts, 21 epistles and the books of the Revelation. Heb. MSS. of the 9th cent. A.D. and Gk. MSS. of the 3rd-4th cent. are extant. The Septuagint is a Gk. version of the Heb. books prepared at Alexandria by Jewish scholars of the 3rd-2nd cent. B.C. The Vulgate is a Lat. version of the Bible prepared by Jerome in the 4th cent. A.D. The first complete Eng.tr. of the Vulgate was by John

Wycliffe, c. 1380: the first tr. out of the orig. tongues of the N.T. and the Pentateuch was by William Tyndale, 1525-34. Miles Coverdale Pub. the first complete Eng. Bible in 1535. The Eng. tr. or Authorised Version which has been in general use for over 350 years and is remarkable for the beauty and divinity of its language, was prepared in the time of James I, issued 1611. In 1952 the Revised Standard Version was first pub. in U.S.A. In 1961 the Oxford and Cambridge University Presses pub. jointly the New English Bible New Testament.

Biological Warfare. The use of living organisms, such as bacteria, viruses and fungi, in warfare; to kill incapacitate or damage people or animals, or to harm crops. The Biological Weapons Convention 1972, an agreement banning germ warfare signed by Britain, the U.S.A. and the U.S.S.R. came into force in 1975.

Bipartisanship. Refers to the situation arising from the mutual support of two or more countries, organizations or political parties for each other's general or specific policies.

Black Death. Plague which caused many deaths in the 14th cent. It was called black because of the dark colour of the bodies after *d.* It appeared in Europe in 1348 and soon invaded Eng. The total no. of victims in Eng. was prob. *c.* 500,000. the plague may have been bubonic. That of 1665 was similar.

Black Muslim. A member of an exclusively black group chiefly in USA that professes Islamic religious belief and advocates a strictly separate black community.

Black Nationalist. A member of a group of militant blacks who advocate separatism from the whites and the formation of self-governing black communities.

Black Panther. A member of an organization of militant American Blacks.

Black Power. An economic, political and social movement of black people, esp. in the USA, to obtain equality with whites. The term was coined in 1965 by radical groups discontented with the failure of the Civil Rights movement to obtain satisfactory legislation by means of non-violent action.

Black Shirts. The members of a Fascist organization, esp. of the Italian Fascist party before and during WWII.

Blitzkrieg. (Ger., 'lightning war'). The term applied to a style of attack perfected by German generals in France in 1940. Essential elements has been speed and surprise of attack (*e.g.* using tanks and dive bombing) resulting in shock and disorganization among enemy forces.

Blockade. The Isolation by a warring nation of particular enemy area (*e.g.*, a port) by means of troops or warships to prevent passage of people or supplies; *broadly* a restrictive measure designed to obstruct the commerce and communications of an unfriendly nation.

Blum Leon. (1872-1950), French socialist statesmen. He became leader of the Socialist Party (1925) and the country's first socialist PM (1936), but held office for only a year, returning to power for a few weeks in 1938. He was put on trial during WWII be the Vichy Government as a scapegoat for the country's military inadequacies, and was imprisoned by the Germans in concentration camps. Freed in 1945, he headed an economic mission to the USA (1946) and was PM (1946-47).

Boers. Dutch farmers of S. Africa. They settled there *c.* 1652 and later founded the state of the Transvaal and the Orange Free State. Boer War—war in S. Africa which broke out in 1899. Its causes were chiefly the Boers' demand for indep. made possible by the removal of the Zulu menace and the Boers' irritation at the Brit. Government's indecisive policy. After the Jameson Raid, 1896, the Boers began to arm, and Oct. 1899, laid siege to Ladysmith, Kimberley and Mafeking. The war began disastrously for Brit. but Roberts defeated Cronje, French relieved Kimberley, Buller raised the siege of Ladysmith and a force from Rhodesia relieved Mafeking. Pres. Kruger sued for peace, which Lord Salisbury, the Brit. Premier, granted, on condition that the Orange Free State and the Transvaal came under Brit. rule again. General Smuts, Botha and De Wet continued hostilities, but Lord Kitchener prosecuted the war with such vigour that peace was made in 1902, when Brit. promised to restore independent government.

Boer War. (1899-1902). The term used for a conflict between the British and the Boers (descendants of Dutch settlers) in South Africa caused by Boer resentment of British colonial policy, which it was feared would terminate the Transvaal's independence. After the British victory, the Treaty of Vereeniging (1902) transferred sovereignty over the Boer republics of the Orange Free State and the Transvaal to Britain.

Bohemia. Region and former prov. of Czechoslovakia; an ancient kingdom, formerly part of Austria-Hungary. It consists of ancient rocks, forming a basin-shaped plateau, surrounded by higher land. Drained by the Elbe, it is a fertile area, producing cereals, sugar beet and hops. Lignite is mined, and used in industry; manufactures include glass, porcelain and textiles. Prague is the main city and industrial centre.

Bolas. Weapon used by S. Amer. Indians, esp. those of Patagonia and consists of a length of hide 8 ft long to each end of which is attached a stone ball. The weapon is swung about the head and then hurled at the quarry, entangling the legs of the animal and bringing it down.

Bolshevism. Social and political. movement that arose in Russia during World War I. The word means great, and was given to those who formed the majority in the Communist Party, individually called Bolsheviks, the minority party being called Mensheviks. After 1917, under Lenin and Trotsky and eventually Stalin, its principles were carried out ruthlessly. They included nationalisation of the means of production, disestablishment of the Ch. and in general the abolition of capitalism. The term is now superseded by Communism.

Bombard. A cannon used in late medieval times chiefly to hurl large stones.

Bonaparte. Surname of the family made famous by Napoleon. Carlo Bonaparte, a public official at Ajaccio, Corsica, mar. Laetitia Ramolino and had 5 sons. These were Napoleon Joseph (1768-1944), for a short time king of Naples and then king of Spain : Lucien (1775-1840); Louis (1778-1846), king of Holland; and Jerome (1784-1860), king of Westphalia. Napoleon's family became extinct when his only son *d.* in 1832. Louis was the father of Napoleon III, and his male line became extinct when the Prince Imperial was killed in S. Africa in 1879. In 1926, Jerome's great-grandson, Louis Napoleon, became the head of the family. The

Amer. Bonapartes are descended from Jerome's Ist marriage with Elizabeth Patterson of Baltimore.

Boom. A period of high economic growth which is characterized by rising wages, profits and prices, full employment, and high levels of investment, trade and other economic activity. It is usually followed by a Depression.

Borneo. Large Is. in the E. Indies, lying across the Equator. Divided into Indonesian Kalimantan, the former British colonies of Sabah and Sarawak (now part of Malaysia) and the British protectorate of Brunei. The main mt. system runs parallel to the N.W. coast, terminating in Kinabalu (13,450 fit). The pop. is chiefly Dyak, Malay, Negrito, Bugi and Chinese. Rubber, tobacco, rice, diamonds and oil are the most important products. Area : 287,400 sq.m. Pop. *c*. 743,000. North Borneo. N. part of the Is. of Borneo. The interior is mountainous, rising to 13,450 ft. in Mt. Kinabulu, and forested. Rubber is produced in the narrow coastal plain. Jesselton, Kudat and Sandakan are the chief towns. From 1942-45 it was occupied by the Japs. A Brit. colony until 1963 when it joined the Fed. of Malaysia as the State of Sabah.

Borough. A medieval fortified group of houses forming a town with special duties and privileges 2. A town or urban constituency in Britain that sends a member to Parliament.

Bose, Subhash Chandra. (1897-1945). Born January 23, in Cuttack, Orissa. He assaulted Principal (Oates) for making anti-Indian remarks and rusticated; Passed B.A. from Scottish Church College, Calcutta; and proceeded to England and was successful in the I.C.S. examination (1920). He resigned from I.C.S. (1921); joined Gandhiji's fold, who placed him under Chittaranjan Das (magnetic national leader) with whom he remained till the latter's death (1925). He organised boycott of visit of Prince of Wales (1921) and imprisoned for 6 months in consequence; after release joined *Swaraj* Party of C.R. Das and Motilal Nehru. He was appointed chief executive officer of Calcutta Corporation but arrested of anti-British views, etc., deported to Mandalay prison; on release (1927) on account of serious illness, he went to Switzerland; on return elected president of Bengal Provincial Congress Committee. He was invited by Jawaharlal Nehru to Lucknow Congress session and on return was arrested at Bombay; released (1937) on the eve of introduction of provincial autonomy; went back to Europe because of ill-health; elected President, Indian National Congress, Haripura session (1938); formulated a scheme for establishment of national planning committee and stressed possibilities of revolutionary potential in Congress being used; again elected president of Indian National Congress (1939) Tripuri session. He resigned in disgust and disappointment (April, 1939). He escaped from India (Jan 26, 1941, and known to have gone to Berlin from where from Jan. 1942, his broadcasts could be heard; arrived in Singapore (1943) in a submarine and took up from Rashbehari Bose the reins of Indian Independence movement in East Asia: organized the *Azad Hind Fauj* (Indian National Army) of which he was the Supreme Commander (Aug. 15, 1943). He proclaimed government of *Azad Hind* (Free India) on Oct. 21; liberated Andaman and Nicobar Islands from British rule naming them Shaheed and Swaraj Islands respectively; after shifting INA to Rangoon (1944) the Army crossed the Indo Burmese border into India (March 18, 1944) and entered Kohima and Imphal with the battle-cry "Delhi Chalo" (onward to Delhi) on its lips taking one British out-post after another; but with Japan's defeat it had to retreat; hailed by the INA and nearly the whole of India's civil population as 'Netaji' (Leader). He was reported killed in aircrash over Taiwan on August 18, 1945 (Adopted from 'India').

Botha, Louis. (1862-1919). South African general and statesman who fought for the Boers in the Boer War and then strove for reconciliation with his old enemies. He was PM of the Transvaal (1907-10) and first PM of the Union of South Africa (1910-19).

Botha, Pieter Willem. South African statesman. As PM (1978-84) and President he has pursued a policy of moderate reform, while resisting internal and external pressure for the complete dismantling of Apartheid.

Botswana. Landlocked republic in S. Africa, formerly known as Bechuanaland. Most of the population work in agriculture, though minerals are very important for the economy, with diamonds and copper-nickel matte as major exports Droughts are frequent. The most important tribes are Bamangwato, Bakgatla, Bakwena, Bangwaketse, Batawana, Bamalete, and Batlokwa. Gaborone is the Capital. Bechuanaland came under Brit. influence in 1885 in 1895 agreements were made whereby each chief should rule his own people under the protection of the sovereign represented by a resident commissioner. Botswana became fully independent within the Commonwealth in 1966. Area : 231,800 sq.m. Population 8,20,000.

Bourbon. A member of a French dynasty founded in 1272 to which belong the rules of France from 1589 to 1793 and from 1814 to 1830, of Spain from 1700 to 1808, from 1814 to 1868, from 1875 to 1931, and from 1975, of Naples from 1735 to 1805, and of the Two Sicilies from 1815 to 1860.

Bourbon. The term used for the European family that gave kings to Fr. and Spain. The name is taken from Bourbon I' Archamabault not far from Vichy in C.Fr. These lands came by mar. to a son of St. Louis (Louis IX). Antony, a later duke, was the father of Henry who, in 1589, became the 1st Bourbon king of Fr. He and his descendants ruled until 1789 and again from 1814-48. The Bourbons were also kings of Spain from 1700 to 1931, ruled Naples, 1735-1860, and Parma, 1748-1859.

Bourgeoisie. (*a*) Refers to the middle classes, (*b*) in Marxist philosophy. This term refers to the ruling class of the two basic classes of capitalist society, the other being the proletariat (working class). The bourgeoisie includes bankers, capitalists, manufacturers and other employers, owning the most important of the means of production, with which it exploits the proletariat.

Bourguiba, Habib Ben Ali. Tunisian statesman. He became PM (1956) when Tunisia gained independence, and President (1957-87). His moderate socialism found favour in France, and a close trading relationship get developed between both countries.

Boxers. Organisation in China prior to 1900. Its aim was to drive exploiting foreigners from the country. In 1900 the 'boxers' marched on Peking, where they assailed the foreign legations. On Aug. 14 a relieving force entered Peking and the Rising was put down. The rebellion proved to the Chinese the necessity of reform, and China became a Republic, 1911.

Brahma. First person of the Hindu Trimurti (Brahma, Vishnu, Shiva), the Creator, Brahmanism. Hindu religion. It is a modification of Vedaism which is of very ancient origin. Its scriptures comprise 4 sacred inspired books, *viz*: the *Rigveda, Samaveda, Ajurveda*, and *Atharvaveda*. Two fundamentals of doctrine have been (1) *Karma* (causation) the law by which the individual reaps the results of his actions, good, or evil; (2) *Reincarnation*, the doctrine of progressive re-birth, *viz*; that the soul uses not one but many physical bodies in its progress from savage to sainthood, and that reincarnation ceases only when the soul is merged in a greater consciousness.

Brahmanism. The orthodox Hinduism adhering to the pantheism of the Vedas and to the ancient sacrifices and family ceremonies.

Brandt Willy. German statesmen. Mayor of West Berlin from 1957 until 1966, when he became the first Social Democratic Chancellor of the Federal Republic of Germany. He remained in this post until 1974. The Brandt Report set a world development programme, and in 1971 he was awarded the Nobel Peace Prize for trying to improve relations with the countries of E. Europe.

Brandt Report. (1979). A paper prepared by the Independent Commission of International Development Issues, under the chairmanship of Willy Brandt. The investigation leading to the Report was carried out by a group of international statesmen and leaders from many spheres from 19 countries, the UK's representative being Edward Heath.

The long and complex Report detailed long-term reforms required by 2000 and priority programmers for the 1980s in order to avert an imminent economic crisis. It proposed a new approach to international finance and development of the monetory system, and emphasized the anomalous situation created by the vast expenditure on armaments taking resources away from the urgent needs to Third World countries which have been desperately improverished and have millions living below starvation level. Energy, food and trade were all discussed emphasis being placed on the mutual interests of the industrialized and Third World nations, and the Report put forward proposals to reverse the decline in trade and the revival of the world economy.

Brazzaville Declaration (1944). It got resulted from a meeting in the French Congo between members of the Fighting French (see Free French) and Frence's African colonies for discussing postwar relationships. The Declaration was including proposals for the establishment of assemblies in each colony; the indivisibility of the empire; colonial participation in elections for the French parliament; equal rights of colonial subjects as citizens of the French Republic; economic reforms; and the progression of native populations in public services.

Brest-litovsk. Treaty of (1918). The term used for the peace agreement between the Central Powers and Bolshevik Russia, under which the Russians lost Finland, Poland, the Baltic States, the Caucasus, the Ukraine and White Russia. The treaty got invalidated later in the year by the ending of WWI.

Bretton Woods Conference (1944). The agreement reached in New Hampshire, USA, by 28 nations for establishing a World Bank and an International Monetary Fund (IMF), with the object of preventing financial crisis developing like those which had taken place in the interwar years. The Bank was to advance loans for major projects designed to aid a country's development. The Fund was to operate a system of cash reserves on which members states could rely to meet balance-of-payments deficits.

Brezhnev, Leonid (1906-82). Soviet statesman who remained President of the Supreme Soviet from 1960 to 1964 when he succeeded Khrushchev as First Secretary of the Communist Party emerging as principal ruler of a collective leadership. He resumed the Presidency (1977), retaining his party offices and policy-marking role.

He established the principle called the 'Brezhnev Doctrine' in defence of the Soviet invasion of Czechoslovakia (1968), stating that a socialist state must intervene in another socialist state's affairs must its socialism gets threatened by internal or external attack or subversion. His period of office was notable for the growth of Detente in the 1970s, and its decline following the Soviet invasion of Afganistan (1979).

Briand, Aristide. (1862-1932). French statesman who was originally a socialist but, on entering parliament (1902), inclined towards radicalism. He happened to be responsible for the separation of church and state (1905) and remained 11 times PM between 1909 and 1929, but such was the instability of government during this period, his tenureship of the office only totalled 58 months.

Brigade. 1. A large body of troops; 2. A lactical and administrative millitary unit composed of a headquarters, one or more fighting units (*e.g.*, of infantry battalions or armoured regiments) and supporting units.

Britain. Name for Eng. Wales and Scot. form Rom, times to the coming of the Angles and Saxons in the 5th cent. It comes prob. from the Brythons, a Celtic people, and in the form Britannia was given to the land by the Roms. See England; Scotland; Wales; N. Ireland. Britain, Battle of German air offensive begun on August 8, 1940, against S.E. Eng., and London and intended to prepare the way for a seaborne invasion. The Brit. defending force was outnumbered, but the German air losses were so heavy that the operation was abandoned. Speaking in Parl., on Aug., 20, the P.M (Winston Churchill) said: "Never in the field of human conflict was so much owned by so many to so few".

British Commonwealth of Nations. The Free association of U.K. and ex-colonies. Includes Australia, New Zealand, Canada, India and many African and Asian states. Some territories (including Gibraltar, Hong Kong and Bermuda) and U.K depedencies.

Briton. A member of any of the peoples inhabiting Britain before the Anglo-Saxon invasions.

Bronze. General name for copper-tin alloys, which include gun metal, bell metal and speculum metal. The colour and properties vary according to the proportions of the constituents, but ordinary bronze is harder and stronger than brass and is easily worked. Bronze age—Period between the Stone Age and the Iron Age when man used bronze for his tools. In the E, it may have begun *c*. 5000 B.C. and in the W. perhaps *c*. 2000 B.C. and continued until *c*. 1000 B.C.

Bronze Age. The period of human culture between the Stone Age and Iron Age characterized by the use of bronze or copper tools and weapons.

Bruning, Heinrich. (1885-1970). German statesman, Chancellor (1930-32). His expertise as an economist prompted President Hindenburg to appoint him Chancellor in an effort to stabilize the economy and halt the rise in popular appeal of the Nazi Party. Without a Reichstag majority he governed by Presidential decree, thereby undermining the democratic process and favouring the progression to power of the Nazis who forced his resignation.

Brutus. Cognomen of several Roms. The word means fool, and was given to Lucius Junius because the pretended to be mad in order to save his life. He drove the unpopular Tarquin kings from Rome. He sentenced his own sons to *d*., for conspiring to restore the Tarquins. A later Brutus (Marcus Junius) was one of the munderers of Julius Caesar. When civil war broke out the sided with Pompey. Induced by Cassius to join in the plot against the dictator, he helped in the murder. He was one of the leaders of the force defeated by Caesar's friends at Philippi, and committed suicide (42 B.C.).

Buckingham Palace. Royal residence in London. George III brought it, 1761, and, 1825, its reconstruction was begun by Nash. Sir Astion Webb designed a new front , 1913.

Buddha. Siddhartha Gotama also called Sakyamuni, the founder of Buddhism. It is a generic title, for there have been many Buddhas, of whom Gotama was the latest, but not necessarily the last. He was the son of the Chief of the Sakyas, and was *b. c.* 621 B.C. At the age of 28 he experienced a profound religious change which caused him to leave his wife, and child, and devote himself to a life of poverty and asceticism. He became a full Buddha in 592 B.C., began to teach and soon gained disciples. Buddhism-Religious system and philosophy taught by the Buddha. The dominant religion of Sri Lanka, it is still found in parts of India, in the Lamaism of Tibet, in S.E. Asia, in China, and in Japan. Man is conceived to be an individualised self-conscious being linked irrevocably to the One Universal Cause. The aim of Buddhism is the achievement of *Nirvana* and the kernel of its ethics has been the Buddha'a Noble Eightfold Path, namely—(1) right comprehension (freedom from prejudices illusions and superstitions), (2) right resolution (pressing forward to the higher goal), (3) right speech (kindly, faithful, true), (4) right conduct (peace-loving, honest, pure), (4) right living (harmless livelihood, hurting no living thing), (6) right effort (perseverance in well-doing), (7) right meditation (intellectual activity, always directed to Rule and Doctrine), (8) Right rapture (intense reflection, the mind being wholly withdrawn from things of time and sense). As in Hinduism, the first of the two doctrines fundamental to Buddhism is that of *Reincarnation*. The second important doctrine is that of *Karma*. Thoughts and actions react upon the individual soul according to whether they have been energised constructively or destructively, and reward and punishments are of man's own making according to whether he serves the forces of good or evil.

Buffer State. A small and usually neutral country between two rival powers, *e.g.* Poland prior to WWII acted as a buffer state between Germany and the USSR.

Buffer Zone. A neutral area separating conflicting forces; *broadly* an area designed to separate.

Bulganin Nikolai. (1895-1975). Soviet soldier and politician. He organized Moscow's defence against the German onslaught (1941) and was created a Marshal of the Soviet Union at the end of WWII. In 1946 he succeeded Stalin as Minister of Defence. He was Vice-Premier (1953-55) and PM (1955-58) when he was deposed by Khrushchev. Later that year Bulganin was dropped from the Party Presidium and became chairman of the State Bank.

Burg. An ancient or medieval fortress or walled town.

Bushman. A member of a race of nomadic hunters of southern Africa.

C

Cabinet. (*a*) The executive and policy-making body of a country, consisting of senior ministers, (*b*) The advisory council to a head of State.

Cabinet Minister. A minister who is a member of the cabinet.

Cacique. 1. An Indian chief in areas dominated primarily by a Spanish culture. 2. A local political boss in Spain and Latin America.

Caesar. 1. Any of the Roman emperors who succeeded Augustus Caesar-used as a title. 2. Gius Julius 100-44 B.C. Roman general, statesman, and historian. Caesar conquered Gaul (58-50 B.C.). invaded Britain (55-54 B.C.), and ignoring the senate's order to relinquish his military command crossed the Rublicon and invaded Italy (49 B.C), defeating Pompey's army at Pharsalus. He became dictator in 48 B.C. and was made dictator for life, 44 B.C. Caesar began the reconstruction of the state after the civil war, enlarged the senate to include the provincials, began a digest of Roman law, founded colonies along the Mediterranean coast, restructured the calendar, introduced public libraries, and wrote a history of his wars in Gaul which is admired as a model of dignity and clarify of style. Brutus and Cussius murdered him in the Senate on 15th March.

Caesariam. The political absolutism; dictatorship, imperialism.

Caetano, Marcelo (1906-80). The Protuguese politician. He was President of the National Union, the only permitted political party, Deputy PM (1955-58), and succeeded Salazar as PM (1968-74). He was removed from power by a military coup.

Cairo Conference (1943). The meeting between Chiang Kai-shek, Churchill and Roosevelt during WWII when war Aims for the Far East were approved. These included Japanese unconditional surrender and the surrender by Japan of territories acquired since 1894, which would either be restored to China or become independent. At the Conference strategic discussions also occurred between Churchill and Roosevelt and these were resumed after the Teheran Conference.

Calendar. Systematic division of the year into months and days. Assuming a 365- ¼ day year, Julius Caesar introduced the Julian calendar in 45 B.C. distributing 365 days as at present and inserting an additional day every 4th year as did the ancient Egyptians. The solar year is actually short of this by 11- ¼ mins.; in 1582, therefore, the Old Style was inaccurate by 10 days. Gregory XIII then suppressed the surplus days and ordained that no closing year of a cent.-should be bissextile unless divisible by 400. This Gregorian or New Style was adopted by Britain in 1752. New calendar were introduced in the France Revolution and in Russia in 1929. The Christian calendar starts from the alleged birth-year of Christ; the Mohammedan from the Hegira, or flight of Mohammed to Medina, in the 622nd year of the Christian era.

Calendar Year. A period of year beginning and ending with the dates that are conventionally accepted as marking the beginning and end of numbered year (*e.g.*, January 1 and December 31 in the Gregorian calendar).

Caliph. Title applied first to Mohammed's successor Abu Bekr, as head of the Islamic state and defender of the faith, A.D. 632 Omayyad rulers in Spain, 755-1031, and Fatimide rulers in Egypt, 909-1171, called themselves caliphs. The title passed to Turkey *c.* 1362. In 1924 it was abolished by the national assembly at Ankara.

Cambrian (of or being). The earliest geological period of the Palaeozoic era or the corresponding system of rocks marked by fossils of every great animal type except the vertebrate and by barely recognizable plant fossils.

Cameralism. The mercantilism of a group of 18th-century German public administrators emphasizing economic policies designed to strengthen the power of the ruler.

Campaign for Nuclear Disarmament (CND). The organization founded (1958) to agitate for the UK's unilateral abandonment of nuclear weapons. In the early years it attracted considerable radical, and mostly youthful, support, largely devoted to public demonstrations which annually culminated in a march from the Atomic Weapons

Research Establishment at Aldermaston, Berkshire to a rally in Trafalgar Square, London. After the signing of the Nuclear Test-Ban Treaty (1963) the CND's popularity waned, although a revival in strength started in 1980.

Campbell-Bannerman, Sir Henry (1836-1908). British statesman, Liberal PM (1905-8). His administration initiated trade-union legislation and land reforms, and followed a policy of reconciliation following the Boer War, granting the Boers self-government in the Transvaal and Orange Free State.

Camp David Agreement (1978). The accord reached at the US President's Maryland retreat between Egypt's President Sadat and the Israeli PM, Begin, promoting a Middle East settlement on which was based a peace treaty signed in Washington (1979). President Carter of the USA acted as mediator.

The agreement provided for the signing of a treaty within 3 months; the establishment of diplomatic and economic relations; for phased Israeli withdrawal from Sinai and demilitarized security zones along the frontier; and the development of a degree of Palestinian autonomy on the Jordan's West Bank within 5 years.

Camp Follower. 1. A civilian, *esp* a prostitute, who follows a military unit to attend or exploit military personnel. 2. A follower who is not the main body of members of adherents; *esp* a politician who joins a party or movement solely for personal gain.

Cannan. (O.F) Name of one of Noah's grandsons (Gen. 4), and of the land later called Palestine.

Cananite. A member of a Semitic people inhabiting ancient Palestine and Phoenicia from about 3000 B.C.

Cantonment. (A group of temporary structures for) the quartering of troops.

Canute. Name of several Danish Kings. Canute I, called the Great, became King of Denmark in 1014 and claimed the throne of Eng., won by his father, Sweyn. After a struggle with Edmund Ironside he became king.

Cape Coloured. A person of mixed black and white ancestry South Africa.

Capitalism. The term used for an economic system which is based on private ownership of the means of production, distribution and exchange (capital), characterized by the freedom of the owners of capital (capitalists) to manage to operate their property for profit in competitive conditions.

Caporetto, Battle of (1917). The scene of an Italian defeat by Austro-German forces on the River Isonzo. It was one of the greatest disasters suffered by the Allied armies during WWI, some 300,000 Italians being taken prisoner and even more deserting.

The village of Caporetto was Austrian until the end of WWI, when it became Italian. It was ceded to Yugoslavia (1947) and renamed Kobarid.

Capsian. Of a Palaeolithic culture of northern Africa and southern Europe.

Caractacus. King of the Silures, a British tribe. After defying Rome for 9 years, he was defeated near the Wrekin *c.* A.D. 50. He took refuge with the Queen of the Brigantes, who, however, gave him up.

Carib Indians. Race of S. Amer. Indians. They inhabited the southern W. Indies at the time of Columbus (1492). Tall and of ruddy-brown complexion, they are now confined to the shores of the Caribbean Sea.

Carlos I. (1863-1908) King of Portugal. In 1907 he suspended the constitution and the next year was murdered in Lisbon. His younger son, Manoel, was deposed in 1910, when a Repub. was proclaimed.

Carol. Name of 2 kings of Rumania. Carol I (1839-1914). In 1966 he was elected Prince of Rumania and was made king, 1881. Was succeeded by his nephew Ferdinand. Carlo II (1893-1953) the son of Ferdinand. He twice renounced his claim to the throne. mar. Princess Helen of Greece, 1921, of which was *b.* a son, Prince Michael. In 1926 he again renounced the right to succession but changed his mind, returned to Rumania, 1930, deposing his son who had reigned since 1927, and was accepted King. He abdicated, 1940.

Carolingian. A member of a Frankish dynasty dating from about A.D. 613 and including among its members the rulers of France from 751 to 987, of Germany form 752 to 911, and of Italy from 774 to 961.

Carter, James ('Jimmy') (1924-). US Democratic President (1977-81). In the Presidential election he defeated Gerald Ford, but was himself defeated in 1980 by Ronald Reagon. He was successful in mediating between Egypt and Israel, resulting in the Camp David Agreement. He was a champion of human rights abroad, and continued the policy of detente until the Soviet invasion of Afaghanistan (1979).

Casablanca Conference (1943). The meeting between Churchill and Roosevelt during which plans got discussed for the termination of the war in N. Africa; the invasion of Sicily; and the increase in the bombing of Germany; the transfer of UK war resources to the Far East after the surrender of the Axis powers, which was to be unconditional and not subject to negotiations; and preparation for a second from later in the year.

Casimir. 1310-1370. The Great King of Poland (1333-70) who codified the country's laws.

Cassius Longinus, Gaius. Rom. gen. and politician. He led the conspiracy against Caesar and was present at his association, 44 B.C. Defeated by Antony at Phillippi, he compelled his servant to slay him, 42 B.C.

Caste. Any of the hereditary social groups in Hinduism that restrict the occupation of their members and their association with the members of other castes.

Castro, Fidel (1927-). Cuban Communist politician. He came to prominence when he led an unsuccessful uprising against Batista's oppressive regime (1953). He fled to the USA and Mexico where he organized a revolutionary movement, returning secretly to Cuba (1956) with a group which included Guevara Waging guerrilla warfare he became something of a legendary figure, attracting more and more followers and achieving increasing successes over Batista's forces.

After capturing Havana he became PM and Minister of the Armed Forces (1959). He introduced far-reaching reforms in agriculture, education and industry and strengthened ties with China and the USSR, as well as endeavouring to promote revolutions in Latin America and encouraging Africa liberation movements, notably, in Angola where thousands of Cuban troops are based.

Catherine. The name of 1st, 5th, and 6th wives of Henry VIII of England: Catherine of Aragon 1485-1536; Catherine Howard

1520?—1542; Catherine Parr 1512-1548.

Catherine I. (1684-1727). Empress of Russia. She became the mistress of Peter the Great and in 1711 his wife. When Peter *d.* she was raised to the throne (1725). Catherine II (1729-96) Empress of Russia. In 1745 she mar. Peter, heir to the Russian throne. In 1761 Peter became Czar, but in 1762 was murdered and his widow took his place. Catherine greatly increased the area and power of Russia. She carried out many humanitarian reforms.

Catherine II (1729-1796). *The Great* empress of Russia (1762-96).

Caucasian. The white race of mankind as classified according to physical features.

Cella. The principal chamber of a Roman temple containing the shrine to the divinity; *broadly* the main body of any classical building-compare Naos.

Celt. 1. A member of a division of the early Indo-European peoples distributed from the British Isles and Spain to Asia Minor. 2. A modern Gael, Highland Scot, Irishman, Welshman, Cornishman, or Breton.

CENTO. See Central Treaty Organization.

Central Intelligence Agency (CIA). US security organization which has been established (1947) to conduct and coordinate espionage and intelligence operations. Responsible to the National Security Council, it also plans secret operations for such purposes as the overthrow of government or the downfall of persons hostile to the US and its allies. Successes as in Guatemala, Iran (both 1953-54), and Chile (1973) have been matched by disasters, such as the Bay of Pigs, the failure to predict in 1973 Arab-Israeli War and the 1974 Cyprus crisis, and the Watergate Affair, which revealed that the CIA, among other government agencies is having infringed civil liberties.

Central Powers. The collective term for Austria-Hungary, Germany and Italy, founder members of the Triple Alliance, established in 1882, joined in 1883 by Romania and during WWI by Bulgaria and Turkey, but left by Italy in 1914 and by Romania in 1916.

Although the number of Alliance members fluctuated during the War and finally resolved itself into a membership of 4, the term was retained to differentiate members of the Alliance from Britain, France and Russia, members of the Triple Entente. Italy and Romania eventually joined the Triple Entente members in fighting against their old allies of the Triple Alliance.

Before 1914 the Triple Alliance and Triple Entente had effectively divided Europe into 2 armed camps, thereby nurturing an atmosphere of secrecy and suspicion which developed into a contributory cause of WWI.

Central Treaty Organization (CENTO). The economic and military alliance formed by Iran, Pakistan, Turkey and the UK in 1959, with the US as an associated member. It superceded the Baghdad Pact, which got dissolved following Iraq's withdrawal. Iran, Pakistan and Turkey withdrew in 1979, and the organization was effectively dissolved.

Cetewayo, Cetywayo (1836-1884). Zulu chief who defeated the British at Isandhlwana (1879).

Chad. Republic of equational Africa, former Fr. Possession. Indep. 1960. Cap. Ndjamena. Area : 495,800 sq.m. Population. 4,309,000.

Chadwick, Sir James. F.R.S. (1891-1974). Physicist. Master of Gonville and Caius Coll., Camb. He discovered the *neutron* (*q.v*).

Chaffinch. (*Fringilla coelebs*) British songbird which breeds throughout British and North Europe. The ashy-brown female, usually migrates South without the male. The male, 6 in. long, with reddish breast, forked tail-feathers, has sharp or sweet call notes.

Chalcedony. Semi-previous stone. A cryptocrystalline quartz mixed with opline silica. This commonest of gem stones occurs as agate, bloodstone, carnelian, chrysoprase and onyx.

Chaldea. Biblical place name. It denoted in O.T. times the marshy sealand S.E. of Babylonia. Later a Chaldean or neo-Babylonian dynasty was estab, by Nabopolassar *c.* 625, and throughout this period, Chaldea denoted all Babylonia.

Chaliapin, Feodor Ivanovitch. (1873-1938). Russian operatic singer B. Kazan. First appeared in St. Petersburg in 1894. He won fame as the greatest of all Russian singers.

Chalk. White, earthy variety of limestone, containing 94-98% of calcium carbonate. It comprises mostly minute shells laid down in shallow waters across Europe during the Cretaceous period. It is burned for lime used in making Portland cement and, when levigated, whiting. The Downs and other hills in the south of England are of chalk.

Chalmers, Thomas. (1780-1847). Scot.divine. In 1815 he removed to Glasgow, where he wrote his *Problems of Poverty*. A leader of the Disruption in 1843, he became the first moderator of the Free Ch.

Chalons-Sur-Marne. Cap. of Marne Dept. *c.* 100 m.E. of Paris, on the Marne. It is a centre of the champagne trade Nearby in A.D. 451,. the Huns, under Attila, were defeated by the Roms. and Visigoths. Population 55,700.

Chamberlain Joseph. (1836-1914). England statesman. M.P. for Birmingham (Radical, later Unionist), 1876-1914; President of Local Government Board, 1886; resigned to form Lib. Unionists; Colonial Sec. 1895-1903. Mayor of Birmingham, 1873-76, he did much for the development of the city. He broke with Glandstone over Irish Home Rule. In 1895 he became Salisbury's Colonial Sec. His action in declaring for Tariff Reform split the Unionist party, and he resigned in 1904. His son was Arthur Neville (1869-1940) England statesman M.P. (Cons), 1918-40; Director of Nat. Service, 1916; Chancellor of the Exchequer, 1923-24 and 1931-37; P.M. 1937-40. On following Baldwin as PM in 1937 he had to deal with the threatening internat. situation. His negotiations with Hitler in 1938, and his general policy of 'appeasement' have been variously judged. His government fell in 1940, but for the remaining months of his life he served under Churchill.

Chambery. Capital of Savoiet Dept., E. Fr. A tourist centre, it manufactures silk and lace. Population: 54,000.

Chameleon. Family of lizards differing from true lizards in their telescopic tongues, eyeballs moving independently, opposable toes and prehensile tails. They are famed for their power of changing olour according to the environment. The common species, 12 in. long, ranges the African and Asiatic Medit. coasts.

Chaminade, Cecile Louise Stephanie. (1861-1944). Fr. composer, *b.* in Paris. Best known compositions are her songs and piano pieces.

Chamois. (*Rupicapra*). Animal of the Alps and other mt. areas of Europe and Asia Minor. Intermediate between antelopes and goats and remarkable for its jumping powers. Its average ht. is *c*. 2 ft. The skin is used for gloves etc.

Champagne. Prov. of Fr. before the Revolution, now comprising the depts. of Seine-Marne, Aube, Marne, Ardennes and Haute-Marne. The chief towns are Reims and Troyes. Champagne White sparking wine produced from blended wines and grapes grown in the Champagne district. of Fr. Fermentation takes place after the bottle has been sealed, hence the effervescence.

Champlain. Lake in the U.S.A. and Canada, between Vermont and New York States, discovered by the Fr. explorer Samuel de Champlain in 1609.

Chancellor. Name of several high officials. The chancellor in England became important about the time of Edward I, when he took the place of the justiciar as the chief min. When his duties were confined to legal matters he became Lord High Chanc. The exchequer had a chanc., at first a subsidiary official under the Lord High Treasurer. Other chances, are those of the Duchies of Lancaster and Cornwall. The Chanc. of a British University is usually a person of distinction in public life, while its vice-chancellor is the acting head. Chancery, Court of the Lord Chanc. dating from the time of Edward the Confessor. In 1873 the court was made 1 of the present 3 divisions of the High Court of Justice. It has jurisdiction over actions in which redress cannot be obtained at common law.

Channel Islands. Group of Islands off N.W. Fr. comprising Jersey, Guernsey (*q.v.*) Alderney, Brechou, Gt. and Little Sark, Herm, Jethou and Lihou. Formerly part of the Duchy of Normandy, they have been attached to England since the conquest (1066). They have a mild climate and fertile soil. Early flowers, fruit and vegetables are grown. Guernsey and Jersey cattle are famous. The chief towns are St. Helier (Jersey), St. Peter Port (Guernsey), and St. Anne's (Alderney). Area : 75 sq.m. Pop : 130,000.

Channel Swimming. The first man to swim the England channel was Capt. M. Webb, and Englishman, who swam from Dover to Calais in 21 hrs. 45 mins. on Aug. 25, 1875. The first woman was Gertrude Ederle in Aug. 1926. First two-way Channel swim by Antonio Abertondo in 43 hrs. 5 mins, (1961).

Channel Tunnel. Proposed tunnel between England and France. In 1876 a Co. was formed to carry out similar idea, but the work was stopped in 1882. In 1930 a committee reported in favour of the project. The Government decided against it. New reports from British and France cos. were put before their respective governments in 1964. Furthers discussions and reports followed.

Chantrey, Sir Francis. (1781-1841). England sculptor. He left £ 150,000 (the Chantrey Bequest) which enables the Pres. and Council of the Royal Academy every year to buy pictures and sculptures for the nation.

Chapel. Place devoted to Christian worship. In caths. and large chs. a chapel is a part of the building railed off from the main part and provided with an alter. Places of worships in colls. and schools are also called chapels. At one time Nonconformists used the word chapel for their places of worship.

Chaplain. Priest or min. officially discharging specific nonparochial duties. He may be attached to the sovereign, his representatives and defensive forces, or to institutions. There are 36 chaplains to the queen at the England court, and she has chaplains in Scot. There are chaplains at schools and colls., at embassies and prisons. There are Anglican, R.C. and Free Ch. chaplains in the British Navy, Army and Air Force.

Chaplin Charles. (1889-1977). Film artist B. London. Entered silent pictures in 1913 and formed his own Co. In 1918. He produced many notable pictures including *The Kid*, The *Gold Rush*, *The Great Dictator*. *Limelight*.

Chapman, George. (*c*. 1559-*c*. 1634). England dramatist and poet. Continued Marlowe's *Hero and Leander* (1598); comedies, as with Jonson and Marston) *Eastward Ho!* (1605); tragedies as *Bussy d' Ambois* (1607), *Revenge of Bussy d' Ambois* (1613). Tr. of the *Iliad* 1611, of the *Odyssey*, 1914-15.

Chapter. Permanent body of canons and prebendaries of the cath. or collegiate ch. presided over by the dean. It meets in the Chapter House.

Char. (*Salmo alphinus*) Salmon-like fish which frequents England lakes and lochs in Scot. and Ireland. It is valued as a table fish.

Charcoal. Residue obtained when carbonaceous material of animal or vegetable origin is burnt or heated to remove volatiles. Wood charcoal, an impure, amorphous form of carbon containing at least 93%, is a porous solid which, when burned as fuel, is flameless and smokeless. It is an ingredient in gun-powder, and serves also as a filter.

Charlemagne. (*c*. 742-814) Frankish king, later Emperor. Elder son of King Pepin, in 771. He became King of all the Franks. He waged war successfully against the Saxons, Lombards and Magyars, less successfully against the Saracens in Spain. He was crowned in 800, at Rome, as the 1st 'Holy Rom. Emperor'. His *Life* was written by his friend and sec., Einhard.

Charleroi. Industrial town in Hainaut prov. Belgium, 22 m.E. of Mons, connected by canal with Brussels and North France.

Chaco War. (1928-35). A conflict between Bolivia and Paraguay over possession of the Chaco Boreal, which is a plain between the Andes and the Paraguay River. The eventual settlement divided the territory more than 2 to 1 in favour of Paraguay but guranteed Bolivia access to the South Atlantic via the Paraguay River.

Chaldean. A member of an ancient Semitic people that became dominant in Babylonia.

Chalukya. A dynasty one should not get confused with Chalukya arising in the 6th century. A.D., centred in Kanarese-speaking country but extending at times as far north as the borders of Kathiawar. The empire lasted in one form or another until the end of the 12th century.

Chamberlain Neville (1869-1940). Conservative statesman, PM (1937-40). He was Chancellor of the Exchequer from 1931 until he succeeded Baldwin as PM (1937). As PM he followed a policy of appeasement towards Nazi Germany, and signed the Munich Agreement (1938). Although intended to avoid war, appeasement in fact encouraged Hitler's aggressive policies which led to WWII. Incompetence as a wartime leader led to his resignation in 1940.

Chanak Crisis (1922). Refers to the situation in Anglo-Turkish relations resulting from the ceding of the port of Smyrna (now Izmir) and Turkey's European territories to Greece by the Treaty of Sevres

(1920), which also got established a neutral zone between Greece and Turkey on the East side of the Dardanelles, the neutrality being subject to an Anglo-French guarantee.

A revolt led by Mustapha Kemal (Ataturk) against the Sultan resulted in Greece trying interfere on the Sultan's side, whereupon the rebels advanced on the Straits, after defeating the Greek army at Smyrna. This made the guarantee into effect but France withdrew its troops and the outnumbered UK force had to negotiate an armistice, resulting in the Turks accepting the neutralization of the Bosphorus and Dardanelles in return for the restoration of Adrtanpole and East Thrace and the ending of the Allied occupation of Constantinople (now Istanbul). The agreement formed the basis of the Treaty of Lausanne.

Within a fortnight of the armistice the UK coalition government remained out of office because the Conservative Party withdrew support, due to what was considered Lloyd George's pro-Greek stance during the Crisis and his irresponsibility in taking the UK to the brink of war with Turkey.

Chanakya (Kautilya). He was the Prime Minister of Chandragupta Maurya and an authority on Political Science during 4th century B.C. He wrote Arthashastra (Economics).

Chand Bibi. Daughter of Husain Nizamshah who got married to Ali Adil Shah of Bijapur, South India; after her husband's death she took over the administration of her state and ran it very smoothly till she remained the victim of an intrigue by her courtiers who imprisoned her in the fort of Satara; fell a marry while opposing the Mughals and was buried in a magnificent tomb at Gulbarga.

Chandidas. The great saint-poet of Bengal of medieval period. He was a devotee of Lord Krishna who sang earnestly for Him and was having a profound influence upon the Vaishnava Samaj of Bengal; a contemporary of Vidyapati and Jaideva; all the three saint poets got influenced by Chaitanya *Mahaprabhu*, the renowned religious thinker and reformer of Bengal.

Chandragupta Maurya (Ruled 321-297 BC). Founder of the Maurya dynasty of Magadha, considered to be the illegitimate son of the last Nanda by the low caste Mura from whom he adopted the designation 'Maurya', killed Nanda king and in 321 became the first king of the new Maurya dynasty, the whole of north India coming under his away. He soon took the remaining Greek provinces (in India) under Seleucos, who left the country but gave Chandragupta his daughter in marriage and Baluchistan and Afghanistan in dowry. What has been known about him and his government comes from the *Arthasastra*, or Treatise on Polity written by Chanakya, whom he made his chief minister and the *Indica* of Megasthenes, who was the Greek ambassador at his court. According to these sources, he was an autocratic ruler with an exceedingly strong army, an organised and disciplined bureaucracy and a rich kingdom with a settled and lucrative commerce. He was having a council of 8 ministers but was the supreme authority. A commissioner was in charge of each of the government departments of the army, finance, irrigation, agriculture and gardens, mint, roads, prisons, justice, religion, foreign affairs, textiles and yarn, shipping, chariots mines, metals, gold, the magazine and trade, etc. There a municipal board of 30 members and 6 city departments-one each for handicrafts (including wages and fraud), strangers and lodging arrangements, births and deaths, retail trade and licences, manufactures and collection of taxes. He has a formidable spy system and sinister methods of destroying enemies. Every section of government and public life was minutely supervised. Special servants were used to taste beforehand whatever he ate and drank to prevent his being poisoned. Jaina tradition says he renounced his throne and went to Belgola (in south India) where he got joined the Jain monk, Bhadrabahu, where he slowly starved himself to death as permitted to Jain monks after having completed 12 years of a truly ascetic life. This would be only a legend.

Chandragupta II (A.D. 380-415). The third ruler of the Gupta dynasty. He inherited the vast and powerful Gupta empire but soon got added the Western Saka satrapy to his domains, an outstanding victory which led him to add 'Vikramaditya' to his name. Fa Hien, the Chinese monk, who visited India during his reign gave an illuminating account of the times and the administration. Buddhism was in flourishing state especially in the north-west; the people were prosperous, happy and contented and were not exploited; there were hardly any official restrictions; laws were just and justice fairly and leniently administered and there was no death penalty; free hospitals for the poor and helpless were maintained in all important towns;

there were hospitals for animals also which were maintained by the Buddhist and Jain communities; free food and lodging was available for all travellers in wayside rest-houses; at Patliputra, the capital the magnificent palace was made of huge blocks of stone, beautifully carved and inlaid in intricate and wonderful designs.

Chandragupta had been a great patron of the arts, sciences, crafts and of learning. The marvellous, rustless iron pillar in the grounds of the Qutb Minar (at New Delhi) which was brought to this site from some unknown place in the 11th century, got associated with Chandragupta. The Sanskrit inscription on it mentions one king Chandra who had conquered Bengal and crossed the Indus and its tributaries and as it is in the early Gupta characters and the style of writing and the time seem to be those of Chandragupta's period, it has been regarded that the inscription refers to him.

Changez Khan (1162-1227). The world famous 13th century Mongol General; known previously as Temuchin, he became the Governor of north Gobi region at the age of 13 but had to face rebellion at the hands of his fellow chieftains; fighting valiently he was declared the Governor of Northern Asia and was given the title 'Changez Khan' (The Greatest Administrator, Emperor of the Humanity); Changez Khan gave the name 'Mongol' to all the tribes under his rule; also undertook the permanent military re-organisation of the Turks-Mongols and prepared a code of laws for the government of the tribes; in 1206 defeated his sole enemy Niaman Polo; organised in 1211 an invasion of China and extended his empire up to there; at the time of his death 1227 his empire extended up to north-west India and China; like Mahmud Ghazni, Changez Khan had been also a builder in addition to destroyer who, beside destroying many cultural centres and liquidating numerous empires, also built up a well-administered empire with an efficient intelligence system; he believed in the basic unity of religion and in the Almighty; his conquests caused the establishment of commercial and cultural contacts between the different regions and countries of Europe and Asia and gave rise to increased geographical knowledge.

Charles. Name of 7 rulers of the Holy Rom. Emp. The 1st was Charles the Great or Charlemagne. The 2nd, his grandson, Charles the Bald. He obtained the W. part of the Frankish realm in 843. Charles IV (*d.* 1378) was also recognised as king in Germany and in 1355 was crowned emperor. Charles VI (1685-1740) was a son of Leopold I. In 1711 he succeeded his brother Joesph as Emperor (Maria Theresa, was his daughter).

Charles. (1433-77). Last Duke of Burgundy called the Bold. Son of Philip the Good, Duke of Burgundy. He waged war against the France kings.

Charles V. (1500-58). Holy Rom. Emperor and King of Spain. B. Ghent, the elder son of Philip, son of the Emperor Maximilian, and Joanna, daughter of Ferdinand and Isabella of Sp. Became Emperor, 1520, the most powerful ruler in Europe. He crushed Francis of Fr. and once imprisoned the Pope. After attempts to reconcile the bitterness of the Reformation in Germany, he broke the power of the German princess. Abdicated 1556, leaving Spain to his son Philip II. Don John, the hero of Lepanto, was an illegitimate son.

Charles. Name of 10 kings of France. The Emperor Charlemagne (*q.v.*), was the 1st and the Emperor Charles the Fat the 2nd. Charles VI reigned 1380-1422. In his reign, Henry V of England conquered France and succeeded Charles as king. Charles VII, *d.* 1464, was crowned king after the victories of Joan of Arc in 1439. Charles VIII, *d.* 1498, a son of Louis XI, became king in 1483. He tried to get possession of Naples and other parts of Italy. Charles X (1757-1836) was a brother of Louis XVI and reigned from 1824-30, when he abdicated.

Charles. Name of 4 kings of Spain. Charles II, a son of Philip IV, was king 1665-1700. On his *d.* without heirs, a European war broke out for possession of his empire. Charles III, a son of Philip V, was king 1759-88. He was the 3rd of the Bourbon kings of Spain.

Charles. Name of 15 kings of Sweden. Charles XII (1682-1718). He defeated the Danes and Russians and made himself master of Poland and Saxony. In 1708 he invaded Russia, but in 1709 was routed at Poltava by Peter the Great. He was killed while attacking a fortress in Norway. In the reign of Charles XIII, Norway was united to Sweden. He *d.* 1818, having recognised the Fr. Marshal Bernadotte as his heir. Charles XIV (1764-1844) King of Sweden and Norway. B. Jean Baptiste Jules Bernadotte, he became a gen. in the France army, attracting the notice of Napoleon. In 1810 he was offered the Swedish throne, and became king in 1818. The present royal family is descended from him.

Charles. (1771-1847). Aust. prince and soldier, younger son of the Emperor Leopold II. He won several victories over the Fr. 1796-99, but was defeated 1799, in Switzerland. In 1809 he defeated Napoleon at Aspern.

Charles. (1887-1922). Last emperor of Austria-Hungary. The murder of the Archduke Francis Ferdinand in June, 1914, made him heir and, on the *d.* of Francis Joseph in Nov. 1916. he succeeded. He abdicated at the end of World War I.

Charles I. (1600-49). King of Gt. Brit. and Ireland, 2nd son of James VI of Scot. (I of Brit.). In 1625 he became king and mar. Henrietta Maria, a France R.C. princess. His wife's religion his friends, extravagance and obstinacy and his attempts to force episcopacy on Scot. made him unpopular. From 1629-40 he ruled without Parl., raising money illegally. In 1642 civil war broke out and after defeat at Naseby, Charles gave himself up to the Scots, who handed him over to Parl. He was tried and beheaded. Two of his sons became king.

Charles II. (1630-85). King of Gt. Brit. and Ireland, 2nd son of Charles I. Went into exile, 1676, on his father's defeat. In 1650, accepted the throne of Scot. and invaded England., was defeated and went again into exile. Issued the Declaration of Breda (1660) and returned to Brit. as king. He is remembered for his mistresses and his interest in art and science. Events included the Great Plague, and Fire of London.

Charles Edward. (1720-88). Called 'Bonnie Prince Charlie'. Stewart prince, known as the 'Young Pretender', and, to the Jacobites, as Charles III. Elder son of James Edward, the 'Old Pretender'. His attempt to recover the throne in 1745 failed, ending with defeat at Culloden.

Chauhan, Prithvi Raj. Also known as Raj Pithora, king of Delhi, Ajmer and Sambhar in 12th century; defeated the Ghuri invader Shihabuddin at the battle of Tarain in A.D. 1192; failed to pursue him; was defeated by Ghuri invader in second battle in 1193 at Tarain and was killed; known for his valour and bravery; his exploits recorded by famous bard Chand Bardai in his work *'Chand Raisa.'*

Cheka. The Soviet secret police organisation between 1917 and 1922.

Chiang Kai-Shek. (1887-1975). Chinese polit. In 1926 he led the Nanking, forces to the capture of Peking. He became Pres., of the Executive Yuan, 1935-45; President of China, 1943; re-elected in 1948, Director-Gen. of the Nationalist Kuomintang Party, 1938, he led the Chinese resistance to Jap. aggression, but was unsuccessful against the Chinese communist forces under Mao Tse-tung, 1951. He withdrew his forces from the mainland to Formosa in 1949. His wife, Madame Chinag Kai-shek, a distinguished sociologist, accompanied her husband on many of his military campaigns. She did much war relief work for women, refugees and the wounded. In 1943 she toured the U.S.A. and Canada making speeches, and took a prominent part in the conference at Delhi in 1942 and Cairo in 1943.

Ching, Ch'ing. A Manchu dynasty in China dated 1644-1912 and the last imperial dynasty.

Chishti, Salim, Shaikh. A great sufi saint of Chishti order; lived during the time of Akbar (1556-1605); prophesied three sons to Akbar who named his eldest son Salim after him; Akbar built a new city near saint's dwelling place Sikri and called it Fatehpur Sikri.

Chou En-lai. (1898-1976). Chinese statesman. He received at Western educ., at Tientsin. After the student riots of 1919 he was sent to prison. In Paris in 1921 took part in forming the first branch of the Chinese Communist Party abroad. In 1931 he joined the Red army in China and became vice-chairman of the Revolutionary Military Council, working with Mao Tse-tung. During the struggle against Japan he held office under Chinag-Kai-Shek in Chung-king (1938-40). In 1949 Chou En-lai became Premier and Foreign Minister of the first all-China Communist government under Mao Tse-tung.

Chrisitian Era. The period dating from the birth of Christ.

Christianity. The religion derived from Jesus Christ, based on the Bible as sacred scripture, and professed by Eastern, Roman Catholic, and Protestant bodies.

Chronology. A system for setting past events in order of occurrence; *specif* such a system for recording historical events that has an epoch (*e.g.* the traditionally accepted date for the birth of Christ) and regular division of time (*e.g.*, years).

Churchill, Sir Winston Leonard Spencer. (1874-1965). England statesman. M.P. (Cons). 1900-6, (Lib) 1902-22, (Cons.) 1924-64; Colonial Under-Sec. 1905-8; Home Sec. 1910-11; 1st Lord of the Admiralty, 1911-15; Munitions Min. 1917-18; War Sec. 1919-21; Chanc. of the Exchequer, 1924-29; 1st Lord of the Admiralty. 1939-40; P.M. and Defence Min. 1940-45; Leader of the Opposition, 1945-51. P.M. 1951-55. In 1906 he left the Unionist Party over the question of Tariff Reform, returning in 1924, having been a successful Lib. min. During the '30's he gave constant warning of the German menace. In 1939 he returned to the Admiralty. On the development of the German W. offensive of 1940 and the Dunkirk Evacuation the Chamberlain Government was replaced by a Coaliation under Churchill. He rallied the nation and led it to victory over Germany and Japan. Created K.G. April, 1953.

The Conservative Party was defeated in the 1945 election, and Churchill did not achieve power again until 1951 when he once more became PM, finally resigning in 1955.

CIA. See Central Intelligence Agency.

Ciano, Count Galeazzo (1903-44). Italian Diplomat politician and Mussolini's son-in-law. As Foreign Minister (1936-43), he developed Italo-German relations but, realizing German war aims, became anti-Nazi. Failing to change Mussolini's policies, he voted against him in the Fascist Grand Council (1943) for which he was tried for treason and executed.

Cincinnatus. Lucius Quinctius 51 ?-435 BC. Roman general and statesman, twice dictator.

Cinerarium *n, pl* **Cineraria.** A place to receive the ashes of the cremated dead.

Circassian. A member of group of people of the Caucasus of Caucasian race but not of Indo-European speech.

Civil Defence. The organizing of civilians to deal with enemy attacks.

Civil Disobedience. (*a*) The refusal to obey laws, pay taxes, etc., (*b*) The non-violent method of protest or attempt to achieve political aims.

Civil Liberties. The rights of individuals to certain freedoms of action and speech, the important of which have been the freedoms of assembly, association, conscience, publication, speech, worship, and peaceful demonstration, petition or protest.

Civil Rights. (*a*) The personal rights of citizens upheld by law in most countries. (*b*) The equality of status between groups or races.

Clattonian. Of a Palaeolithic culture characterized by flint makes with a half cone at the point of striking.

Class. The category or grouping of people according to economic, occupational or social status. In Marxist theory, the term refers exclusively to those persons which a common relationship to material production (see Bourgeoisie and Prolateriat). Traditionally, society has been divided into the upper, middle and working (lower) classes, according to socio-economic status.

Claudius. The full name Tiberius Claudius Drusus Nero Germanicus 10 BC-AD 54 Roman emperor (41-54).

Clemenceau, Georges. (1841-1929). French Radical statesman, PM (1906-09 and 1917-1920). His first ministerial appointment was Minister of Home Affairs (1906) and by the year end he was PM. He was defeated (1909) because of his failure to expand the navy without having achieved many of the reforms he desired.

During WWI he was critical of the way it was being conducted and in 1917 became PM and minister of War. He inspired the armed forces and civilian population to resist the final German onslaught and assume the offensive, and played a major part in negotiating the Treaty of Versailles. His intransigent hatred of Germany contributed to the harshness of the terms of the Treaty, which were possibly contributory factors in the outbreak of WWII.

Cleopatra. (69-30 BC). Queen of Egypt. She became, in 51 BC joint ruler of Egypt. In 48 BC she was driven out, but Caesar restored her. After his *d.* she became the mistress of Mark Antony. This was one of the causes of the war between Antony and Octavian. After Antony's defeat and *d.* Cleopatra killed herself. Cleopatra's Needles have been 2 obelisks erected at Heliopolis *c.* 1500 BC. In 1878 one of these was brought to London and erected on the Victoria Embankment.

CND. See Campaign for Nuclear Disarmament.

Coalition Government. The alliance or union between 2 or more political parties for some specific or temporary reason, usually in order to form a government where no party has an absolute majority.

Cold War. A conflict, esp between nations, carried on by methods short of military action and use without breaking off diplomatic relations.

Cold War. The state of military tension and diplomatic and political hostility between 2 countries or power blocs, esp., that between the US and the USSR and their respective allies since WWII.

The Cold War has been involving propaganda, subversion, threats, etc., and it has been characterized by assertive actions with limited objectives which have not been permitted to develop into direct military conflict, *e.g.*, the invasions of Hungary, Czechoslovakia and Afghanistan; the Suez Crisis; the Cuban Missiles Crisis; the Berlin blockade and wall; the Arab-Israeli Wars; and Lebanon. The attempts by both sides to achieve detente have met with only limited success.

Collaboration. Refers to the act of cooperating with an enemy, esp. one occupying one's own country.

Collective Security. A system of maintaining global peace and security by concerted action on the part of the nations of the world, or in a limited area, by members of an association of states.

Collectivization. (*a*) The organization under collective control; (*b*) a social systèm based on the principle of the ownership of the means of production by a state, *e.g.*, a collective farm (kolkhoz) in a Communist country. The system got opposed in the USSR in the 1930s by the kulaks, former peasant who had been allowed to become medium-sized farm owners before the Revolution. In order to achieve the First Five-Year Plan, Stalin ordered the liquidation of the kulaks and about 10 million have been thought to have died.

Collins, Michael. (1890-1922). Irish politician and Sinn Fein leader who got participated in the Easter Rising. After WWI he organized the Irish Republican Army (IRA) and was a delegate to the London Conferençe (1921) which agreed to the establishment of Southern Ireland as the Irish Free State, of which he became first PM. He got assassinated (1922) by a faction within the IRA which got opposed the Conference agreements.

Colombo Plan. The proposals which were initiated in 1950 at a

Commonwealth ministers' meeting in Colombo, Ceylon (now Sri Lanka) for cooperative economic development of under-developed Commonwealth countries in S and SE Asia. Details got agreed at a Colombo meeting of the Commonwealth consultative Committee (1951) by which the principal recipients of economic advice, financial aid and technical training provided by Australia, Canada, New Zealand and the UK were to be Burma, Ceylon (Sri Lanka), India, Malaya, Malaysia and Pakistan.

Eventually the Plan got expanded to include Japan and the USA as contributors and Afghanistan, Bhutan, Cambodia (Kampuchea), Indonesia, Iran, Laos, the Maldives, Nepal, the Philippines, Singapore, South Korea, South Vietnam and Thailand as recipients.

Colonialism. 1. The control by one power over a dependent area or people. 2. A policy advocating or based on such control colonialist *n* or *adj*. colonialistic *adj*.

Colony. A body of people living in a new territory but subject to control by the parent state; also their territory.

Columbus. Christopher *Italian* Cristoforo *Colombo Spanish* Cristobal *Colon* 1451-1506 Italian navigator who discovered America.

Comanchean. (Of or being the period of the). Mesozoic era between the Jurassic and the Cretaceous or the corresponding system or rocks.

Comecon. Council for Mutual Economic Assistance.

Cominform (Communist Information Bureau). It was established in 1947 for the exchange of information and coordination of activities by the Communist parties of Bulgaria, Czechoslovakia, France, Hungary, Italy, Poland, Romania, USSR and Yugoslavia, with HQ in Belgrade. It got dissolved in 1956 as a condition of reconciliation demanded by Yugoslavia which was expelled in 1948 for deviationist activities.

Comintern. The Communist or 3rd International, a movement which was established (1919) by Lenin to promote revolutionary Marxist international socialism as opposed to the reformist socialism of the 2nd International. In the early years the ideas of Trotsky and Zinoviev prevailed but Stalin's policies gradually took their place and served only Russian interests. The movement got dissolved

(1943), probably to mollify disquiet amongst the Western allies of the USSR.

Comity of Nations. 1. The courtesy and friendship of nations marked esp. by mutual recognition of executive, legislative and judicial acts. 2. The group of nations practising international comity.

Common Agricultural Policy (CAP). EEC scheme for increasing agricultural productivity, stabilizing markets, and assuring the availability or supplies, reasonable consumer prices and fair living standards for the agricultural community.

The policy has been based on stable currency parties, a single market structure of common prices, consensus on administrative, health and veterinary legislation, Community preference, common financing and the stabilization of markets against world price fluctuations by using intervention measures, levies and refunds on exports and imports.

Commonwealth of Nations, British. The association of sovereign states that are, or at some time have been, ruled by the UK, and which acknowledge the British sovereign as Head of the Commonwealth.

Communism. Orig. the doctrine of the common ownership of all property, the term now means that form of revolutionary socialism based on the writings of Karl Marx and esp. strong in E. Europe. It forms the Governments of Russia, Poland, China, etc., Its principles include the nationalisation of the means of production, distribution and exchange. In Russia, strict control of the country's economy was maintained by means of Five Year Plans. During World War II, Communists worked with the Resistance Movements in the occupied countries, and after the war gained power in countries within the Russian sphere of influence. The communist parties of W. Europe sought election in Parl.

Concentration Camps. Prison camps set up by the Nazis to contain German and other nationals opposed to the Nat. Soc. regime or considered to be politically suspect. Camps of the kind were in existence prior to World War II (1939-45), but during hostilities enormous numbers of men, women and children of all ages were incarcerated in such camps without trial. These included Jews, Socialists, Communists and people of liberal and pacifist convictions, both Catholic and Protestant, from all over Europe. The majority of such prisoners underwent incredible hardships. Millions were murdered by shooting, hanging, gassing, etc. When Germany was invaded, the Allies found 80,000 prisoners at Buchenwald, 30,000 at Belsen and 32,000 at Dachau. Thousands were found to be suffering from dysentery, typhoid, tuberculosis and other diseases. It is estimated that at the Polish camp of Oswiecim more than 4,000,000 people, men, women and children, were put to death is gas-chambers, and medical experiments were carried out on living persons.

Concordat. The part or treaty, esp. between the Vatican and a state concerning religious matters in that state. Best known are the Lateran Treaties (1929) between the Vatican and Italy which recognized the Vatican City as an independent state and regulated the position of the RC church in Italy. Indemnity was also awarded to the Vatican for papal possessions seized when Rome got occupied in 1870 during the progression to Italian unification.

Confucian. The Chinese philosopher Confucius or his teachings or followers.

Congress. The US legislature which got established by Article 1 of the Constitution. It consists of the House of Representatives and the Senate. The former, the lower chamber, comprises members elected every 2 years from districts of roughly equal populations. The Senate comprises 2 senators from each state, elected for 6-year terms; every 2 years, a third of the Senate comes up for election.

Congress Party. The Indian political organization known prior to independence as the Indian National Congress. It was founded (1885) to draw together regionally based, well-educated political groups. Between the World Wars Mahatma Gandhi's doctrine of non-violent civil disobedience as a means towards Indian independence dominated the Party, leading members of which were interned (1942-45) because of opposition to India's entry into WWII. Since independence the Party has been in power continuously apart from 1977-80 under the successive leaderships of Nehru, Shastri, and Indira and Rajiv Gandhi.

Conservative Party. British political organization which developed from the Tories of the 1930s. It encourages property ownership, a mixed economy and strong defence, based (since 1945) on Collective security against Communist expansion and subversion. Known from 1866 to 1922 as the Conservative and Unionist Party due to its opposition to Irish Home Rule, it has maintained adherence to established institutions coupled with moderate reforms, and its former imperialism has evolved into an affinity with the Commonwealth concept. Under Thatcher the Party has moved to the right, with a policy more radically in favour of free enterprise.

Constantinople Agreement. (1915). The secret assurances given to Russia by British and France that after WWI Constantinople (now Istanbul), the Bosphorus, the Dardanelles, and their hinterlands would be incorporated into Russia. The agreements foreshadowed the partition of the Ottoman Empire since they also provided for Britain and France acquiring unspecified areas of the Empire, the Russian acquisition being dependent on this happening. After the October Revolution (1917) the Bolsheviks repudiated the Agreements and published the secret texts, making Turkey's resistance to stiffen and inciting liberal protests in Britain and the USA.

Constitution. Assemblage and union of the essential parts of a body or system. It may be of natural origin, as with the universe stars and living bodies, or a system of principles and rules, either recognised by prescriptive usage or written, governing a state or assoc. The Brit. constitution which is unwritten comprises the collective principles of public policy whereby Brit. is governed. The Constitution of the U.S.A. is contained in a document, the terms of which cannot be changed without special procedure.

Constitutional Monarchy. The form of government in which supreme authority is vested in a single, usually hereditary, figure who rules according to a Constitution that defines and limits the sovereign's powers.

Containment. The act of restraining ideological or political power of a hostile country or operations of a hostile military force.

Continental System. The attempt begun by Napoleon in 1806 to blockade Britain.

Corbusier, Le. He was a French architect who planned Chandigarh

Coronation. Ceremony of crowning the sovereign. The rulers of the restored Rom. Emp. were crowned by the Pope.

Council of Europe. Organisation for political and economic consultation set up in 1949. It included Belgium, Denmark, France, Italy, Luxembourg, Netherlands, Norway, Sweden, the U.K., Eire, Greece, Turkey, Germany and Austria.

Country Party. Australian political party founded in 1920 with the objective of giving better representation to agricultural interests in a predominantly urban-orientated parliament. By 1922 it held the balance of power between Labour and Nationalists and was a partner in coalition governments (1922-29, 1934-41 and 1949-71).

Ceolidge, Calvin. (1872-1933). US Republican statesman, Vice-President (1921-23), President (1923-29). On President Harding's mid-term death he succeeded to the Presidency, and set about restoring public confidence after the scandals of Harding's administration. He was a believer in unrestricted freedom in business which led to a rapid growth in commercial monopolies,and followed a policy of conservative Isolationism. After the left office the prosperity engendered by his policies was destroyed in the Wall Street Crash.

Council for Mutual Economic Assistance (COMECON). The organization established (1949) for the improvement of trade between the member states—Albania, Bulgaria, Czechoslovakia, Hungary, Poland, Romania and the USSR. Albania was expelled (1961), but additional members are East Germany (1950), Mongolia (1962), Cuba (1972), and Vietnam (1978).

Council of Europe. It was established (1949) by a decision of the Consultative Council of the Western European Union. Its members have been Belgium, Denmark, France, Eire, Italy, Luxembourg, the Netherlands, Norway, Sweden and the U.K. Greece, and Turkey joined (1949), Iceland (1950), West Germany (1951), Austria (1956), Cyprus (1961), Switzerland (1963), Malta (1965), Portugal (1976), Spain (1977) and Liechtenstein (1978). Greece withdrew (1969) due to opposition within the council to its violation of human rights.

The council's aims are the achievement of greater unity between members states and their economic and social progress, practically the only topic barred from discussion being that of a member-state's national defence.

Coup D'etat. A sudden, violent or illegal seizure of government.

Court Martial. Court for trying soldiers, sailors and airman, both officers and men, for offences incidental to their profession. A court is composed of officers and the procedure is much more direct than in the civil courts. Milit courts martial are either regimental, district or general. Officers can only be tried by a general court martial, which can inflict sentence of death. The others deal with minor offences.

Cromwell Oliver. (1599-1658). English general and statesman who led the parliamentary army to victory over the Rovalists in the English civil war. He urged the execution of Charles I and the abolition of the Church of England and the House of Lords, and crushed remaining Royalist support in Scotland and Ireland. He was made lord protector of England (1653-1658). Cromwell is regarded as one of the greatest generals in British history.

Crusade. Milit. expedition sent under the banner of the cross, esp. those sent out from Europe to recover Palestine for the Christians. Palestine could be overrun by the Saracens in the 7th cent. but Christians were allowed to make pilgrimages to the Holy Places at Jerusalem. In the 11th cent., the Turks occupied the country and pilgrims were maltreated. This gave rise to the First Crusade, preached by Peter the Hermit and ordered by Pope Urban II at Clermont in 1095. Some European princes raised an army in 1097 and this took Antioch, and in 1099 captured Jerusalem, where a kingdom was set up under Godfrey of Bouillon. In 1187 Jerusalem was retaken by Saladin and the Third Crusade got organised. In this Richard I, Frederick Barbarossa and Philip Augustus of Fr. took part. It ended in 1192 in a treaty allowing the pilgrims to visit the Holy Places.

Cuban Missiles Crisis (1962). The sequence of events which brought about a grave risk of nuclear warfare. US aerial reconnaissance showed that weapons being supplied by the USSR to Castro's Cuba were ballistic missiles with atomic warheads capable of reaching any part of the USA. President Kennedy announced that the USA would blockade Cuba and requested the USSR to remove all weapons that had already reached the island and to order vessels carrying more to return home. In exchange for the removal of the weapons the USA pledged to lift the blockade and refrain from invading Cuba. There has been establishment of the NW Frontier Province. He became Foreign Secretary (1919-24) when his main achievement was the conclusion of the Treaty of Lausanne (1923).

Cultural Revolution. A revolutionary movement launched in 1966 to develop the ideological consciousness and revolutionary potential of the Chinese masses.

Cultural Revolution. Period of upheaval (1966-69) in China, under Mao Tse-tung. The aim was to rekindle the revolutionary spirit. Many top Communist Party officials were removed. There were mass rallies and open hostilities.

Curara. (Or curara). Arrow poison used by the S. Amer. Indians, Prepared from various plants, principally species of *Strychnos*, and used to some extent in medicine. From it is obtained the active principle, curarine, in the form of a yellowish-brown powder which paralyses the muscles if injected beneath the skin.

Curzon Line. The proposed border along the 'ethnic line' separating Poles and Russians, suggested by the British Foreign Secretary, Lord Curzon, in 1919. As a result of the Polish Soviet War the boundary was fixed by the Treaty of Riga (1921) well to the E of the Curzon Line. Following the Teheran Conference in 1944, the Curzon Line became the future E border of Poland.

Curzon, Lord. (1859-1925 A.D.). Viceroy of India 1889-1904 and after a brief interim reappointed until 1905. His attempt to partition Bengal in 1905 generated considerable opposition among Indians. His legacies include the reform of the Police, establishment of Farm Credit Societies, expansion of railroads, and the establishment of an Archaeological Department.

Cyrus. Name of 2 rulers of Persia, Cyrus the elder, called the Great, was the founder of the Persian Empire. He captured Babylon, united the Medes and Persians and made Susa his cap. Cyrus the Younger was the 2nd son of Darius, king of Persia. He led an army of Gks. from Asia Minor into Persia and get killed at the Battle of Cunaxa in 401 BC.

Czech. People of Slavic stock inhabiting Bohemia and Moravia. They form, with Poles, Wends and Slovaks, the W. branch of the Slavs, Prob. migrating from the Upper Vistula in the 5th cent. Their speech became differentiated and was kept alive by John Hus, and by the Moravian Brethren. They are closely akin to the Slovaks but have a very different hist.

D

Dadabhai Naoroji. (1825-1917). He was called the 'Grand Old Man of India'. He was a prominent leader of early Congressmen. He was the most distinguished member of Indians.

Dakota. A member of an American Indian People of the northern Mississippi Valley.

Daladier, Edouard. (1884-70), French statesman, Radical Party PM (1933-34 and 1938-40). The governments he led favoured appeasement anna he was a signatory of the Munich Agreement.

Dalai Lama. Chief spiritual head of Lamaism.

Dalhousie, Earl of. (1812-1860 AD). Governor-General of India 1848-1856, who developed a postal system, established a department of public instruction, attempted to abolish human sacrifice, annexed Burma and the Punjab, and whose pursuance of the 'doctrine of lapse' in Oudh helped trigger the 1857 Uprising.

Damocles. A courtier of ancient Syracuse held to have been seated at a banquet beneath a sword hung by a single hair.

Danes. Rovers from the Scandinavian countries who raided Eng. before 1066, also called Northmen. From 790 to 751 raids were frequent and great damage was done by the invaders, who sailed up rivers in search of plunder. In 851 the Danes began to settle in Eng. and Alfred the Great handed over the Danelaw to them. About 922 the Danish ravages began again. Ethelred the Unready raised money, the Danegeld, to buy them off. In 1013 Sweyn, King of Denmark, conquered the N and in 1016 his son, Canute, became King of Eng. He reigned until 1035, and his sons, Harold and Hardicanute, until 1042, when the Danish rule ended.

Dara Shikoh (1614?-1659 A.D.). Eldest and favourite son of the Mughal emperor Shah Jahan, who got defeated and eventually executed by his younger brother Aurangzeb in the succession struggle that broke out during a serious illness of Shah Jahan in 1658. Deeply influenced by a Sufi saint, Dara came to have great sympathy for Hinduism; translated Upanisads himself into Persian with the help of Sanskrit scholars, and even wrote a book drawing parallels between *Sufism* and *Vedantism*.

Dark Ages. The period from about AD 476 to about 800, *broadly* middle ages.

David. 1 (Saint) 520?-600? patron saint of Wales. 2. 1035?-973? BC King of Judah and Israel (1013-973 BC); author of many of the Psalms.

David I. 1084-1153 king of Scotland (1124-53); founder of several monasteries.

Dayan, Moshe. (1915-81), Israeli general and politician. He was Chief of Staff (1953-58), directing the Sinai campaign against Egypt (1956). As a Labour member of the Knesset (Parliament) he served as Minister of Agriculture (1959-64). He was Minister of Defence (1967-74), responsible for the successful outcome of the 1967 and 1973. Arab-Israeli Wars. After becoming critical of the government he joined the opposition and became Foreign Minister (1977-79) in Begin's coalition government.

D Day. A day set for launching an operation; *specif* June 6, 1944, on which the invasion of France in World War II was begun by forces allied against Germany.

Decembrist. One taking part in the unsuccessful uprising against the Russian emperor Nicholas 1 in December 1825.

Declaration. Formal statement of any kind. Outstanding examples are the Declaration of Indulgence, 1687; the Declaration of Rights, 1689; the Amer. Declaration of Indep., 1797 (*q.v.*); the Declaration of Paris, 1856, and the Declaration of London, 1908-9, both on maritime warfare.

Decolonization. (*a*) granting of independence to a colony, (*b*) freeing from colonial status.

De Gaulle, Charles Andre Joseph Marie. (1890-1970) Fr. gen. and statesman. Served in World War I and II Brig-Gen commanding tank brig. 1940. Escaped after Dunkirk and organised Free Fr. Movement. Pres. of Fr. Committee for Nat. Liberation, 1943-44.

Head of Provisional Government 1944. Retired from public life, 1946. Became P.M. 1958 and Pres. 1959, concentrating power in his own hands. Opposed entry of Brit. into European Common Market. His memoirs, *The Call to Honour*, were pub. 1955. Retired after referendum defeat (1969).

Deira. Ancient Anglian Kingdom between the Humber and Tyne. It was united with Bernicia to form Northumbria.

Danarius *n. pl.* **Denarii.** A small silver coin of ancient Rome.

Denazify. To rid of Nazism and its influence.

Dendrochronology. The science of dating past events and variations in environment in former periods by comparative study of growth rings in trees and aged wood.

Depression or Slump. In economic terms a decline in trade and general prosperity. The Great Depression of 1929-34 was worldwide, starting with an agricultural recession followed by financial panic and collapse, known as the Wall Street Crash, in the USA. This is turn affected financial institutions and money markets in other parts of the world and caused a run on the pound in the UK. The result was a decline in internal consumption and exports in industrialized countries, factory closures and massive unemployment.

Dessalines, Jean Jacques. (*c*. 1758-1806) Emperor of Haiti. B. a negro slave, he served under Toussaint L'Ouverture in the wars of liberation. In 1802 he served under Leclerc, but later joined the enemy. Although Toussaint was captured and Leclerc's army decimated by yellow fever, Dessalines again changed sides, led another revolt, and in 1803 the Fr. invaders were defeated. In the following year Haiti declared her indep. and set up her own government with Dessalines as emperor.

Desai, Morarji Ranchhodji. Born at Bhadali (Gujarat) in Anavil Brahmana family; eldest of 8 children; married at 15 to Gujraben; a year after graduation from Wilson College, Bombay, became Deputy Collector at Ahmedabad (1918); resigned (1930) to join Civil Disobedience Movement; imprisoned 3 times in next 4 years for fighting in freedom struggle; member of all-India Congress Committee 1931 onwards; member Bombay Legislative Assembly (1937); Minister for Revenue and Forests (1937-38); participated in individual civil disobedience movement; imprisoned for 3 years in connection with 1942 (Quit India) Movement; re-elected to Bombay Legislative Assembly and become Home and Revenue Minister (1946-52); was Chief Minister of State till 1956; Cabinet Minister (in Central Government) for Commerce and Heavy Industries (1956); Finance Minister (1958-63); resigned under Kamraj Plan; became Finance Minister (1966) and Deputy Prime Minister (1967); resigned (1969) because of differences with Prime Minister (Indira Gandhi); after split in Indian National Congress (1969) became chairman of Opposition Congress Party (Congress 'Organisation') in Parliament (November, 1969); imprisoned for 19 months (1975-77) as a political prisoner; wrote his autobiography in jail (published 1979); does not believe in power being concentrated in hands of higher (or highest) echelons; became Prime Minister after Janata Party was returned at the polls and took office (March 1977); shrewd as political tactician; ; first and last a great patriot; staunch advocate of *swadesi*; spins some (*khadi*) yarn every day; simple, almost austere; habits; vegetarian, non-smoker, teetotlar, naturopath; associated with many social, cultural, educational, religious and academic organisations; liberal minded; front-ranking national leader of integrity, sincerity and honesty; stands for a high moral standard (Adopted from India).

Desegregation or Integration. The policy of ending the forced separation of racial, political or religious groups within a society.

In South Africa, the policy of apartheid opposes racial desegration.

Detente. The easing or relaxing of tension, esp. between nations. More specifically the term is used for the improvement of relations between East and West from around 1969.

Deterrence. The prevention of hostilities by the possession of a weapon or combination of weapons, esp. nuclear, held by a state or allied states, in order to deter attack by another state or states. There is a 'balance of terror' where opposing groupings each possess such weapons, thereby deterring each other between NATO and Warsaw Pact powers.

Devapala. (810-850 A.D.). He was the most powerful of the rulers of Pala dynasty. He successfully resisted the Hun invasion, defeated

Mihirabhoja of Kanauj. He raised Bengal to the highest pinnacle of power and prestige. After him, the Gauda (Bengal) empire disintegrated.

Deviationism. The ideological deviation, esp. from orthodox Moscow-line Communism, such as practised by Yugoslavia since the 1950s and advocated by W European Communist parties.

Devolution. The transfer or allocation of authority, esp. from a central government to regional governments or particular interests; such as certain functions and powers passed to Northern Irish, Scottish and Welsh authorities by the UK government.

Dharmapala. (About 770-815 AD). He was the founder of great *Pala* dynasty, which ruled Bengal. He was defeated by the Rashtrakuta King, Dhruva. He was a Buddhist. For some time, he ruled Kanauj.

Dhingra, Madan Lal. B. in Punjab. He took part in Indian revolutionary activities in Britain; undertook training in the use of fire-arms; shot and killed Col. William Curzom Wyllie, Political A.D.C. in the India Office, at a gathering in the Imperial Institute. London; declared it to be an act of "humble revenge for the inhuman hangings and transportation of patriotic Indian youths". Arrested and tried for murder; sentenced to death; died on the gallows at the Pentonville Prison, London, on August 17, 1909.

Diaz, Bartholomew. (*d.* 1500) Portuguese navigator; first European to round the Cape of Good Hope (1486-88). This voyage opened up the sea-route to India.

Diaz, Porfirio. (1830-1915) Mexican Pres. A lawyer. He led the Maxican Army in the struggle against the Emperor Maximillian and in 1877 was elected Pres. Under his rule, order and prosperity were restored, although the poor we neglected.

Diocletian. (245-313) Rom. Emperor. Gaius Aurelius Valerius Diocletianus, a soldier, who in 284 was proclaimed emperor. He divided the empire with is colleague, Maximian, and later, in 292, with Galerius and Constantius Chlorus. Nicomedia was his cap. He presecuted the Christians.

Dictator. A ruler who is not effectively restricted by a constitution, laws, recognized opposition, etc. Examples incl. Hitler, Mussolini and Stalin.

Dien Bien Phu. The village in North Vietnam, the scene of a decisive victory (1954) by the Viet Minh over the French in the war of independence in Indo-China. The French defeat led to the end of French colonial rule in Indo-China and the partition of Vietnam following the 1954 Geneva Agreement.

Din-i-Ilahi (P). 'Divine faith', an eclectic religion established by the Mughal emperor Akbar in 1582 that included elements of Hinduism (fire sacrifice ceremonies), Zoroastrianism (fire worship), Christian (baptism), as well as Islam. The cult, centering around Akbar himself and stressing a simple monasticism, rapidly faded away after Akbar's death.

Diocletian. The full name Gaius Aurelius Valerius Diocletianus 245-313 Roman emperor (284-305) noted for his persecution of Christians.

Disarmament. The reduction of defensive or offensive fighting capability by an armed force or nation.

Dogger Bank Incident (1904). The event arising during the Russo-Japanese War when the Russian Baltic Fleet was despatced to the Far East. Steaming through the North Sea it encountered what were thought to be Japanese torpedo boats but actually were full fishing vessels. The warships sank one vessel, killing 2 of its crew, thereby rousing such anger in Britain that an armed conflict was barely avoided. International arbitration and Russian acceptance of compensation claims eased tension, and long-term relations between the 2 countries were unimpared.

Dollfuss, Engelbert. (1892-1934), Austrian statesman. After WWI he joined the Christian Social Party, becoming Chancellor (1932-34). Fearing a socialist revolt he suspended parliamentary government (1933), and ordered the army to suppress a demonstration by attacking housing estates in the Viennese suburbs (1934). His introduction of a new and Fascist constitution (1934) brought about his downfall. Hated by the nazis, who wanted Anschluss, and by the Marxists, he was assassinated in the Chancellery by Nazis attempting to stage a coup d'etat.

Domino Theory. The idea that a Communist takeover of a country will lead to Communist takeovers in neighbouring states; an allusion to a line of dominoes, each standing on end, all of which fall when one is pushed. The theory was invoked by those in the USA who opposed withdrawal of US forces from the Vietnam War.

Douglas-Home, Sir Alec, Baron Home of the Hirsel. (1903-). British Conservative statesman, PM (1963-64). He was twice Foreign Secretary (1960-63 and 1970-74). After Macmillan's resignation (1963), Douglas-Home was elected leader of the Conservative Party, and became PM. An experienced politician and diplomat, the success of his 'caretaker' premiership drastically reduced the size of Labour's majority in the 1964 election.

Dravidian. 1. A member of any of the peoples of southern India and Sri Lanka who speak Dravidian language. 2. Any of several languages of India and Pakistan (*e.g.* Tamil and Malayalam).

Dreyfus. Alfred 1859-1935 French Jewish army officer wrongly accused of treason and imprisoned, but eventually exonerated. His case divided France and nearly caused civil war.

Dulles, John Foster (1888-1959). US diplomat and statesman. As Secretary of State (1953-59) he caused tension with America's allies, esp. during the Suez Crisis.

Duma. Russian elective legislative assembly established by Tsar Nicholas II (1905) and overthrown by the Bolsheviks (1917). The upper chamber was the Council of State and the lower chamber, the State Duma, elected on a limited franchise. There were 4 Dumas during the period 1905-17. The Tsar retained the power of dissolution and veto, and ministers were responsible to him and not to the Duma, which was allowed only limited control of the budget.

Dumbarton Oaks Conference (1944). A series of meetings held near Washington by delegates from Britain. China, the USSR and the USA to discuss structural proposals for the United nations Organization, with special reference to the Security Council and the individual members' use of veto powers.

Dunkirk. The port of NW France, scene in WWII of the evacuation of the British Expeditionary Force and the French 1st Army (1940). About 336,000 men were rescued by an improvised flotilla of vessels of all descriptions, strongly supported by the RAF. Shortly afterwards France capitulated, but the success of the evacuation did much to strengthen British morale.

Durnham Report. On 11 February 1839, Lord Durnham submitted his famous reports on the affairs of British North America. He proposed the union of Upper and Lower Canada and the grant of responsible government. According to this report, the imperial government was to retain control only of foreign relations, regulation of trade, disposal of public lands, and the determination of the colonial constitution. In other fields Canada was to be given self-governments. Though the report concerned Canada only, it contained certain fundamental principles on which self-governments developed in other colonies during the 16th and 20th centuries.

Dyarchy. A government in which power is vested in two rulers or authorities.

E

Eagle. Heraldic symbol. It dates from Egyptian, Persian and Roman times, and was used by Charlemagne. Russia, as the successor of the Gk. Empire, and Austria used a double-headed eagle. Germany, which took the symbol in 71, a single-headed one. In Amer, the eagle was used by the Indians, and adopted by the U.S.A as a nat. emblem, with a single head and in its talons arrows and an olive branch.

East India Company. The (English) East India Company was formed in 1600 by a Charter to trade with India. In 1615 they built a factory at Surat with Jehangir's permission. They had to face Dutch and French opposition in the beginning but they successfully overcame them. The company's functions expanded to political ambitions. Robert Clive led the English forces to capture Aroct and other regions Robert Clive *was instrumental in lying the foundation of the British empire in India*. In the *Carnatic Wars* (three battles between the French and the English) the English finally defeated the French in the Battle of Wandiwash to gain control over South India.

Eden, Sir Anthony, 1st Earl of Avon. (1897-1977). British Conservative statesman, PM (1955-57). He was also Foreign Secretary (1935-38, 1940-45 and 1951-55). His administration's handling of the Suez Crisis (1956) aroused widespread opposition and this, coupled with poor health, caused his resignation.

Edmund. (*d.*870) Eng. saint and King of E. Anglia. In 870 he was taken prisoner by the Danes and martyred. The city which grew up round his shrine was named after him, Bury St. Edmunds.

Edmund. (980-1016) Eng. king, called Ironside. Son of Ethelred the Unready, he succeeded his father in 1016. He fought bravely against the Danes, but was beaten and agreed to divide the kingdom with Canute.

Edward. (1005-66) Eng. king called the Confessor, son of Ethelred the

Unready. In 1041 he crossed over to Eng. and was chosen king in succession to his half-brother, Hardicanute. He reigned for 25 years. He built the 1st abbey at West minster, and was canonised in 1161.

Edward (The Black Prince). (1330-76) Eng. prince. Eldest son of Edward III.

Edward 1. (1239-1307) King of Eng. eldest son of Henry III. He fought against the rebellious barons and in 1265 defeated Simon de Montfort at Evesham. Later he went on a crusade and during his absence in 1272 became king. He conquered Wales and made war on Scot. but won his most enduring fame by calling the Medel Parl. of 1295.

Edward II. (1284-1327) King of Eng. Son of Edward I, *b.* at Caernarvon, and created Prince of Wales in 1301, the 1st Eng. prince to bear that title. Coming to the throne in 1307, he made peace at once with Scot. His reign, of 20 years was marked by the dominance of favourites and revolts of the nobles. The king was eventually deposed and murdered in Berkeley Castle.

Edward III. (1312-77) King of Eng. son of Edward II. He became king in 1327, and in 1330 put an end to the usurped authority of his mother Isabella, and Roger Mortimer. His reign was chiefly occupied with the Fr. war and was marked by the victories of Crecy and Poitiers. His reign was notable for constitutional developments, the Black Death (1348), the Statute of Labourers (1351) and the preaching of Wycliffe.

Edward IV. (1442-83) King of Eng., the eldest son of Richard, Duke of York. He began to fight for the Yorkists, and in 1460, on his father's *d.* became their leader. In 1469, owing to the desertion of the Earl of Warwick, he left Eng. but returned and crushed his foes at Barnet and Tewkesbury. In 1464 Edward mar. Elizabeth Woodville. Their son was Edward V (1470-83). In April, 1483, he became king, with his uncle, the Duek of Gloucester, afterwards Richard III, as his guardian. With his brother he was imprisoned in the Tower, where both were murdered.

Edward VI. (1537-53) King of Eng. Son of Henry VIII and Jane Seymour, he became king in 1547, and resigned for 6 years. The chief event was the estab. of the Protestant Ch.

Edward VII. (1841-1910) King of Gt. Brit. and Ireland, eldest son and

2nd child of Queen Victoria and Albert of Saxe-Coburg. He was created Prince of Wales and Duke of Cornwall soon after his birth. In 1863 Albert Edward mar. Alexandra, daughter of the prince who afterwards became King Christian IX of Denmark. Because of the queen's retirement, the Prince and Princess of Wales were for many years the acknowledged leaders of Eng. society. The Prince entered into every form of social activity, but his mother did not allow him and considerable share in affairs of State. On Jan. 22, 1901, the Prince became King and Emperor.

Edward VII. (1841-1910), King of Great Britain and Ireland (1901-10). The eldest son of Queen Victoria, his playboy image weakened Victorian conventions and so earned the Queen's disapproval, with the result that she denied him official responsibilities. However, throughout his 9 year reign he was a popular and well-loved monarch.

Edward VIII. (1894-1972) King of Gt. Brit. and Ireland, 1936. Eldest son of George V and Queen Mary, he was created Prince of Wales in 1911. He had a naval training at Osborne and Dartmouth, studied at Paris and Magdalen Coll. Oxford, and was on active service during World War I. He succeeded to the throne in Jan. 1936. His wish to marry the Amer. Mrs. Simpson roused such opposition that he abdicated in Dec. of that year. He mar. Mrs. Simpson in 1937 and received the title of Duke of Windsor.

Edwin. (*c.* 585-633) King of Northumbria, son of Ella, King of Deira. Driven out by the King of Bermicia, in 617 he killed his foe in battle, and united Bernicia and Deira into the Kingdom of Northumbria. He mar. Etherlburga of Kent, and in 627, under her influence and that of Paulinus, became a Christian. He was killed in battle against Penda, King of Mercia.

E.E.C. (European Economic Community). Sometimes known as the Common Market, the E.E.C. is an organisation of European states with the aim of achieving economic and political integration. Founded (with the European Coal and Steel community and the European Atomic Energy Community) under the Treaty of Rome of 1957, the original members were Belgium, France, West Germany, Italy, Luxembourg and the Netherlands. The United Kingdom, Denmark and Ireland joined in 1973, followed by Greece in 1981. Spain is eager to join. The E.E.C. is governed by a Commission,

Council of Ministers and Parliament. There is also a Court of Justice.

Egbert. (775-839) The king of Wessex (802-839); 1st overlord of England.

Egyptian Civilisation. The Nile valley of Egypt is more like the Indus, and it may be interesting to compare the ancient civilisation of Egypt with that of the Indus. Egypt is called the 'Gift of the Nile.' The first important king of Egypt was Menes, who lived about 3000 B.C., and ruled over the whole of the Nile valley: Historians divide the history of Egypt into three periods: the *Old Kingdom, the Middle Kingdom* and *the New Kingdom.* The Old Kingdom is also called the Age of Pyramids. During this period, Memphis, situated near modern Cairo, was the capital. The civilisation of Egypt with its advances in art, religion and sciences developed during this period (3000-2000 B.C.) and during the Middle Kingdom (1200-1750 B.C.). But in the eighteenth century B.C., Egypt was over-run by invaders called the Hyksos, who came from the east. Their rule was shortlived; soon the Egyptian kings regained their land, and the New Kingdom was founded.

The Egyptian king was called the *pharaoh*. He had absolute power and was looked upon as a god and his statues put in temples. Next to the pharao came priests, officials, artists and craftsmen. Below these people were the farmers who lived beyond the cities and then came the slaves who were generally prisoners of war and owned by the king.

Agriculture was the most important occupation of the people. They appear to have used oxen to draw the plough as early as 3000 B.C. Like the people of other early civilisations, the Egyptians domesticated animals—goats, dogs, pigs, geese etc. The horse was brought to Egypt by the Hyksos and used to draw war chariots. While the Mesopotamians wore woollen clothes, the Egyptians and linen garments. The Egyptians made beautiful stone vases which they exported. They produced glassware of graceful shapes and made beautiful furniture inlaid with ivory and precious stones. Internal and foreign trade was controlled by the king. The Nile was used as a waterway. The Egyptians worshipped the sun; they also worshipped the god of floods, and the moon god. They believed in life after death. The *mummy* was put in a wooden box and buried. The pyramids were the tombs of great kings.

Pyramids and the Sphinx are the two specimens of Egyptian architectural excellence. The Sphinx is a mythological animal with the body of a lion and the head of a man. Each Sphinx was carved out of a single solid stone. Egyptian temples are also remarkable buildings.

The Egyptian scrip is known as *hieroglyphic*, which means sacred writing. it consisted of 24 signs, each of which stood for a single consonant. Vowels were not written. Later, the Egyptians started using syinbols for ideas and the total number of signs rose to about 500. They made significant advances in many fields of knowledge and developed a decimal system of numeration. They also developed the Solar calendar.

By about 1000 B.C. the great days of Egypt were over. In quick succession Egypt was conquered and became part of the empires of Assyrians, Iranians, Greeks and Romans.

Egyptology. The study of Egyptian antiquities.

Eisenhower. Dwight David 1890-1967 American general and president of the USA (1953-1961); commander-in-chief of the Allied forces in Western Europe (1943-1945).

Eisenhower Doctrine. The principle recommended by President Eisenhower to Congress (1957) that US forces should be used to protect any state in the Middle East subject to aggression by any nation 'controlled by international Communism'.

Military advice and economic aid to any state in the area which considered its independence threatened was also proposed. The Doctrine was withdrawn (1959) owing to the fact that those countries it was designed to assist believed it was against the principles of Arab nationalism.

Eleanor. Name of 3 Eng. queens including the daughter of William, Duke of Aquitaine, who in 1137 mar. Louis VII of Fr. The marriage being dissolved, she became the wife of Henry II of Eng. She was the mother of Richard I and John, and *d.* 1204, Eleanor, a daughter of Ferdinand III, King of Castile. In 1254 she mar. Edward, later Edward I, and with him went on crusade. She *d.* 1290.

Elijah. Heb. prophet (1 Kings 17-21; 2 Kings 1-3). He led the life of a hermit, emerging to proclaim the wishes of God. Finally he disappeared in a fiery chariot.

Eliot, T.S. (1888-1965). Poet, critic and dramatist. Won the Noble Prize for Literature in 1948. His two most successful plays were *Murder in the Cathedral* and *Cockail Party.*

Elizabeth. (1709-62) Empress of Russia, daughter of Peter the Great and Catherine I, she appeared in 1741 at the head of the party that deposed the young Tsar, Ivan VI. She became empress and ruled Russia until her *d.* Much of her reign was occupied in fighting against Frederick the Great. She founded the Univ. of Moscow.

Elizabeth. Eldest daughter of James I, mar. Frederick, later King of Bohemia. Mother of Sophia whose son was George I.

Elizabeth. (1533-1603) Queen of Eng. and Ireland, daughter of henry VIII and Anne Boleyn. She succeeded to the throne in 1558. The first part of her reign was occupied with the estab. of the C.of E. Then hostility between Eng. and Sp. became open war. Plots were discovered to kill the Queen and replace her by Mary, Queen of Scots. The execution of Mary in 1587 put an end to one danger, and the defeat of the Sp. Armade in 1588 made Eng. supreme on the seas. The last years of the reign were troubled by risings in Ireland and by the queen's reluctance to name a successor. She refused to mar. Philip II of Sp.; she toyed with the idea of marrying Henry III of Fr. or a Fr. prince, but these were only moves in the polit. game.

Elizabeth. Queen of Gt. Brit. Lady Elizabeth Bowes-Lyon, daughter of 14th Earl of Strathmore, mar. April 26th, 1923, Prince Albert Frederick Arthur George, Duke of York, 2nd son of King George V. On the abdication of Edward VIII, 1936, the Duke and Duchess of York became King and Queen.

Elizabeth II. Queen of Great Britain and Northern Ireland. She married Philip Mountbatten in 1947 and succeeded her father George VI in 1952. Her reign has been characterized by closer relationships with her subjects both at home and overseas than that of any previous monarch, and she has maintained and developed Commonwealth ties and relationships between the UK and foreign countries.

Ellenborough, Earl of. (1790-1871 A.D.) Governor-General of India 1842-1844, especially concerned with Afghan wars; also annexed Sind; later served as President of the Board of Control of the East India Company.

Elphinstone, Mountstuart. (1779-1859 A.D.). British civil servant who held several key administrative posts in India, including the Governorship of Bombay, and championed strong state and local educational institutions. Author of a history of India, he twice declined the Governor-Generalship of India.

Emir. A ruler of any various Muslim states, esp in former times a male descendant of Muhammad.

Emperor. The supreme ruler of an empire.

Empire. 1(*a*) A major political unit having a territory of great extent or a number of territories or peoples under as ingle sovereign authority; *esp* one having an emperor as head of state; (*b*) the territory of such a political unit. 2. Imperial sovereignty, rule, or dominion.

Empress. 1. The wife or widow of an emperor. 2. A women having in her own right the rank of emperor.

Enosis. The union of Cyprus and Greece.

Entente Cordiale. A term first used in the 1840s to denote the friendly relationship between France and Britain; nevertheless severe strains have been imposed upon the friendship from time to time.

Epaminondas. (*c*.418-362 B.C.). A Theban general and statesman. In 371 he was one of the generals at the Battle of Leuctra; in 370 he invaded Peloponnesus, where he founded Messene and Megalopolis. In 362 he invaded it for the 4th time, and was killed gaining a brilliant victory over the Lacedaemonians at Mantinea.

Ephesus. In ancient geog. the chief of the 12 Ionian cities on the coast of Asia Minor. It has numerous interesting ruins, including the famous temple of Diana (Artemis) built in the 6th cent. B.C. Ephesians, Epistle to the. Tenth book of the N.T. Written during St. Paul's first imprisonment in Rome, A.D. 62, it was apparently a circular letter addressed to the churches of Asia Minor.

Epic Age. The great epics of the Aryans were the *Ramayana* and the *Mahabharata*. The *Ramayana* is the oldest and the most popular epic of the Hindus. It consists of 7 books and 2,400 couplets; it was written by Valmiki.

The *Mahabharata* consists of 18 books and about 10,000 couplets. It is believed that it was written by Vyas. The epics are the

Vedas of the masses. The *Mahabharata* recounts feud between the wily and aristocratic *Kauravas* and the fierce *Pandavas.* Lord Krishna takes a prominent part in the struggle in aid of Arjuna, the most valiant among the Pandavas. Noteworthy within the epic is the *Bhagavadgita* (Song of the Lord), which urges personal love and devotion (*bhakti*). The *Mahabharata* seems to have been written around the 2nd century B.C.

The theme of the *Ramayana* is the conflict between Rama and Ravana who can be take to be representatives of the Aryan and non-Aryan civilisation respectively. Unlike the *Ramayana*, and *Mahabharata* describes a conflict among the Aryans themselves. The Mahabharata war at Kurukshetra affected all the Aryan kings of India who were ranged on either side. The Pandavas had their allies from Kashi, Kosala, Magadha, Matsya, Chedi and the Yadus of Mathura. The allies of the Kauravas were the Yavanas, Sakas, Madras, Kambojas, Kaikeyas, Sindhus, Sanviras, Bhojas, Andhrakas etc.

During the epic period many new castes came into existence as a result of the inter-marriages between the different castes. Polygamy and polyandry were both practised. Dashratha had three wives. Ravana also had many wives. Draupadi married the five Pandavas. Shudras occupied a very low position in the society. Women were not allowed much freedom in the matter of matrimonial alliances. The system of 'Sati' existed in Punjab. The cow was a sacred animal. Vagetarianism was popular. People used cotton and silk. The Kshatriyas kept long hair but the Brahmanas shaved their heads and chins. People liked ornaments of gold and silver. The rich were addicted to drinking and gambling, prostitution was a recognised institution. Sanskrit was the spoken language of the people, but Prakrit was also making a beginning. People studied philosophy and rhetoric. Music and dancing were among the accomplishments for young girls. Astronomy had made considerable progress.

Agriculture and the breeding of cattle were still the main occupations. The merchants were organised in guilds which were controlled by the Mahajans. Although the village or *grama* was a popular unit of economic life, there are references to the towns or *nagaras* in the epics.

The Vedic gods were superseded by Brahma, Vishnu and Shiva; and Indra, Surya and Varuna were relegated to the background. The *avtaras* or the doctrine of the various incarnations of Vishnu became popular. Rama and Krishna came to be worshipped as the incarnations of Vishnu.

There were a large number of states in India. The ordinary form of government was kingship. The king was not an autocrat. He was required to rule according to the principles of justice and morality. The people had the right to depose a wicked king. There were also republics.

The king levied taxes but they were not oppressive. The army was regularly paid. The army consisted of infantry, cavalry, elephants and chariots. The foot soldiers were armed with swords or spears. Strong bodied persons used the *gada* or mace. Archery rached the zenith of its glory. It was the age of chivalry; it was shameful for a Kshatriya to run away from the battlefield.

Erie. A member of an American Indian people of the Lake Erie region.

Essene. A member of a monastic brotherhood of Jews in Palestine from the 2nd century B.C. to the 2nd century A.D.

Essex, Earl of. (1566-1601) Eng. courtier. Robert Devereux, favourite of Queen Elizabeth. He was sent to Ireland as governor-general in 1599. Executed for his part in a rebellion. His son, Robert Devereux (1591-1646) was restored to the earldom in 1604. In 1642 he was C.-in-C. of the parl. army.

Ethelred. Name of 2 Eng. kings. Ethelred II (968-1016) was a son of KIing Edgar. He began to reign when only 10, and was on the throne for nearly 40 years. His inability to deal with the Danish peril won for him the neame of the Unready. He began the payment of Danegeld.

Ethnarch. The governor of a province of people (*e.g.*, of the Byzantine Empire).

Eugenie. (1826-1920) Empress of the Fr. She mar. Napoleon III in 1853. From 1853-70 she was the centre of a brilliant and luxurious court; from 1871 she was an exile in Eng.

Eunuch. A castrated man placed in charge of a harem or employed as a chamberlain in a palace.

Eurocommunism. A term denoting the liberalized form of Communism as practised by Western European Communist parties since 1975 when the French and Italian parties issued a joint policy declaration. This recognized the right of other parties to exist, advocated democratic elections, guaranteed civil liberties and the right of opposition, and abandoned the principle of the dictatorship of the proletariat.

European Parliament. The originated (1952) as part of the European Coal and Steel Community and was expanded by the Treaties of Rome (1957) to cover EEC and Euratom affairs. It became (1967) one of the constituents of the European Community. Until 1979 the Parliament comprised members nominated by the national parliaments of the member states. It was then decided that every 5 years the electorate of each state should elect its own representatives. The membership is split on party lines similar to those prevailing in the national parliaments.

Exarch. 1. A viceroy in a Byzantire empire. 2. An Eastern bishop ranking below a patriarch and above a metropolitan; *specif* the head of an autocephalous church.

Extradition. The surrender of an alleged criminal, sue under the provisions of a treaty or statute, by one state or other authority to another having jurisdiction to try the charge.

Ezekiel. A Hebrew priest and prophet of the 6th century B.C.

F

Fabian. Of or resembling the Roman general Quintus Fabius Miximus known for his defeat of Hannibal in the Second Punic War by the avoidance of decisive contests.

Fabian Society. An association of British socialists (founded 1884) advocating the establishment of democratic socialism by gradual reforms within the law. Notable early members were George Bernard Shaw and Sidney and Beatrice Webb.

Fa-Hien. Famous Chinese traveller who visited India from A.D. 401 to 410 and went to holy places of Buddhists. He wrote a beautiful account of the people and the country; praised Indian rulers and their concern for the welfare of the people.

Fabius Miximus. Quintus *d* 203 Roman dictator and general famous for his delaying tactics in the war against Hannibal.

Fakhar-ud-din Ali Ahmad. (Dec. 13, 1905-Feb. 11, 1977); 5th President of Republic of India. He practised law at Calcutta for a while; gave up lucrative practice to join national movement and went away to Assam where he joined Indian National Congress (1931); returned to Assam Assembly (1935). In 1958 he became minister in charge of finance, law, community development, panchayat and local self-government; re-elected to State Assembly (1962). He got elected to Rajya Sabha (1966); Central Cabinet Minister for Irrigation and Power (January 1966); Education Minister (December, 1966); elected to Lok Sabha in general elections of 1967 from Assam. He became Cabinet Minister for Industrial Development and Company Affairs. He became Minister for Agriculture (1970) which he continued to remain after his election to Lok Sabha in general elections (1972). He became ill while on State visit to Malaysia on Feb. 8, 1977; cut short his visit abroad and returned to India; suffered massive heart attack on Feb. 11 and died that morning. He was a staunch nationalist throughout his life; had wide-ranging interests; was a sportsman, a man of culture and of humility; had uncompromising faith in secularism and was liberal minded and forward looking.

Falange. Fascist movement founded in Spain in 1933 by Jose Antonio Primo de Rivera (1903-36). It was the only legal party under the Franco regime.

Falangist. 1. A member of the fascist political party that ruled Spain after the civil war of 1936-39 until the death of Franco in 1975. 2. A member of a right-wing Christian faction in the Lebanon.

Falchion. A broad-bladed slightly curved sword of medieval times.

Falkland Islands, (Span. *Islas Malvinas*). Crown colony of the UK, in S. Atlantic Ocean.

Settled by British colonists in the 19th cent., the islands have long been claimed by Argentina. In April 1982 Argentinian forces occupied the islands. Attempts by the USA and UN to bring about a diplomatic solution were unsuccessful, and UK despatched a task force to retake the islands. After heavy fighting, the UK force eventually recaptured the Islands in June 1982. Argentina has continued to claim sovereignty, which the UK continues to refuse to negotiate.

Fascism. The ideology and political system of Benito Mussolini, which encouraged militarism and extreme nationalism, organizing Italy along right-wing hierarchial authoritarian lines fundamentally opposed to democracy and liberalism. The term is also applied to any ideology or movement inspired by such principles, *e.g.*, German National Socialism and the Spanish Falange.

Fascista *pl* **Fascisti.** A member of the fascist political party under Mussolini that ruled Italy from 1922 to 1943.

Fatehpur Sikri. Capital city of the Mughal empire from 1569 to 1584 A.D. during the reign of Akbar, about 25 miles west of Agra. Its architecture, largely planned by Akbar himself and executed in red sandstone, shows both Hindu and Muslim styles, initially abandoned for lack of an adequate water supply, Fatehpur Sikri was finally deserted after Akbar's death.

Fedayee. A member of an Arab commando group operating esp against Israel.

Federal Bureau of Investigation (F.B.I.). Detective branch of the U.S. dept. of justice, Estabd. in 1908 to investigate crimes against federal law, as distinct from those against the laws of individual states, the F.B.I. enforces laws against espionage, white-slave traffic, blackmail, racketeering, etc. During World War II, F.B.I. detachments accompanied U.S. armed forces on counter-espionage duties, and since 1945 the bureau has been prominent in anti-Communist activities. The detectives are known as G-men from the dept.'s code letter "G".

Feisal. (1885-1933) King of Iraq, 2nd son of Hussein, Sharif of Mecca (*q.v.*) Educ. in Constantinople, he was one of the group that deprived Abdul Hamid II of his throne in 1909. In 1918 he helped the Brit. to conquer Palestine and Syria, and he attended the Peace Conference in Paris in 1919. In August, 1921, he was elected and proclaimed King of Iraq. Until 1932 Iraq was governed in assoc. with Brit. along mandatory lines. He Was succeeded by his son Ghasi (1912-39), and by his grandson Feisal II (1935-58), who was assassinated. See Irao.

Ferdinand. Name of 7 kings of Spain. Ferdinand V (1452-1516) became King of Aragon, 1470. Previously he had mar. Isabella, who became Queen of Castile, 1474. Under their rule Spain became a single kingdom with an immense empire overseas, as the Moors were crushed and the New World discovered. His grandson was the Emperor Charles V.

Feudalism. 1. A medieval system of political organization having as its basis the relationship of lord to vassal with all land held in fee and as its chief characteristics homage, the service of tenants under arms and in court, wardship, and forfeiture. 2. Any of various political or social systems similar to medieval feudalism.

Fifth Column. A group of Falangist sympathisers within Madrid during the Spanish Civil War who aided the 4 columns of rebel troops marching on the city. The term is now applied to any group of hostile or subversive infiltrators.

First Round Table Conference 1930. Seeing that the report of the Simon Commission had been condemned by every political party and there was a great deal of unrest in the country, the British Government called a Round Table Conference in London in Nov. 1930, to draw up a constitution for India. Representatives from British India and Indias States, together with English politicians took part in this conference but the Civil Disobedience Movement was going on and the Congress refused to send representative. The recommendations were not found satisfactory.

First World War. See World War One.

Fizherbert. Marie Anne 1756-1837 nee *Smythe*; wife of George IV of England.

Five-Year Plan. In socialist economies a government plan for economic development over a period of 5 years. In the USSR Stalin introduced a series of 3 such plans, starting in 1928, which involved rapid industrialization and the collectivization of agriculture.

Flag of Truce. A white flag carried of displayed to an enemy as an invitation to conference or parley.

Fourteen Points. A peace programme to follow the end of WWI, outlined by President Woodrow Wilson to the US Congress in 1918.

The points were: (1) renunciation of secret diplomacy; (2) freedom of the seas; (3) removal, where possible, of economic barriers; (4) reduction in armaments; (5) impartial adjustment of colonial claims; (6) Germany and its allies to leave USSR territory; (7) restoration of Belgium; (8) liberation of occupied France, and the return to France of Alsace-Lorraine; (9) Italian frontiers to be adjusted along clearly recognizable lines of nationality; (10) autonomous development for the peoples of the Austro-Hungarian Empire; (11) occupation forces to withdraw from Romania, Montenegro and Serbia, with Serbia receiving access to the sea; (12) self-development for non-Turkish peoples within The Ottoman Empire, and free passage of the dardanelles; (13) formation of an independent Poland with access to the sea; (14) the creation of a general association of nations to guarantee the political independence of all states.

The majority of these points were implemented at the Paris Peace conference, and point (14) led to the foundation of the League of Nations.

Fourth of July. American Independence Day.

France Third Republic (1871-1946). It was established after the overthrow of the Emperor Napoleon III in the Franco-Prussian War. Because of a fear of authoritarian, anti-republican rule, its constitution favoured weak and unstable governments—for example between WWI and WWII there were 44 governments, led by 20 different PMs. The Franco-Russian Alliance (see Triple Entente) let to France's involvement in WWI, and the instability of its governments led to near-defeat. However, with the Allied victory, France regained Alsace-Lorraine from Germany.

In the 1930s, France, like Britain, pursued a policy of appeasement towards Hitler, and the instability of its governments was again a factor in its defeat (1940) and occupation by Germany in WWII, when the collaborationist Vichy Government came to power (1940-44). De Gaulle and the Free French, together with resistance groups in France, continued to oppose German occupation until the liberation (1944).

The Fourth Republic. (1946-58) was just as unstable as the Third Republic, 23 governments holding power in 12 years. Under the Republic, the economy was revitalized after the ravages of war, and France became a founder member of the EEC. The unsuccessful attempt to hold onto the French colonies in Indo-China discredited the Republic, and its plans for the independence of Algeria led to a threatened rebellion by French settlers in the colony and by elements in the army. The crisis led to the return to power of De Gaulle, and his establishment of the Fifth Republic (1958).

The Fifth Republic. gave extensive powers to the President, and put an end to government instability. As President, De Gaulle, having survived an army rebellion in 1961, eventually settled the Algerian problem when independence was granted in 1962. In the late 1950s and early 1960s France also granted independence to most of its other colonies, principally in Africa, but it has maintained close economic, political and cultural links with them.

De Gaulle's ambition was to establish France as leader of a united Europe independent of US and Soviet influence. He withdrew French forces from NATO (1966), and twice blocked the UK's application to join the EEC (1963 and 1967), fearing that France's dominant position might be usurped. He insisted that France develop its own nuclear deterrent, and in foreign affairs followed an independent line, *e.g.*, by visiting Warsaw Pact as countries, and by opposing Western policies in conflicts such as the Middle East and Vietnam. At home, crisis developed over the value of the franc and over a lack of educational and social investment. These, combined with substantial wage demands, culminated in a general strike and the Paris student demonstrations (1968).

De Gaulle resigned following a referendum defeat in 1969, and was succeeded as president by Pompidou (1969-74), Giscard D'Estang (1974-81), and Mitterand. French opposition to expansion of EEC membership was dropped, and France has been more amenable to cooperating with the West's political and economic policies, although still opting for an independent military approach.

Franchise or Suffrage. The right to vote, esp. for representatives in a legislative body.

Francis. Name of 2 Emperors. Francis II (1768-1835) Emperor of Austria and the Holy Rom. Empire, was the brother of Marie Antoinette, and from 1792-1814 was often at war with Fr. His daughter, Marie Louise, became Napoleon's wife, but in 1813 he joined the allies and assisted in the final defeat of the emperor. Francis was the last emperor of the Holy Rom. Empire, which was dissolved in 1806, and the first Emperor of Austria.

Francis. Name of 2 kings of Fr. Francis I (1494-1547) mar. in 1514, Claude, daughter of Louis XII, and succeeded to the throne in 1515. His reign was largely occupied by his wars against the Emperor Charles V. His son became Henry II. Francis II (1541-60) Eldest son of Henry II and Catherine de Medici. He mar. Mary Stuart in 1558 and in 1559 succeeded as king.

Francis Joseph. (1830-1916) Emperor of Austria and king of Hungary. He was the eldest son of the Archduke Francis, a grandson of the Emperor Francis II and a member of the house of Habsburg. His 60 years' reign was one of nat. and personal misfortune. The defeat of Austria by Prussia in 1866 was the end of her long dominance in German affairs. With innate stubbornness the emperor held on, and towards the end took the fatal step of attacking Serbia, after the murder of his nephew and heir, Francis Ferdinand.

Franco, Francisco. (1892-1975), called el Caudillo, Spanish General and statesman. He was Commander-in-Chief of the nationalist rebels in the Spanish Civil War (1936-39), defeating the republican socialist government with German and Italian military aid and establishing a dictatorship. He kept Spain neutral during WWII, and afterwards made a pact with the USA for military bases in Spain in return for economic aid. He prepared the country for a return of the monarchy and the restoration of democracy after his death. *See also* Spain.

Franco-Prussian War. Struggle in 1870-1 between Fr. and Prussia. There was some tension because Napoleon III, then ruling Fr., objected to the selection of a German prince as king of Spain. Bismarck, who wished to weaken Fr., precipitated the struggle by altering and publishing a telegram from Ems which made it appear that the King of Prussia had insulted the Fr. Ambassador. War was declared by Fr. on July 19. German victories forced a large Fr. army to take refuge in Metz. The decisive Battle of Sedan ended in the surrender of Napoleon and his army. The Germans then besieged Paris from Sept. 20 until its surrender in Jan. 1871. Fr. agreed to surrender Alsace-Lorraine and to pay a huge indemnity. At versailles, Jan. 18,1871, William I of Prussia was declared Emperor.

Franks. Name given to some European tribes, first heard of in the 3rd cent. along the lower courses of the Rhine. By the 4th cent. these were collected into 2 groups, the *Ripuarian Franks* and the *Salian Franks*. Under the leadership of Clovis, the Salian Franks moved into what is now Fr. and in 481 he was made their king. In the 9th cent. when their land had extended in all directions, the Franks again broke into 2 divisions. The W. Franks remained in Fr. whilst the E. Franks founded what later became Germany.

Frankpledge. An Anglo-Saxon system under which each adult male member of a tithing was responsible for the good conduct of the others; also the member himself or the tithing.

Franz Josef I. (1830-1916), Emperor of Austria (1848-1916) and King of Hungary (1867-1916). His autocratic reaction to the 1848 revolutions led him to distrust all forms of party government and adhere to bureaucratic administration, under a benevolent dynasty, at the expense of constitutional rule. The last years of his reign were marked by WWI.

Frederick. Name of 2 Holy Roman Emperors. Frederick I (1124-90) known as Barbarossa (Redbeard) belonged to the Hohenstaufen family. In 1155 he was crowned Emp. in Rome. To Germany he was a strong had resolute ruler, cruching the Dukes who opposed him. In Italy he was involved in quarrels with the Papacy. In 1189 he set out on a Crusade, and was drowned. Frederick II (1194-1250) son of the Emperor Henry VI, was chosen German King in 1196. In 1212 he was crowned king but had to fight to estab. his position. In 1220, in Rome, he was crowned Emperor by the Pope, and in 1228, having spent some years in Sicily, he went on a Crusade and was crowned King of Jerusalem. His sons, henry and Conrad bad in turn risen against him. Brilliantly versatile, he was known as *Stupor Mundi*—Wonder of the World.

Frederick. (1596-1632), King of Bohemia. Son of Frederick IV, Elector Palatine of the Rhine. In 1613 he mar. Elizabeth, daughter of James I, and in 1619, being a Protestant, he was elected King of Bohemia. His enemies were too strong for him. From 1623 until his *d.* Frederick was an exile. Among his children were Sophia. Electress of Hanover, mother of George I.

Frederick IX. (1892-1972), King of Denmark, son of Christian X; succeeded to the throne 1947. He mar. Ingrid, grand-daughter of Gustavus V of Sweden, and had 3 daughters. He was succeeded by his daughter Margarethe.

Frederick II. (1712-1972), King of Prussia called the Great. B. Berlin, son of Frederick William I. He had a very unhappy childhood, and was a virtual prisoner for some years. Later he mar. a princess of Brunswick, corresponded with Voltaire, read much in Fr. In 1740, Frederick became king, and almost at once made war on Austria. His aim was to obtain Silesia. In 1756 the Seven Years' War began. The odds against Prussia, aided only by Brit. were immense, but her king performed miracles both as general and administrator. His country was utterly exhausted when peace was made in 1763. For the rest of his reign, ruling as an absolute monarch, he did much to restore its prosperity. The king wrote a great deal, always in Fr. and his waitings have been pub. in 33 vols.

Free French. The name given in 1940 to supporters of General De Gaulle during WWII. The movement represented a political alternative to the Vichy Government as well as a rallying-point for French patriots. It was renamed the Fighting French in 1942.

Free Trade. The international trade that is free of such government influence as import quotas, export subsidies, protection tariffs, etc. The opposite to free trade is protectionism.

Free World. The part of the world where totalitarian or Communist political and economic system do not prevail.

French Revolution. The French Revolution was a great event in the history not only of France and Europe but also of man-kind. It gave to humanity new ideas of liberty, equality and fraternity. The most important cause of the French Revolution was the social inequality. French society was divided into the privileged and the unpriviledged. The privileged were those who belonged to the nobility and the clergy; they enjoyed all facilities. But the condition of unprivileged classes was deplorable. A peasant had to work for his landlord from sunrise to sunset. He was bound to grind his corn at the mill. The peasants paid taxes to the Church as well as to the King. But the privileged classes were exempted from these taxes. The bourgeoisie or the middle-class also belonged to the unprivileged part of French society. The bureaucracy was corrupt and harassed the people. The class relations were highly strained. The medieval feudal society oppressed the serfs, the peasants and artisans. The country was passing through financial bankruptcy because of the wars of Louis XIV and XV. The intellectual background for the Revolution was prepared by the preachings of the three intellectual giants of the age—Montesquieu, Voltaire and Rousseau. Rousseau's *The Social Contract* and the theory of General Will supplied the text and lit the fire of revolution. It started with the fall of Bastille and freeing of prisoners who had been held by the monarch. The French Revolution stood for "Liberty, Equality and Fraternity." King Louis XVI and his Queen Marie Antoinette were beheaded. Napoleon, after some time, emerged as the strong man of France.

The Continental System. Napoleon tried hard to bring England to her knees but failed in the battle of Trafalgar in 1805. He called England a 'nation of shopkeepers'. He thought that the best way to conquer England was to destroy her trade and commerce. And since Napoleon had defeated Austria in the Battle of Austerlitz (December 1805), Prussia in the Battle of Jean (1806) and Russia in the Battle of Friedland (1807), he felt that he was in a position to attack England at a point where she was vulnerable. He issued the Berlin and Milan decrees which declared the British Isles to be in a state of blockade. He declared in the famous Berlin decree: "The British islands are henceforth blockaded. All commerce with them is prohibited; letters and packages with an English address will be confiscated as also every store of English goods on the Continent within the border of France and her allies; every piece of English goods, all English vessels, and those laden with staples from English colonies will be excluded from all European harbours, including those of neutral states." The Milan decree provided that even neutral vessels sailing from a British port or from a country occupied by British troops, might be seized by French warships. The decree went so far as to order the confiscation or public burning of all British-manufactured goods in the French Empire. The British Government also hit back by orders-in-Council of 1807. According to these Orders, all vessels trading with France or her allies were liable to be captured. In certain cases, neutral vessels were to touch at a British port before proceeding to any part of Europe.

Napoleon failed in his objective. The application of Continental System was a physical impossibility. Trade was dislocated. The prices of the articles of common use rose high. The system added to the sufferings of the people of Europe. Napoleon was termed as a merciless dictator. The Continental System not only roused the people of Europe against Napoleon, he also lost the confidence of the French middle class. The efforts of Napoleon to enforce the Continental System crippled the resources of France and alienated many of his allies. The Continental System was a grand economic endurance test and Great Britain won it.

Fronde. Civil war that took place in Fr. (1648-53). The first Fronde was due to a quarrel between Mazarin and the Parl. of Paris about taxation. Helped by troops under the great Conde, Mazarin put down the rising and peace was made in March, 1649. The second Fronde was a rinsing in 1652-53. Conde had quarrelled with Mazarin and raised a revolt which Mazarin quelled.

Fronde. Either of two rebellions against the policies of the chief minister, Cardinal Mazarin, during the minority of Louis XIV, the first (1648-49)led by the parliament of Paris, and the second (1650-53) led by the princes.

G

Gaddafi, Col. Mu'ammar. Libyan political leader. Seized power in 1969, overthrowing the monarchy and establishing a repub. He has promoted the use of Libya's great oil wealth to involve Libya in the affairs of other nations, supporting revolutionary and resistance movements such as palestinian guerrilla forces.

Gandhi, Indira. (1917-1984) Indian politician, Prime Minister 1966-77 and from 1979. She is the daughter of Nehru and succeeded Shastri as leader of the Congress Party. She lost the election of 1977, after declaring a state of emergency in 1975 and suppressing many civil liberties. She subsequently faced corruption charges, but still had a spectacular success at the polies in 1979, when she was re-elected. She was assassinated by her security guards.

Gandhi-Irwin Pact (1931). On March 5, 1931, Mahatma Gandhi and Lord Irwin arrived at an understanding and concluded at Delhi what is known as the Gandhi-Irwin Pact, or 'Delhi Pact'. Mahatma Gandhi called off the Civil Disobedience Movement. Lord Irwin released all political prisoners and the salt laws were amended so that people could collect salt from the seacoast for their personal use. Mahatma Gandhi also agreed to take part in the Second Round Table Conference.

Gandhi, Kasturba. Born 1869 in a merchant family of Porbandar, married to M.K. Gandhi in 1882; a devoted wife remained in forefront throughout her husband's eventful career; spent many years in jail; arrested along with Gandhi during Quit India Movement; died while suffering imprisonment at Poona in 1944.

Gandhi, Mohandas Karamchand. (1869-1948) Hindu polit. leader and saint (Mahatma). Barrister-at-law, Inner Tample, London. He practiced passive resistance in India after World War I in order to overthrow Brit. rule, and was frequently imprisoned. Pres. and chief influence in Indian Nat. Congress, 1924-33. Very influential because of asceticism and popularity. Undertook several fasts to end commercial riots after partition of India (1947). He was killed by a Hindu fanatic, 1948.

Gandhi, Rajiv. (1942-1991), Indian statesman. He became PM 1984-) following the assassination of his mother Indira. He has had to deal with the problems of Sikh separatists in the Punjab and the civil war in Sri Lanka. He also initiated a major crackdown on corruption.

Gang of Four. The radical faction within the Chinese Communist Party, consisting of Jiang Qing (Mao-Zedong's widow). Zhang Chunqiao, Wang Hongwen and Yao Wenyuan. It emerged as a political force (1976) but was denounced 6 months later by Party Chairman Hua Guofeng for leading the excesses of the Cultural Revolution, and was again denounced at the Party's 11th congress (1977). The members of the gang were brought to trial and sentenced to life imprisonment. The term has also been applied to the founders of the UK Social Democratic Party.

Gaza Strip. An area of about 160 sq km on the E Mediterranean coast around Gaza. Formerly part of a British Mandate for Palestine it was administered by Egypt (1949-56), and frequently used as a base for terrorist missions against Isreal. Isreal occupied it during the 1956 Arab-Isreali War, and it was placed under UN control (1957-67). It was occupied during the 1967 War by Israel which subsequently administered it as 'occupied territory'.

General Agreement on Tariffs and Trade (GATT). The multilateral International treaty signed by 86 states in 1948. It was designed to expand international trade and promote economic development, esp. by the elimination or reduction of import quotas and tariffs. Special attention is given to the trading problems of developing countries.

Since its inception, 7 rounds of negotiations have been concluded, and participation countries now account for some 80% of world trade. In addition to its members the Agreement has 31 de facto adherents who participate under special arrangements.

Geneva Convention. A series of 4 international agreements, signed as a group (1949) by 59 governments, for the protection of war victims. The oldest (1864) set out regulations for the care of sick and wounded. Naval combatants were covered in 1907, treatment of prisoners of war in 1929, and treatment of non-combatants in 1949.

George I. (1660-1727) King of Gt. Brit. and Ireland. His mother, a granddaughter of James I of Gt. Brit. was made heir to the throne in 1701, and George became king of Brit. on the *d.* of Queen Anne in 1714. He spoke no Eng. and left the admin. of the country to his ministers, a practice which initiated the system of Cabinet Government.

George II. (1683-1760). King of Gt Brit. and Ireland. Son of George I, he was created Prince of Wales in 1714. In 1727 he succeeded to the throne and followed his father's policy of ruling through his ministers, esp. Sir Robert Walpole, the first P.M. In 1743 he led his army against the Fr. at Dettingen. During his reign occurred the Jacobite Rebellion of 1745, and was with Fr. His family consisted of 2 sons and 5 daughters, but as his eldest son Frederick, Prince of Wales, *d.* before him, he was succeeded by Frederick's son, as George III.

George III. (1738-1820) King of Gt. Brit. and Ireland. His father *d.* in 1751. In 1960, George succeeded his grandfather, George II. In 1762 he made Bute P.M., but in 1763 the earl resigned. In 1770, having formed in Parl. a party known as the King's Friends, he was able to put Lord North at the head of affairs. For 12 years George and North were responsible for the government a period marked by the loss of the Amer. colonies. In 1788, the king's mind gave way, and his son George was appointed regent. He became permanently insane in 1811, and for the rest of the reign his son was regent. George mar. in 1761, Charlotte, princess of Mecklenburg-Strelitz and had 15 children, 7 of the 9 sons survived.

George IV. (1762-1830) King of Gt. Brit. and Ireland, eldest son of George III, he was made Prince of Wales in 1762. In 1795 he mar. Caroline of Brunswick but soon quarrelled with his wife. As Prince of Wales, George was notorious for his extravagance and profligacy. He became the central figure of the Whig opposition to the government, Fox and Sheridan being among his friends. He acted as regent during his father's insanity in 1788. In 1811 he was again regent, and retained the office until he became king in Jan. 1820. Mrs. Fitzherbert was his morganatic wife from 1785 until her *d.* 1813.

George V. (1865-1936), King of Great Britain and Ireland (1910-36). His reign was marked by the Parliament Act, WWI, the Irish troubles, the General Strike, the Great Depression, the choice of Baldwin as PM, and the formation of a National Government (1931).

George VI. (1894-1952), King of Great Britain and Northern Ireland (1936-52). His reign was marked by the aftermath of his brother Edward VIII's abdication, WWII, the formation of the first Labour government with an overall majority, and the start of the dissolution of the Empire.

Gestapo. Nazi Germany's secret state police, headed by Himmler, and notorious for its ruthless interrogation methods.

Ghaddar Party. (1913). The Ghaddar Party was founded in 1913 by some Indian Revolutionaries living in Canada and America. The party also had its branches in other countries. Among its leaders were also Ras Bihari Bose, Raja Mahendra Pratap, L. Hardayal, Abdul Rehman, Madam Cama, etc. Sikh peasantry and soldiers formed its membership. The party decided to send a shipload of arms to the Punjab were some regiments were to revolt on 21 February, 1915. However, the secret leaked out. The regiments were disbanded. The ship and the leaders were arrested.

Ghana. English. Cap: Accra.

The original Gold Coast was established as a British colony in 1874 after being purchased from the Dutch in 1871. Ashanti and the Northern Territories were incorporated in 1901 and the former German colony of Togoland was incorporated as a mandated territory after the WWI peace settlements.

The country became independent as Ghana in 1957, with Nkrumah as P.M. In 1960 Ghana became a republic within the commonwealth, and in 1964 Nkrumah established a 1-party state. He was overthrown by a millitary coup in 1966, since when the country has been ruled by a succession of civilian and military governments, which have, however, failed to deal with the problems of widespread corruption.

Geazni, Mahmud of (d. 1030 A.D.). Muslim ruler who came to power in Afghanishan in 997 A.D. and soon began invading India. After defeating a confederacy of Hindu princes in 1008, he launched a series of raids into the heart of North India, establishing Muslim rule at Lahore in 1020.

Ghory Dynasty. (1186-1206). See Mohammad Ghori.

Gibraltar. The self-governing British crown colony at the W end of the Mediterranean Sea, at the S end of the Iberian Peninsula.

The Rock was captured from Spain by the British (1704), possession being confirmed by the Treaties of Utrecht (1713). Paris (1763) and Versailles (1783), but Spain has constantly pressed for its return. The inhabitants voted overwhelmingly in a referendum to stay British (1967) and Spain closed its frontier and severed communications with the colony in 1969 until 1985 when anglo-Spanish relationships improved. Gibraltar was of great strategic importance during WWII.

Giri, Varahagiri Venkatigiri. (1894-1980). Born at Behrampur in prosperous Brahmana home; followed father's nationalistic proclivities (was member of Swaraj Party in ninteen twenties) and interested in Bengal-Nagpur Railway Workers' Federation; educated in home town; entered Dublin University for higher education; greatly influence by De Valera and freedom struggle of Irish and Irish Trade Union Movement; became associated with Sinn Fein Movement and many leading Irish nationalists; called to Bar; returned to India (1916); started law practice in home town; took active part in national movement and keen interest in labour movement; joined Home Rule League and Indian National Congress; gave up lucrative practice and joined non-co-operation movement; arrested and imprisoned for a short while; one of founders of Indian Railwaymen's Federation (1923); President, Trade Union Congress (1926 and 1942); as leading trade unionist, attended International Labour Conference, Geneva, (1927); attended Second Round Table Conference, London, as workers' representative (1931-1932); played prominent part in organising trade unions in support of national movement; member, Indian Legislative Assembly (1934-37) where was forceful speaker; as Congress candidate won general election from Babbili against raja of that place whose stronghold it was ; became Cabinet Minister for Labour in Congress ministry, Madras (1937) and again after general elections of 1946; India's High Commissioner in Srilanka; member, Lok Sabha (1952-57); member of Union Cabinet with portfolio of Labour (1952-54); Governor, Uttar Pradesh, Kerala and Karnataka; President, Indian Conference of Social Work (1958); Vice-President of India (1967);

(fourth) President of India (1969-74); uncompromising believer in parliamentary form of democracy for India;some of his schemes he had in mind were for providing gainful employment through self-employment, land colonisation linked with network of cottage and village industries; advocated procurement of foodgrains at Panchayat level and organisation of honest and efficient public distribution system; a thorough-going socialist, has always held a brief for the millions; had a practical and human outlook; tow of his important books are *Industrial Relations and Labour Problems in Indian Industry* and one of his publications, *Jobs for the millions*.

Giscard D'Estaing, Valery. French statesman, President (1974-81). As leader of the Independent Republicans (allied to the Gaullists), he became the youngest President of France since 1848, and was faced with difficult economic circumstances with mounting inflation and uncertain political support, esp. from his Gaullist PM Jacques Chirac. Giscard maintained a strong French position within the EEC and on defence matters.

Glasnost. (Russ.) openness. The term is applied to the Soviet policy of political and social liberalization embarked upon under Gorbachev since 1985.

Glorious Revolution (1688). James II was a Roman Catholic. His tactless attempt to secure freedom of worship for Catholics united the Whigs and Tories of the Anglican Church against him. People tolerated the rule of James II, because they thought that he would be succeeded by his daughter Mary who was a Protestant. But a son was born to James II. The knowledge that James' policies might be continued by a son to be brought up as a Catholic turned against him many Tories hitherto loyal. So a few leading men—Whigs as well as Tories—despatched an invitation to William of Orange, ruler of Holland, to succeed to the English throne and save England from Catholic tyranny. William accepted the invitation and came to England for this purpose. James, throwing the great seal into the Thames, fled to France. This event is known as Glorious or Bloodless Revolution in England. The despotic rule of the Stuarts ended; the supremacy of Parliament was established. A series of measures made the constitutional adjustments necessitated by the Glorious Revolution. The system of requiring estimate and accounts for supplies and, of specific appropriations—which is the nucleus of modern budgetary system— now became fixed. The Bill of Rights settled the problem of succession; it also laid the provision that no Roman Catholic can wear the Crown.

Godesberg Meeting (1938). The discussion between the British PM Neville Chamberlain and Hitler, at which Chamberlain refused to agree to the German occupation of the Sudetenland, the German-speaking area of Czechoslovakia. A week later, Chamberlain, with Daladier and Mussolini, signed the Munich Agreement, agreeing to the German occupation.

Goebbels, Joseph. (1897-1945). German Nazi politician. He was an early follower of Hitler, and controlled the party propaganda machine from 1929. From 1833 to 1945 he was Minister of Enlightenment and Propaganda, and his control of press, radio and cinema contributed enormously to the establishment of totalitarian Nazi state. He committed suicide with his family in 1945 in Hitler's bunker.

Georing, Herman. (1893-1946). German Nazi politician, Luft-waffe officer. An early Nazi, he joined with Hitler in the Munich Putsch. In 1932 he became President of the Reichstag, and form 1933 he was Minister of Aviation, building up the Luftwaffe (German air force) into a formidable fighting machine, used with great success in the Blitzkrieg tactics of WWII. Following the victories of 1940, he was created Reichsmarshal, but thereafter his influence declined. He committed suicide after the Nuremberg Trials (1946) i which he had been sentenced to death for war crimes.

Golan Heights. The range of hills astride the NE Israeli and SW Syrian frontier N of the Sea of Galilee. This strategic area was the scene of heavy fighting between the two countries during the 1967 Arab-Isreal War, and was finally occupied by Isreal. After the 1973 War it was occupied by UN forces.

Gomukla, Wladyslaw. (1905-82). Polish Communist politican. He became General Secretary of the Communist Polish Workers' Party (1943). He was Vice-President in the Postwar government, but his nationalist deviation from orthodox Stalinist Communism led him to be dismissed from office and imprisoned (1951-55).

He was rehabilitated in 1956 and, admist growing political unrest, later in the same year became the country's leader as First Secretary of the Party, a position he held until replaced by Gierek (1970). Economic stagnation, and serious rioting which arose from substantial food price increases, contributed to his downfall

Gokhale, Gopal Krishna. Born May 9, 1866 in a village Kotluk in Ratnagiri district of old Bombay Presidency; graduated from Elphinstone College, Bombay: Professor of History and Political Economy in Fergusson College, Bombay; came in close touch with Justice Ranade whose influence enabled Gokhale to make no compromise on principles; adherence to truth, willingness to admit mistakes, honesty of purpose and respect for moral standards became his watchwords; appointed Hony. Secy. of Deccan Sabha; in 1889 joined Indian National Congress; elected to Bombay Legislative Assembly (1899); opposed principle of communal representation; elected to Supreme Legislative Council in 1902, continued up to 1911; constitutional fight against bureaucracy; did not preach direct action; advocated free press and compulsory education; elected Secretary of Congress (1904); President Banares Session of Congress (1905); founded Servants of India Society in 1905; took up cause of Indians settled in South Africa; member of Royal Commission to inquire into public services in India; prepared draft constitution for India; wanted dominion status of India; died February 19, 1915.

He was the most gifted member of Moderate Party and was the greatest statesman of his time. He was the founder of servants of India society. He was the political Guru of Mahatma Gandhi.

Goths. Teutonic people, who prob. came N. Europe. They were dwelling on the shores of the Baltic in the 1st cent. Soon they were divided into 2 branches, in the E. the Ostrogoths and in the W the Visigoths. They were converted to Christianity by the preaching of Ulfilas. *c*.400, under Alaric, a warlike and ambitious leader, they began to move. They marched W., reached Italy, and in 410 captured and plundered Bome. In a short time they estabd: a Gothic kingdom in Fr. and Sp.; first king was Theodoric. In Fr. they were overthrown by the Franks under Clovis early in the 6th cent. In Spain they conquered the Vandals and occupied a dominant position until their last king, Roderic, was killed in battle with the Moors in 711. After the Visigoths had moved W. the Ostrogoths were temporarily conquered by the Huns. About 520 they marched into Italy, as the emissaries of the Empire at Byzantium. They estabd. Themselves there under their leader, Theodoric, who made Revenna his capital.

Soon after his *d.* in 526, Justinian sent Belisarius against the Ostrogoths. A long struggle took place, ending only when Narses, the succesor of Belisarius, destroyed the power of the Ostrogoths.

Gottwald, Klement. (1896-1953). Czechoslovak Communist politician. He was General Secretary of the Party (1929-53). He became PM of a coalition government (1946) and established a 1-party state by using the police and workers' militia to effect a coup d'etat (1948), since when the country has been Communist controlled. Gottwald succeeded Benes as President (1948-53).

Governor-General of India and Acts

Warren Hastings (1774-1785) introduced several reforms, established civil and criminal courts, and courts of appeal. He passed *The Regulating Act*, 1947, giving a legalised working Constitution to the Company's dominion in India. It envisaged a Council of Ministers under the Governor-General. *The Pitt's India* Act, of 1784 put the Company's affairs in Parliament control of the British Parliament.

Lord Cornwallis (1786-1793) introduced a new revenue system under the *Permanent Settlement of Bengal* in 1793. In the third Mysore War, Tipu Sultan was defeated in (1792). He introduced Civil Services in India.

Lord Wellesley (1798-1805) made an Alliance with the Nizam. Tipu was defeated in the Fourth Mysore War and killed. Wellesley prepared the *subsidiary system of alliances*. In this system, the states joining it lost independence.

Lord Minto (1807-1813) Treaty of Amritsar in 1809 with Maharaaja Ranjit Singh, defining the latter's boundaries to the west of the Sutlej.

Marquess of Hastings (1813-1823). War with Nepal resulted in Nepal ceding Grahwal and Kumaon to the Company. Marathas completely routed. He completed the work of Wallesley and made the Completely the paramount power in India. Reforms include introduction of Ryotwari system, special attention to education, building of roads, bridges and canals.

Lord William Bentick (1828-1835) is famous for the social

reforms he introduced, such as abolition of *sati*, suppression of *thuggee*, suppression of female infanticide and human sacrifices. Indians were employed to higher posts but on lower salaries. Law courts were reformed. He also made a treaty with Maharaja Ranjit Singh, the Sikh ruler of the Punjab. In 1833, with the *Charter Act*, the Company ceased to be a trading company and became administrative. The Governor General of Bengal was termed the Governor General of India, and it was declared that no Indian could be debarred from holding any post under the Company on racial grounds.

Sir Charles Metcalf (1835-1836) is notable for removing restrictions on the Press.

Load Hardinge (1844-1848) brought about reforms in forming a railway scheme for India, extending education, preparing a project for the Ganga canal. *The First Sikh War* took place in 1845-46 in which the English took advantage of chaotic condition of Punjab after Maharaja Ranjit Sing. The *Treaty of Lahore* was made.

Lord Dalhousie (1848-1856). *The Second Sikh War* in which the Sikhs were defeated, by treachery and Punjab was annexed.

The second Burmese war resulted in the English getting control of the whole coastline from Chittagong to Singapore. Dalhousie rigidly followed *Doctrine of Lapse* by which the British would get those states whose rulers died without a son to inherit. He abolished titles and pension of native rulers. He annexed Berar and Oudh (which was an act of aggression). The *Charter Act* of 1853 paved the pay for the Crown to take over administration of India. It also set up the first Legislative Council at the centre. Reforms include setting up of P.W.D., improvement of Post and Telegraph on modern lines, Railway laid (1853), education given special attention, passing the Widow Remarriage Act (1856).

Gowon Yakubu. (1934-). Nigerian politician and general. He emerged as head of state (1866-75) after a millitary coup. He introduced a new federal system of 12 states, later increases to 19. In the Biafran War (1967-70) Grown successfully crushed the rebel forces. In 1975 he was remove by another army group.

Grand Alliance. (1688-97) Known also as the war of the League of Augsburg, it was the third of the wars waged by Louis XIV against Spain, the Empire, Brit. and Holland. In 1988 Louis sent his troops into Germany. The Leauge of Augsburg took up the challenge and, converted into the 'Grand Alliance, by the addition of new members in 1689, waged war against Louis. Treaty of Ryswick ended the war.

Great Leap Forward. (1958-61). The slogan used to describe the massive upheaval in China aimed at transforming the country, economically and politically,. to the level of advanced nations.

Inspired by Mao Zedong it had radical aims: to sweep away backwardness by the condemnation of old customs and usages; to establish a commune system encompassing agriculture, education, industry, local defence, trade and welfare; to diversify industry and the economy; to reduce consumption; to establish a truly communistic society; and to mobilize the population' latent talents.

It failed due to a variety of causes: a series of national disasters; managerial difficulties; withdrawal of Soviet technological advice; bureaucratic opposition; Party pragmatism; and substandard harvests.

(The) Greek Civilisation

Greece is the southernmost part of the Balkan Peninusla that dips into the Mediterranean Sea in the south-east Europe. On the east, the Aegean Sea Divides Greece from Turkey sometimes called Anatolia as well as Asia Minor. Much of the early Greek history consists of tales of conflict between the Cretans and the Greeks. The Cretan civilisation dates back about 4000 years. In the sixteenth century B.C. came waves of Greek invaders to overwhelm the Cretans completely. The Greeks came from the north, probably from the Danube river valley. They spoke an Indo-European language. Each wave or group that came into the Aegean region had its own name—Achaeans, Ionians and Dorians. Soon all began to call themselves *Hellenes*, which means Greek.

The early Greeks lived in tribes, each group of tribes having a king. They had many gods whom they imagined to be like human beings. Zeus was the god of the sky and hence caused thunder. Poseidon was the god of the sea, Apollo, the sun god, Athena, the goddess of victory and patroness of the arts and Dionysus was the god of wine. The Greeks thought their gods lived on Mt. Olympus, a mountain in northern Greece. They had no priests and the head of the family performed the sacrifices, or the king performed them for the entire community. Homer provides a great deal of information about the life and institutions of the early Greeks. His *Iliad* is the story of the siege and destruction of the city of Troy, on the western coast of Asia Minor. His *Odyssey* describes the travel adventures and homecoming from Troy, of a great Greek hero Odysseus.

Around 800 B.C., group of Greek villages began amalgamating into large units to form city-states. Many city-states grew up all over Greece on a number of islands—Sparta, Athens, Macedonia, Corinth, Thebes and others. At first the city-states were ruled by monarchs. Then wealthy owners took over political power and abolished the monarchy. Most of the states established either a kind of democracy, or an *digarchy*—ruled by a few rich men. There were many clashes between the city-states, but due to difficulties to travel and communication, they could not be unified in a single state. Philip of a *Maced Onia* conquered most of the states. Then his son, Alexandar, compelled all Greece to accept his leadership and conquered the Achaemenid empire, the largest and the most powerful at the time. This brought him to the Borders of India where he defeated Kings Porus on the Jhelum in 326 B.C. He died at the age of 32 in 323 B.C. When Alexandar died, his generals divided his empire among themselves. Ptolemy, a general of Alexander, became ruler of Egypt, Palestine and Phoenicia. Alexander had founded the city of Alexandria which became a seat of Greek culture and education for a long time. In Alexandria, Ptolemy built a temple to the Greek goddess of art literature and learning, which is known as the *Museum*. It had an observatory and a library. Euclid, the father of geometry lived in Alexandria; Eratosthenes, the geographer, calculated the circumference of the earth there; Archimedes, whose principles children still study at school, worked at the Muse.

Between 146 and 30 B.C., as a result of the Roman onslaught almost the entire territory of the Greeks and their empire became a part of the Roman empire.

For Greek citizens life was easy and simple—simple houses, clothing, food and religion. There were daily sports for men and exercises, and an evening meal with wine and music and serious conversation about life and politics, truth and beauty. There were festivals and holidays to celebrate marriages and honour gods and Goddesses. The world still celebrates one of them—the Olympic games. This event, to honour the god Zeus, was held every four years, then as now. In the field of literature, the Greeks have given us epics, poetry, drama and history. Homer, wrote the *Iliad* and the *Odyssey*, the two great epics of the world. Sappho, the great woman poet, sang of the beauty of love and nature. Pindar, a lyric poet, wrote poems to honour victorious athletes. The founder of Greek tragedy was Aeschylus, author of *Prometheus Bound*. Sophocles, the greatest of the Greek tragedians, wrote *Oedipus Rex, Aetigone* and *Electra*. Other dramatics are Euripides and Aristophanes. Herodoutus, Thucydides and Plutarch are the Greek historians. The most famous philosophers of Greece are Socrates, Plato and Aristotle. The Greeks made a massive contribution to science and mathematics. Hippocrates laid the foundations of modern medicine. The Greeks excelled in art and architecture also.

Guevara, Ernesto ('Che'). (1928-67), Argentinian revolutionary. He joined the exiled Castro in Mexico where he was planning the Cuban revolution. They fought together in Cuba to oust Batista, and Guevara became Minister of Industries in the new regime. His revolutionary ideals did not contain him for long and he left Cuba to rouse Bolivian tinminers to insurrection, but was captured by the army and executed. His guerrilla techniques have influenced revolutionary movements elsewhere.

Guinevere. Wife of King Arthur. She was unfaithful to him. This led to the break-up of Authur's court and the *d.* of the king.

Gulf War. A conflict between Iran and Iraq. The war started in 1980 with an Iraqi attack in pursuit of disputed territory Enormous offensives by both sides have resulted in huge numbers of casualties, but no resolution to the conflict has been achieved, despite diplomatic efforts by other states. The hostilities have also involved attacks on neutral shipping in the Persian Gulf.

Gupta Dynasty (320-550 A.D.). The Gupta period is known as the golden period of Hindu India. The Guptas freed the country from the foreign domination. During their rule, people were happy and prosperous. Art, science and literature were cultivated with success and distinction. *Ajanta caves* were built during Gupta period.

Chandra Gupta Maurya (320-330 B.C.). He was the founder of Gupta dynasty. He established a new era from 320 A.D.

Samundragupta (330-375 A.D.). He was one of the most powerful and ablest of Hindu kings. He was a great scholar, poet and musician. He is known as Indian Napoleon on account of his conquests. He was a great poet and musician. He was worshipper of Vishnu but tolerant of Buddhism. He erected Allahabad Pillar.

Chandra Gupta II (375-413 A.D.). He is generally identified with legendary Vikramaditya. He was a great ruler and conqueror. During his reign Gupta empire was at the height of its power. He was liberal patron of art and literature. The Chinese pilgrim *Fahein* visited India during his time. Fahein says the country was rich and the people led a moral land honest life.

Kumar Gupta I (413-455 A.D.). He was the son of Chandragupta II. Towards the end of his region, he was attached by the Pushyamitras (from the west) and the Huns and with him ended the golden age of Guptas.

Skandagupta (455-477 A.D.). He was the last ruler of the dynasty. His reign was short and stormy as the huns made their fierce raids in his times.

Gustav V. (1858-1950) B. and *d.* Stockholm. King of Sweden, son of Oscar II, whom he succeeded, 1907. He mar. in 1881, had 2 sons, Crown Prince Gustav Adolf and William. A democratic king, he refused to wear his crown and was never crowned.

Gustav VI. (1882-1973) King of Sweden, son of Gustav V, whom he succeeded , 1950. Mar. (1) Margaret, daughter of the Duke of Connaught, who *d.* 1920. (2) In 1923, Lady Louise Mountbattan, Queen Louise of Sweden (*d.* 1965). Eldest son, Prince Gustav Adolf, was killed in a Copenhagen air crash, 1947. He was succeeded by his grandson, Carl Gustav (*b.* 1946).

Gustavus Adolphus. (1594-1632) Gustavus II, King of Sweden. A son of Charles IX, he succeeded his father in 1611. Though much of his reign was spent in warfare he found time to improve the state of his the then very poor country. He made the Swedish Army into a most efficient instrument, winning back Swedish land from Denmark, and defeating Russia and Poland. In 1630 he entered the 30 Years' War on the side of the Protestants. For 2 years he dominated the scene. His greatest victories were Breitenfeld, 1631, and Lutzen, 1632, but in the latter battle he was killed. His only child, Christina (*q.v.*), succeeded him.

H

Haakon. Name of 7 kings of Norway. Haakon VII (1872-1957) was a son of Frederick VIII, King of Denmark. In 1905, on the separation of Norway from Sweden, he was chosen king and crowned in June, 1906. In 1940, having refused to surrender to the invading German forces, he fled to Eng. and led the Norwegian fight from London. He was succeeded by his son, Olav V.

Hadrian. (76-138) Rom. emperor. A soldier and administrator selected by his friend and patron, the Emperor Trajan, as his successor. He visited Brit. Where he was responsible for the wall called after him. Hadrian's Wall. Defensive wall extending from the Solway Firth across Eng. to Wallsend-on-Tyne. It was built *c.* A.D. 122, was 73 m. long and its course may still be traced.

Hague Peace Conference. (1907). The assembly attended by delegates from 44 countries to discuss international arbitration and disarmament. Its declaration against the arms race was ineffectual and it achieved very little, except that a proposition to establish an international court came to fruition in 1920 (see International Court of Justice) having been postponed by the outbreak of WWI.

Haile Selassie. (1892-1975) Emperor of Ethiopia. Through his influence many reforms were carried out, including the modernising of the educ. system, and the abolition of slave-trading. In 1930, he was officially crowned Emperor. In 1935 Ethiopia was invaded by Italy and overwhelmed. Haile Selassie strongly protested to the League of Nations against the Ital. aggression, but it was not until the outbreak of World War II that liberation became possible. In 1936 he escaped to Eng. He recovered his throne in 1941. He finally abolished slavery and set up an advisory two-chamber Parl. In 1974, a military coup deposed him.

Hammarskjold, Dag (1905-61). Swedish politician. He was Secretary-General of the UN (1953-61), and was internationally respected for the impartial and skilful manner in which he carried out his duties, particularly during the Suez Crisis and the turmoil arising from the granting of independence to the Belgian Congo (Zaire). He was killed in an air crash in Zambia while dealing with the Congo Crisis, and was posthumously awarded the Nobel Peace Prize (1961).

Hammurabi. (*c.* 2100 B.C.) King of Babylon. He dominated the Sumerian and Akkadian city states, and made Babylonia a single monarchy. He left valuable latters, and a Semitic code of laws.

Har Dayal, Lala. B. October 14, 1884, at Delhi; son of Gouri Dayal Mathur; M.A. in English literature; after a brilliant academic career, he joined St. John's College, Oxford, England, in 1905 on a Government scholarship; his revolutionary ideas, however, came into conflict with his studies and he had to give up the Government scholarship in 1907; left Oxford and associated himself with the anti-British activities of Shyamji Krishna Varma in Paris, France; visited India and organised revolutionary activities against British rule ; returned to Paris in 1908 and tried to convert Shyamji Krishna Varma to his ideas of violent revolution against the British in India; reached the USA in 1911 and joined Stanford University as a Lecturer in Indian Philosophy; forced to give up his job at the University due to his revolutionary activities; devoted himself completely to propagating revolutionary ideals among the Indians settled in the USA. Addressed meetings of Indians at several places on the Pacific Coast in 1913; his brilliant oratory and convincing logic made him the leader of the Indian community. Elected General Secretary of the Hindustani Association, which came to be known as the Ghadr Party with its headquarters at San Frncisco; carried on his anti-British propaganda through the party's journal *Ghadr* and a large number of books and pamphlets. Served with a warrant of arrest on March 25, 1914, by the U.S. Police on the complaint of the British Consul; released on bail; slipped out of the USA and reached Geneva, Switzerland; resumed his work by publishing a magazine named *Vande Mataram*. Went to Berlin and organised the Indian Independence Committee; successfully enlisted the moral and material help of the German Government; defeat of Germany in the Second World War, however, disrupted his plans and put an end to his activities; died in exile in the USA on March 4, 1939 (Adopted from India).

Harold. Name of 4 kings of Norway. Harold I reigned 872-930. He was at first a chieftain, one of several, in Norway, but succeeded in bringing the whole land under his own rule. Harold III, called Hardrada, invaded Eng. in 1066 and was killed at Stamford Bridge.

Harold I. (*d.* 1040) Eng. king called Harefoot. A son of Canute the great, he claimed the throne on his father's *d.* 1035. It was also claimed by his half-brother, Hardicanute. Harold II (*c.* 1022-66) Eng. king, son of Earl Godwin. In 1051 Godwin and his sons were banished. By 1053 Harold had returned and succeeded his father as Earl of Wessex. In 1066, on Edward's *d.* the Witan chose him as king and he was crowned at Westminster. Shortly afterwards, Harold, King of Norway, together with Tostig, a rebellious brother of the Eng. king, invaded Eng. Harold II defeated them at Stamford Bridge, Sept. 25, and then led his army S. where William of Normandy had landed to claim the crown. At Hastings he met the Normans and there he was killed.

Harsh Vardhana (606-647). He was a strong king of Northern India. He is considered to be the last Hindu king of India. He was a great devout follower of Buddhism, which flourished in his reign. *Hieun Tsang*, a Chinese pilgrim visited during his reign and left interesting account for the conditions of India at that time.

Hasting, Warren (1732-1818 A.D.). First Governor-General of Bengal from 1774-1785. During his tenure, he consolidated and expanded the Company's position in India despite opposition from his own Council for several years. After his return to England, he was first tried and later exonerated and honoured for his actions in India.

Heath, Edward Richard George. Brit. Cons. statesman, P.M. (1970-4). Lord Privy Seal (1960-3), headed Brit. delegation at Common Market negotiations (1961-3). Elected leader Cons. party (1965) and led it to victory in Gen. Election (1970) 1. In 1974, a Labour government was voted into power, and in 1975 Edward Heath was replaced as Conservative party leader.

Hegemony. The ascendancy or domination of a power or state within a group of neighbouring states, a confederation, league, etc., or of one social class over others.

Hejira. Arabic word used for the flight of Mahommed from Mecca to Medina, in 622. From it the Moslems date their era and their year, which begins on July 16.

Helena (*c.* 248-328). Saint and Rom. empress. Her son was Constantine the Great. In her old age she made a pilgrimage to Jerusalem. A legend says that she discovered the Holy Sepulcher and the true cross.

Helsinki Conference. The assembly attended by delegates from 35 countries to discuss security issues, with the aim of reducing international tension. The initial stage of the negotiations took place in Helsinki (1973) and the process was continued intermittently at Geneva (1973-75). Agreements were reached on: economic and technological cooperation ; the upholding of human rights, coupled with closer links between peoples of different states; and measures aimed at preventing accidental confrontation between opposing power blocs. A separate agreement was reached on Mediterranean problems.

Henry. Name of 7 German kings. Henry IV (1050-1106) became king in 1056. In 1069 he began to rule as well as reign, and he passed a long life mainly in a quarrel with the Ch. In 1074 he submitted to Gregory VII at Canossa, but the struggle was soon renewed.

Henry. Name of 4 kings of Fr. Henry I was a grandson of Hugh Capet. He ruled from 1031-60, fighting William, Duke of Normandy, and other of his vassals. Henry II, a son of Francis I, reigned from 1547-59. He is known as the husband of Catherine de Medici and the father of 3 kings, Francis II, Charles IX and Henry III. His daughters mar. Philip of Spain and Henry IV of Fr. He was also the lover of Diane de Poitiers. Henry IV (*q.v.*) reigned from 1589-1610.

Henry. (1394-1460) Prince of Portugal, called the Navigator, son of John I and a grandson of John of Gaunt. He provided money for voyages of exploration to the Asian and African coasts.

Henry I. (1068-1135) King of Eng. 4th son of William I. In 1100, after his brother, William II's *d.*, he ascended the throne. He reigned for 35 years and is regarded as the founder of the Eng. system of justice. He also quarrelled with the ch. Henry mar. Matilda, daughter of Malcolm, King of Scot. His only legitimate son, William, was drowned in the White Ship in 1120; consequently he left the throne to his daughter, Matilda or maud.

Henry II. (1133-89) King of Eng., son of Matilda, daughter of Henry I. In 1153 a treaty was made by which Henry was recognised as

Stephen's successor on the throne. He became king in 1154, 2 years after he had mar. Eleanor, Duchess of Aquitaine, the divorced wife of Louis VII of Fr. In Eng. he restored order after the anarchy under Stephen and introduced legal reforms. This led him into a quarrel with the Ch. and Thomas a Becket, whose murder led to the king's humiliation. In Fr. Henry was chiefly occupied in fighting King Louis and his own rebellious nobles. In 1173 he had to face a rebellion in Eng. in which his eldest son, Henry, took part. His other sons, Richard I, John and Geoffrey, also rebelled against him.

Henry III. (1207-72) King of Eng., son of King John and Isabella of Angouleme. He was only 9 years old when he became king. As a ruler he was influenced by favourites and his mar. in 1236 with Eleanor of Provence led to the arrival of many needy foreigners. The barons, in 1258, compelled Henry to hand over the government to themselves, with Simon de Montfort as their leader. War broke out, Henry was defeated and made prisoner at Lewes in 1264. In 1265 his son Edward defeated the barons at Evesham.

Henry IV. (1367-1413) King of Eng. Eldest son of John of Gaunt, Duke of Lancaster. In 1398, he was sent into exile by Richard II and on Gaunt's d. the king seized his lands. Henry returned, collected a small army in Yorkshire, and Richard being in Ireland, he had no difficulty in securing the throne. His title to it was admitted by Parliament and he began to reign in 1399. The reign, which lasted for 13 years, was marked by rebellions.

Henry IV. (1533-1610) King of Fr., son of Jeanne d'Albret, Queen of Navarre. Although a Protestant he was educ. at the court in Paris and in 1572, just before the Massacre of St. Bartholomew, he mar. Margaret, daughter of the King, Henry II. In 1572, also, he became King of Navarre. In 1589, when Henry III was murdered, he was crowned King. He defeated the Catholic faction in battle at Ivry and Arques, took Paris and then declared himself a R.C. In 1598 he granted the Protestants toleration by the Edict of Nantes.

Henry V. (1387-1422) Kings of Eng., eldest son of Henry IV. He was made Prince of Wales in 1399 and began to take part in public affairs. In 1413 he became king and claimed the throne of Fr. and went with an army to make good his right. In 1415, he won the great victory of Agincourt, and between then and 1420 he conquered the whole of Normandy. In 1420 the Fr. king agreed to the Treaty of

Troyes by which Henry was made regent, or recognised as the next king. He mar. Catherine, a daughter of the King of Fr. and left an only son, Henry VI.

Henry VI. (1421-71) King of Eng. Only son of Henry V, he became King of Eng. and Fr. in 1422. In 1445 he mar. Margaret of Anjou, but before then the faction fights which led to the Wars of the Roses had begun. Henry was quite unable to keep order between the factions, esp, after 1453, when he became insane. Richard, Duke of York was named protector and in 1455 the civil war began. The cause of Henry was championed by his wife, but in 1460 he was made a prisoner. York then claimed the throne, but it was decided that Henry should rule during his lifetime, his rival and not his son, succeeding. War was soon renewed. York was killed at Wakefield and his son made himself king in 1461 as Edward IV. In 1465 Henry was again taken prisoner, but in 1470, by a sudden reversal of fortune, due to Warwick, he was restored for a few months. Edward IV returned from exile., crushed the Lancastrians and put Henry to *d*.

Henry VII. (1457-1509) King of Eng., son of Edmund Tudor and Margaret Beaufort, a descendant of John of Gaunt, Duke of Lancaster. In 1485 he claimed the throne. He collected an army, defeated Richard III at Bosworth and was crowned. Parl. accepted him and he mar. Elizabeth, daughter of Edward IV. He laid the foundation of the Tudor monarchy, by husbanding his revenues, keeping the peace, and crushing the last remnants of baronial indep. His sons were Arthur and Henry VIII. His daughter, Margaret, mar. James IV, of Scot. and their great-grandson became first king of Gt. Brit. in 1603.

Henry VIII. (1491-1547) King of Eng. 2nd son of Henry VII. He became heir to the throne when his brother, Arthur *d*. 1502. He became king in 1509 and at once mar. Catherine, daughter of Ferdinand and Isabella of Spain, and widow of his brother Arthur. The emperor, Charles V, and Francis I of Fr. both sought his aid, and he defeated the Scots at Flodden in 1513. At this time Henry had for his adviser Thomas Wolsey, Archbishop and Cardinal. *C*. 1526, Henry fell in love with Anne Boleyn. To marry her he had to divorce Catherine, which could only be done at the expense of a breach with Rome. In 1529 a Parl. met, which made Henry supreme head of the Ch. in Eng. The work of reform was completed by the dissolution of the monasteries. This led to the abortive rising called the Pilgrimage of Grace. In 1536, Anne Boleyn, charged with crimes against the king, was executed and Henry mar. Jane Seymour. She *d.* very soon, and he took, for his 4th wife Anne of Cleves. She was soon divorced, this leading to the execution of the king's adviser, Thomas Cromwell, in 1540. Henry's 5th wife was Catherine Howard, a niece of the Duke of Norfolk, who was beheaded for infidelity. The 6th was Catherine Parr, who survived him. Henry left 3 children, Edward VI, Mary and Elizabeth, children of Jane Seymour, Catherine of Aragon and Anne Boleyn resp.

Herodotus. Gk. historian (*c.* 484-424 B.C.) B. Cappadocia in Asia Minor. The hist. of Herodotus is in 9 books. It deals with the early hist. of Persia, Lydia and Egypt, but its main theme is the struggle between the Gks. and the Persians.

Herriot, Edouard (1872-1957). French Radical-Socialist statesman. He was PM (1924-25). His government recognized the USSR, championed the cause of disarmament, Collective Security and the League of Nations, and withdrew troops from the Ruhr. Internal economic problems brought down the government, but Herriot again became PM in 1926 (for 2 days) and in 1932. He was imprisoned by the Vichy Government and the Nazis during WWII, and elected President of the National Assembly (1947-53) and afterwards for life.

Hess, Rudolf (1894-1987). German Nazi politician. He joined the Nazi Party and became Hitler's political secretary in 1920 and in 1923 participated in the Munich Putsch. He became deputy Party leader (1934) and successor-designate to Hitler after Goering (1939). He flew alone to Scotland (1941) to try to arrange a negotiated peace settlement of WWII, but was interned for the rest of the War. He was sentenced to life imprisonment at the Nuremburg Trials and from 1966 was the sole remaining prisoner in Spandau Gaol, Berlin, the Russians having consistently rejected pleas by the Americans, British and French for his release.

Hirohito (1901-1989). Emperor of Japan. He became a constitutional monarch, May, 1946, by order of the Occupying Powers, and renounced war. He signed the treaty ending the state of war between Brit. and Japan in 1951. (*See* Japan)

Hiroshima. Japanese port on the island of Honshu. It was destroyed (1945) by the USA by means of an atomic bomb, the first wartime use of a nuclear weapon. A second bomb was dropped in Nagasaki 3 days later, which led to Japan's unconditional surrender to the Allies.

Hitler, Adolf (1889-1945). German dictator. B. Austria; corporal in World War I. Joined German Workers' Party, 1919, and became its leader in 1921, renaming it the National Socialist German Workers' Party. In 1923 he was sentenced to 9 months in prison where he wrote *Mein Kampf.* In 1932 he polled 7 million votes against Hindenburg in the pres. election. On the fall of Papen's government in 1933 he became Chanc. and soon seized dictatorial powers. His policy was that of world domination. He became Further and He of the State in 1934. The Rome-Berlin Axis became an official alliance in 1937. Germany signed a non-aggression pact with Russia on Aug. 12, invaded Poland on Sept. I and World War II began on Sept. 3, 1939. Denmark, The Netherlands, Belgium, France and Norway were overrun. On June 22, 1941, Germany attacked Russia and by Dec. German troops were within 25 m. of Moscow. The German armies were finally driven from Russia in the great offensive of 1943. The Allied landing in Normandy on June 5-6, 1944, sealed the fate of the German forces. By April, 1945, the Russians were occupying a large part of Berlin. Hitler and his wife committed suicide on April 30, 1945, and their bodies were burned in the garden of the Chancellery. See *Hitler* by Alan Bullock (1952).

Hittites. Ancient people in Asia Minor. The Biblical names Heth and Hittite indicate a people almost unknown until exploration from 1870 onwards revealed distinctive monuments. Prof. Sayce announced in 1880 the discovery of a Hittite empire. Their federation took place about 1400 B.C. They disapperared about 1200 B.C. Hittite language. Prob. branch of Indo-European with which it shares vocabulary and inflectional system. Found in hieroglyphic clay-tablet archives at Boghazkeui (Turkey), prob. of the 2nd millennium B.C.

Hiuen Tsang or Yuan Chwang. Chinese Buddhist monk who visited India in A.D. 630 to collect sacred Buddhist literature; stayed India for about 13 years; left a detailed account of his observations on persons, places and customs and manners of people; his book translated into English "*Travels or Records of Western Lands.*"

Hoare-Laval Pact (1935). The proposals for terminating Italo-Abyssinian hostilities prepared by the UK Foreign Secretary, Sir Samuel Hoare, Viscount Templeweed (1880-1959), and the French PM, Pierre Laval, at the request of the League of Nations.

Ho Chi Minh (Vietnamese, 'Seeker of Englightenment'). The orig. Nguyen Van Thann (1892-1969), Vietnamese Communist politician. He founded the Communist Part in Indo-China (1930). After an abortive uprising against the French (1940) he fled to S China and founded a resistance movement of Communists and Nationalists (Viet Minh) to fight the Japanese, then occupying Vietnam during WWII.

After the Japanese surrender the French returned and Ho Chi Minh then led the Viet Minh in successful operations against them (1946-54) having managed to establish a provisional government (1945). He continued to fight for independence in the jungle and, after finally succeeding, became PM (1954-55) and President of North Vietnam (1955-69).

After his victory in the North, Ho Chi Minh set about gaining control of South Vietnam by sending supplies along a secret route through the jungle (the Ho Chi Minh Trail) to the Viet Cong nationalists still fighting for independence. After the US military intervention in support of the South (1965), he despatched regular army units to support the rebels.

In spite of the devastation and turmoil of War, Ho Chi Minh introduced drastic land reforms, increased heavy industrial output in the North and was a highly popular leader among his own people.

Holocaust. The term used to describe the genocide to European Jewry by the Nazis during WWII. See concentration camps.

Holy Roman Empire. A revival of the Ancient Rom. emp. of the W. founded by Charlemagne in 800, under the sanction of the Pope. The epithet Holy was first annexed to the title by Frederick Barbarossa in 1156. Rudolph, the first Hapsburg Emp, Was elected in 1273, and thereafter the empire was a German institution. After the 30 Years' Warm, its centre shifted to Austria (1648), and it was dissolved in 1806 by the resignation of Francis II, Emp. of Austria following the unsuccessful struggle against Napoleonic France.

Home Rule Movement. Mrs. Annie Besant started Home Rule Movement in 1916 to secure home rule for the Indians. She was interned. The movement dissolved when Lord Montague, Secretary of State for India, made his August Declaration in 1917 promising self-government by stages for India.

Hoover, Herbert (1874-1964). US Republican President (1929-33). His administration was uneventful apart from the Wall Street Crash (1929). He was rejected in favour of F.D. Roosevelt at the 1932 election because of the effect the depression was having on the country and because of his refusal, despite increasing hardship, to allow the government to assume responsibility of the unemployed.

'Hot Line'. The direct telephone, teletype, or other communications link between heads of government for emergency use. The 'Hot Line' between the President of the USA and the leader shop of the USSR was established in 1963 following the Cuban Missiles Crisis.

Hoysalas of Dorasamudra. This dynasty ruled the Mysore area at the beginning of the 12th century in subordination to Chalukyas but helped much in the revival of Hinduism (Vaishnavism). Many temples were built by them. Finally the dynasty ended with the sack of Dorasamudra by Malik Kafur, the general of Alla-ud-din Khilji.

Humayun. Second Mughal Emperor, ruled from A.D. 1530 to A.D. 1540 and again 1555-1556; not a strong ruler; defeated by Afghan Sher Shah Suri who became king in 1540 and his successors continued to rule upto 1555 when Humayun reconquered his empire after defeating Sikander Shah Suri; died soon afterwards in 1556.

Hundred Days. Name given to the period between Napoleon's escape from Elba and his surrender after Waterloo, March 20, to June 28, 1815.

Hundred Years' War (1337-1453). Struggle between Eng. and Fr. It began when Edward III claimed the throne of Fr. The Eng. won victories at Crecy and Poitiers, and in 1360 peace was made at Bretigny. The war began again in 1369 and lasted until 1396. By the treaty of 1396 the Eng. lost many of their possessions. In 1415 Henry V claimed the throne of Fr. He won the Battle of Agincourt, conquered Normandy, and in 1420 was recognised as Regent and future King of Fr. Part of the nation refused to submit and the war went on until 1429, when the tide turned on the arrival of Joan of Arc. The Eng. then steadily lost ground and the struggle ended in

1453, all Fr., except Calais, being lost.

Huns. The Huns, a wild nomadic tribe of Central Asia, invaded India in the middle of the 5th century. *Tormanana*, their leader conquered Malwa and Gujarat. Eventually Huns were absorbed into the Rajput population.

Huns. Horde of Asiatics who invaded Europe in the 4th cent. After a career of conquest under Attila they were defeated in 451 at Chalons by Theodoric, King of the Visigoths and disappeared.

Hussein (ibn Talal). King of Jordan. He has maintained a robust and highly personal rule necessitated by the political unheavals inside the country and in the surrounding states. He has sought to keep on good terms with other Arab states, while at the same time maintaining friendly ties with the West, particularly the UK.

His antipathy to Israel resulted in Jordan signing a defence agreement with Egypt (1967). Israel, surrounded by hostile states, included Jordan in its offensive action during the 1967 Arab-Israeli War and occupied E Jerusalem and the West Bank.

In addition Hussein had to contend with his country being used as a base by the Palestine Liberation Organization for terrorist attacks on Israel and elsewhere. Finally, after bitter fighting, Hussein put a stop to these activities by expelling the PLO (1970).

Hyder Ali. (1722-1782 A.D) Father of Tipu Sultan, opponent of the English in the first two Anglo-Mysore wars until his death in 1782.

Hyksos or Shepherd Kings. Name given to the leaders of a group of Semitic tribes who seized power in Egypt after the downfall of the 13th dynasty, *c.* 2300 B.C. and were expelled when the Theban kings regained the ascendancy, *c.* 1829 B.C.

I

Ibn Saud. Abdul Aziz Ibn Rahman Al Feisal, G.C.B., G.C.I.E., (1880-1953). King of Saudi Arabian. Originally rulers of the Nejd, Ibn Saud's family was deposited and took shelter at Kuwait; he won his capital Rijadh, with 40 followers (1901); was king of Hejaz and Nejd (1927); changed name of kingdom to Saudi Arabia in 1932. Ibn Saud took a leading part in founding the Arab League, 1945. He was succeeded by his eldest son, Emir Saud (1953), who abdicated in favour of his brother Faisal, 1964. Faisal was assassinated by a nephew in 1975 and was succeeded by his half-brother Khaled.

Imperial Conferences (1911-13). The meetings in London of the PMs of the UK and the Dominions. Under the little of Colonial Conferences, 4 similar meetings had taken place earlier, and since WWII such gatherings have been called Commonwealth Conferences.

Imperialism or Colonialism. The policy or practice of extending a state's rule over other territories, and of incorporating such colonized territories into an empire.

Since WWII, the European powers have gradually granted independence to most of their colonies (see Decolonization), though the economic domination of the Third World by the developed countries has been called 'neoimperialism'.

Imperial Preference. The economic arrangement between members of the British Empire, and later the Commonwealth, by which preferential Tariffs were operated between them.

Independence Act 1947. India was to be partitioned and two independent and sovereign states of India and Pakistan were to be formed on 15 August 1947 according to the Mountbatten Plan agreed upon by the Congress and the League. It also provided for partition of Punjab and Bengal. The princely states were given the choice of joining either of two new states keeping in view certain principles. India became free on 15th August 1947.

Indian Council of Historical Research. Set up in New Delhi, in 1972, the Council enunciates and implements a national policy of historical research and encourages scientific writing of history. It gives grants for holding of seminars, publication of research works and Journals. It also operates research projects, offers fellowships and grants to scholars in the fields of history.

Indian Historical Records Commission, New Delhi. Government sponsored; advisory body for preserving, acquiring and utilising historical records, promoting surveying, salvaging and listing or records, formulating policy and recommending steps for guidance of government, universities, other bodies, etc.; publishes proceedings, index to papers, records, books, resolutions, etc.

Indian Mutiny. (1857-59) Revolt against Brit. rule in India, attributed partly to an order stating that in future Bengali soldiers were liable to service overseas, and partly to the annexation of Oudh in 1856. The mutiny proper began at Meerut of May 10. There, some native regts, murdered their officers with their families, marched to Delhi, and restored the old Mogul Empire. Other centres of revolt were Cawnpore and Lucknow, and at both places Brit. garrisons were besieged. On June 27, Cawnpore surrendered, and, in spite of a safe conduct, all men, women and children were murdered by order of Nana Sahib. Sir Henry Havelock fought several battles on his way to Cawnpore. From there he marched towards Lucknow which he reached on Sept. 23. The mutiny at Delhi had meanwhile been crushed. Sir Colin Campbell, and then with 8,000 men relieved the garrison at Lucknow. The capture of Jhansi and Gwalior in the summer of 1858 marked the end of the major operations.

Indian National Army. Shri Subhash Chandra Bose, now remembered as 'Netaji' (the leader) was true patriot of India. The British Government had interned him in his own house at Calcutta. Towards the end of January, 1941, he was found that he had mysteriously disappeared. In 1942, he found his way to Burma which had by that time occupied by the Japanese. The Japanese had captured large numbers of Indian soldiers as prisoners of war. Out of these men, Netaji organized a regular army of about twenty thousand Indians in 1943, in Singapore, and called in the Indian National Army or Azad Hind Fauj. He himself became Commander-in-Chief and gave it the slogan 'Jai Hind'. After the reoccupation of Burma by the British, many officers and men of the I.N.A. were captured and brought to India. Some of them were prosecuted. The Indian National Congress openly espoused the cause of these officers, and thus it became still more popular in the country. The INA officers (General Shah Nawaz, Colonel Sehgal and Major Dhillon) were released. Netaji is said to have been killed in an air accident in 1945.

India Under the Crown. The Queen's Proclamation, on the 1st November, 1858, transferred the government of India from the Company to the British Crown. As a result, (*i*) Viceroy was appointed. (*ii*) Princes were given the right to adopt sons. (*iii*) Treaties were to be honoured. (*iv*) Religious freedom was given. (*v*) Equality of treatment was promised. (*vi*) Promise of progress. The proclamation was called the *Magna Carta of India liberties*.

Indo-China. The former French dependency in SE Asia comprising the colonial territories of Cochin China and the protectorates of Annam, Cambodia (Kampuchea), Laos and Tonkin. The Indo-China union lasted from 1887 until 1949 when Vietnam was established by the merger of Annam, Cochin China and Tonkin. The French connection was broken when Cambodia, Laos and Vietnam became independent states in 1954.

Indus Valley Civilization. The excavations at Mohenjo-daro (Sind), Harappa (W. Punjab). Rupar (E. Punjab), Kalibangen (Rajasthan) and *Lothal* (Gujrat) have testified that on advanced urban civilisation flourished between 3000-1500 B.C.

(*a*) *Political life* : The historians feel that there was a centralized government. The weapons of war like axes, spears, daggers,bows and arrows, maces and slings were made of stone.

(*b*) *Social life* (*i*) *Food* : The people of Indus Valley used wheat, rice, barley, milk dates, fish, eggs, animal flesh. (*ii*) *Dress:* They used both cotton and woollen cloth. (*iii*) *Ornaments* were of gold, silver, ivory, copper, precious stones for the rich, and for the poor made of shell or terracotta. (*iv*) *Amusements*: The Indus Valley people amused themselves by hunting, fishing, and rearing of animals and birds as pets. (*v*) *Education* : The Indus Valleys people knew the art of reading and writing.

(*c*) *economic life* (*i*) These people were *good traders* whose transport on land was the bullock cart, while boats were used on the rivers and the sea. (*ii*) These people were *depending upon agriculture* as they grew wheat, barley, rice, dates, cotton. (*iii*) *Animals rearing* was another source of income as they domesticated cattle, camels, elephants, pigs, fowls and dogs.

(*d*) *Art and Architecture*. (*i*) *Great Builders: Their drainage* system was *par excellent*. They built many planned cities (*ii*) *Crafts*: Potters used to paint pottery children's toys like rattles, and whistles. Other crafts included spinning, and weaving of cotton and wool.

(*e*) *Religious life*. The Indus Valley people worshipped Mother-Goddess, Siva and stones, trees and animals.

Industrial Revolution. By Industrial revolution we mean the progress made by England in the field of industry. The invention of the various kinds of machines—such as steam engine, spinning and weaving machines etc. brought about a transformation in the economic condition of England. There was all-round industrial development; England, an agricultural country was now turned into a manufacturing country. The production increased manifold. Things were available at cheaper rates. Improved methods of communication followed. The economic progress and industrialisation of England influenced the social and cultural life of the people. It had far-reaching effects on the political history of England.

Indus Valley Civilization. The valley of the Indus is a vast plain in the shape of a irregular triangle about 1500 kilometers long and 1100 kilometers wide. It was watered by the Saraswati (which has dried up now) in the east and the Indus with its tributaries on the west. The Indus Valley civilization, or the Harappan culture, is not the oldest of the river valley civilizations, but it is the first known civilization in India. It seems to have flourished about 2500 B.C. and extended over a larger area than any of the other contemporary civilizations. Evidences of this civilization are found in areas between Baluchistan and West Uttar Pradesh on one side and Gujarat on the other.

Harappa and Mohenjodaro were well planned and thickly populated cities of the Indus Valley civilization. Most of the people during this period were farmers who grew wheat, barely, peas and cotton, and kept domesticated animal like humped and humpless cattle, goats and buffaloes, and possibly elephants. The people used metal for their implements and utensils. They had efficient government. Dead bodies were either buried or cremated. It is believed that the Harappan culture came to an end by 1500 B.C.

Intermediate Nuclear Forces Treaty (INF) Treaty. The treaty signed in 1987 by the USA and USSR banning all short and medium-range land-based nuclear missiles.

International Brigades. The volunteer units organized to fight in the Spanish Civil War (1936-39) against Franco's forces. All were imbued with anti-Fascist ideals and many were communists. The volunteers totalled some 40,000 men draw from most European countries and the America.

International Socialism. The concept of worldwide fraternity and solidarity between working-class peoples, first propounded by Engels and Marx (1848). The Second International (founded 1889) still survives as a loose association of social democratic parties. The Third International was the Comintern.

Iranian Civilisation. Even though settled life in Iran began almost at the same time as in the neighbouring Mesopotamia, the growth of culture there was rather slow. In the middle of the sixth century B.C., a powerful empire was established in Iran. It lasted over two centuries and is known as the Achaemenid empire. The founder of this empire was Cyrus with his capital at Pasargadae. In 539 B.C., Cyrus defeated the Babylonians and extended his empire over a vast territory up to Asia Minor. His successor, Darius I (522-486 B.C.) further extended the empire up to north-western India. He built a new capital at Persepolis. This period saw the flowering of ancient Iranian art and architecture. Darius and his successors were involved in wars with the Greek states. Alexander dealt the empire a final blow during the reign of Darius III. The Geeks destroyed the city of Persepolis.

In third century A.D., a new and powerful empire arose in Iran-the Sassanid empire. This empire founded by Ardashir in A.D. 226 held sway in Iran up to middle of the seventh century. An efficient system of centralized administration helped to maintain its stability. However, their long and costly wars with the Roman empire and later with the Byzantine empire weakened them. The Arabs who emerged as a strong power after the rise of Islam, conquered Iran in A.D. 651.

The main religion of the ancient Iranians was Zoroastrianism founded by Zarathustra, or Zoroaster, who believed in the concept of one God. The ancient Iranians also had a number of minor gods—Indra, Vayu, Mithru, Naon-Raithya and Verethraghna—who can easily be identified with the Vedic gods.

Irgun Zvai Leumi. The revisionist Zionist underground organization founded (1937) for the defence of Jewish settlers against Arab attacks in Palestine. It was subsequently in opposition to the British mandated forces, though it declared a true in 1939 leading to the breakaway of the Stern Gang. It resumed hostilities in 1944 and blew up, with the loss of 91 lives, Jerusalem's King David Hotel (1946) while it was being used as the British administrative HQ. Begin was its leader before it was absorbed into the Israeli Army.

Irish Republican Army (IRA). Irish irregular military organization founded (1919) as the armed wing of Sinn Fein. Its purpose was to carry out guerrilla operations against British institutions and troops. Its successes contributed to the formation of the Irish Free State (1921) but it then split into factions that either accepted or refuted the Anglo-Irish Treaty (1921).

Iron Age. In archaeology a cultural phase marked by the use of iron. In Europe and W. Asia it usually followed the copper-using or bronze-using phase or age; in Africa it directly succeeded the stone age. In Europe iron working became general in the Med. region *c.* 1000 B.C. The two periods are characterised esp. by finds as Hallstadt and La Tene respectively.

Iron Curtain. The term used by Churchill (1946) to describe the ideological division and physical barriers preventing interchange of people and ideas between the West and the Soviet-dominated countries in Eastern Europe, which later became members of the Warsaw Pact.

Isabella. (1292-1358) Queen of Edward II of Eng. a daughter of Philip IV of Fr., she mar. Edward in 1308. The union was not happy, and *c.* 1324, having become the lover of Roger Mortimer, she escaped to Fr. In 1326 they returned and secured the throne for her son, Edward III, Edward II being murdered.

Isabella. Name of 2 queens of Spain. Isabella I (1451-1505) was a daughter of John of Castile. In 1469 she mar. Ferdinand. The two conquered the Moors and united Spain into a single monarchy. Isabella II (1830-1904) was a daughter of King Ferdinand VII. In 1843 she began to reign and in 1846 mar. for reasons of state, a cousin, Francis. After a series of insurrections, the queen was deposed in 1870, her son, Alphonso XII, becoming king.

Isolationism. A policy of non-participation in, or withdrawal from, international affairs, esp. as practised in the USA. The concept has been adhere to during much of the 20th cent.

Ivan. Name of 4 rules of Russia. Ivan III, called the Great reigned 1462-1505. He made his territory indep., extended its areas, issued laws, made treaties with rulers and took as his emblem the Rom. Ivan IV, who reigned 1547-84, was the first to take the title of Tsar. He earned the epithet of 'Terrible' by his cruelties. It is said that he *d.* of sorrow for his eldest son, Ivan, whom he killed, 1580.

J

Jackson, Andrew. (1767-1845) 7th Pres. of the U.S.A. He led the Amer. forces against the Brit. in the war of 1812. In 1821-23 he was Gov. of Florida. In 1828 he was elected Pres. and was re-elected in 1832. He left office in 1836.

Jahangir. Born in 1569; eldest son of Emperor Akbar whom he succeeded in 1605; ruled till his death in 1627; extended the empire by conquering Ahmadnagar (1616) and Kangra (1620); Bengal and Mewar, too, submitted; however, lost Qandahar to Persia in 1622; completely came under the influence of his wife Nur Jahan who virtually ruled in his name; it led to rebellion by his son Prince Khurram (later on Shahjahan) and his general Mahabat Khan; however, these rebellions were crushed; great patron of fine arts; a generous and just king.

Jai Hind. (Victory of India)—Watchword given to Indian National Army by Subhash Chandra Bose which he organised in Malaya in 1942; slogan became in india in almost every walk of life and after Independence used almost universally by defence forces.

Jainism. It is a non-Brahmanical system. Its founder is supported to be Mahavira. The chief doctrines of the Jainism is Tri Ratna or *Three Jewels i.e.*, every Jain must bold faith in three things : (*i*) Right faith; (*ii*) Right knowledge; (*iii*) Right conduct. They believe in the doctrine of non-violence. They are silent about the existence of God. According to them, the highest aim of life is *Nirvana*. It is divided into them, the highest aim of life in *Nirvana*. It is divided into two acts : Svetambara (white-clad) and Digambara (sky-clad).

Jallianwala Bagh. A park in Amritsar where occurred a tragic yet glorious event of supreme nationalism and sacrifice. On April 9, during the regime of the anti-Indian Lieutenant-governor of Punjab, Micheal O'Dwyer, when two national leaders, Saifuddin Kitchlew and Satyapal, were deported from Amritsar, people came out in a procession to protest and were met with police firing. Martial Law was also declared but peasants and other coming to the city for the *Baishakhi* festival did not know this and when a public meeting was held in the park on the 13th. (General) Dyer's troops opened fire on them without any warning and 375 were killed. This massacre was 'avenged' by Udham Singh, the nationalist revolutionary, who shot O'Dwyer dead in England on March 13, 1940.

James. Name of 6 King of Scot. James I (1394-1437) was son of Robert III. James III(1451-88) was the eldest son of James II. In 1488 urged on by the nobles, his young son rebelled against him, and after a fight near Stirling, the king was killed. James IV (1473-1513) became king on his father's *d.* He mar. Margaret, daughter of Henry VII, had a comparatively peaceful reign of 25 years, and *d.* at Flodden. James V (1512-42) became king when under 2 years old. In 1530 he began to rule for himself. In 1542 the Eng. defeated his troops at Solway Moss and on Dec. 14 of that year he *d.* at Falkland. James mar. Mary, daughter of the Duke of Guise, and their only child was Mary, Queen of Scots. Her son was James VI, who later became James I of Gt. Brit. (*g.v.*).

James I. (1566-1625) King of Gt. Brit. B. Edinburgh, the son of Mary, Queen of Scots, and Lord Darnley, he was proclaimed King as James VI in 1567. His minority, Axis Powers, 1940, and attacked the U.S. base, Pearl Harbour, Dec. 1941. A large part of S.E. Asia was occupied by the Japanese troops. After 2 atom bombs had been dropped on Hiroshima and Nagasaki (Aug. 1945), Japan surrendered unconditionally. A new constitution, by which the Emperor is divested of his divinity, came into force, May 1947. The *Diet* is composed of a house of representatives and a house of councillors. The Peace Treaty was signed Sept. 1951.

James II. (1633-1701) King of Gt. Brit. The 2nd surviving son of Charles I. In 1660, as Lord high Admiral, he commanded the fleet in battles with the Dutch. Later is Scot, he took part in the suppression of the Covenanters. His conversion to the R.C. Ch. led to the formation of a strong party determined to exclude him from the throne, but in 1685 he became king. The rebellion led by Monmouth having been crushed, James endeavoured to make Eng. a R.C. country. Only 3 years after his succession, an invitation was sent to William of Orange to come and take the crown. James found himself unable to defend his throne and fled to Fr. In 1690 he was in Ireland, where despite Fr. help, he was defeated at the Battle of the Boyne, James mar. Anne Hyde, daughter of the Earl of Clarendon. Their children were Mary, who mar. William of Orange (1677), and Anne. His 2nd wife was Mary, daughter of the Duke of Modena, by whom he had a son, james Edward, known as the Old Pretender.

Jawaharlal Nehru. (1889-1964). He was the Prime Minister of India from 1947 to 1964. He worked in closed collaboration with Gandhi for India's independence.

Jaziya. The the tax upon the non-Muslims levied in India (and in other Muslim countries) during the Muslim period; levied for the first time in india is Sind by Muhammad Bin Qasim (A.D. 712-13); Akbar, the Mughal Emperor, abolished it in 1564; Aurangzeb re-imposed it in 1679 which led to much discontent, corruption and disorder; finally abolished by the Muhammad Shah in 1713.

Jefferson, Thomas. (1743-1826) 3rd Pres. of the U.S.A. B. in Virginia. He helped to draw up the Declaration of Indep. in 1776. He went to Paris to help to make the peace treaty with Brit. in 1784. in 1797 he was elected Vice-Pres. and in 1801, Pres. He was again elected Pres. in 1805, but retired in 1809. During his term of office, Louisiana was brought from Fr. (1803).

Jinnah, M.A. Founder of Pakistan; born in Karachi in 1876; studied law and called to Bar; disciple of moderate Congress leader Gokhale; elected President of Muslim League in 1916; sponsored Congress-League scheme of reforms which included Lucknow Pact; condemned Gandhi; Non-Cooperation Movement; championed right of self-determination for Muslims; in 1940 demanded partition of india on religious grounds; rejected Cripps proposals; Gandhi's efforts for reconciliation failed; on transfer of power in 1947 became Governor General of Pakistan; died at Karachi in September 1948.

John. (1167-1216) King of Eng., youngest of the 5 sons of Henry II. He revolted against his father, and was also disloyal to his brother Richard. In 1199, John's disastrous reign began. A war with Fr. ended in the loss of normally; a quarrel with the Pope brought on an interdict and a humiliating surrender; the wrath of the barons forced him to sign Magna Carta in 1215. He left 2 sons, Henry III and Richard, Earl of Cornwall.

Johnson, Lyndon Baines. (1908-73), US Democratic President (1963-69). He became Vice President (1961) and after Kennedy's assassination succeeded him as President (1963), retaining the position after the 1964 election.

Josephine. (1763-1814). Empress of the Fr. B. Martinique. In 1779 she mar. the Vicomte de Beauharnais. In 1794 he husband was guillotined. In 1796 Josephine mar. Napoleon Bonaparte. In 1809 she was divorced.

Juan Carlos. (1938-) King of Spain. He assumed the throne on the death of Franco in 1975, having been heir-designate since 1969.

Julian. (331-63) Rom. emperor, nephew of Constantine the Great. In 355 his cousin, the Emperor Constantine, made him joint ruler.

Juliana.(1909-) Queen of Netherlands. She mar. Prince Bernhard of Lippe-Biesterfeld. After a year as Regent, Juliana became Queen, 1948, when her mother, Wilhelmina, abdicated. In 1980, Queen Juliana abdicated in favour of her daughter Beatrix.

Junta. A ruling group of officers in a military government, esp. after a coup d'etat or revolutionary seizure of power. The term is also applied to an executive or legislative council in several Latin American states.

Justinian. Name of 2 E. Rom. Emperors. Justinian I (483-565) was a nephew of Justin I, who reared him. In 527 he became emperor at Constantinople. His reign was marked by the victories of Belisarius and Narses over the Persians, Vandals and Ostrogoths. His wife was the Empress Theodora. Justinian is remembered for the codification of Rom. law which he organised. Its influence on the development of the legal systems of Europe can hardly be exaggerated.

Jutland, Battle of (1916). An important naval engagement between the Royal Navy and the German High Seas Fleet. The British lost 14 vessels to Germany's 11. As the Germans were able to return to port, despite British dominance in ships and firepower, the battle was tactically indecisive. However, Jutland was regarded as a strategic victory for Britain since the German High Seas Fleet never again ventured to seek out the British fleet.

K

Kalinga War (261 B.C.). It was fought between Ashoka and the ruler of Kalinga, in which Ashoka was successful after great bloodshed and gave up the idea of conquest through the force of arms. He embraced Buddhism and used the resources of his mighty empire to spread Buddhism in various parts of Asia.

Kampuchea. The republic of SE Asia; formerly known as Cambodia and the Khmer Republic.

The country was part of Indo-China from 1887 until it achieved independence from France in 1954. Prince Norodom Silhanouk dominated political life until 1970 when he was deposed as a result of the country's increasing economic difficulties and intensifying indirect involvement in the Vietnam War.

After the establishment of the Khmer Republic (1970), Marshal Lon Nol became PM and, in 1972, President. A civil war developed between the US-backed Republic and the Communist Khmer Rouge backed by China and North Vietnam. After their victory in 1975 the Khmer Rough, led by Pol Pot, imposed a several regimented regime, expelled all foreigners, cut off contacts with the rest of the world and compelled the urban population to undertake agricultural work.

War with Vietnam broke out in 1977, and Vietnamese troops occupied the capital in 1979. A puppet regime was established, but Khmer Rouge forces continue fighting in remote parts of the country.

Kaffir. Name adopted by Dutch and Brit, settlers for African negroid peoples who constitute, with the Zulus, the Zulu-Kaffir division of the S. Bantu peoples. Following a war in 1809 there was almost constant trouble breaking out into serious wars in 1834, 1836, 1850-53, 1858 and finally 1877-78. The Kaffirs form a considerable element in the population of S. Africa, and are largely employed on the land, in the gold mines, etc. Kaffir Bread. Native farinaceous food, derived from the spongy pith of the stems of a S. African cycad, *Encephalartos caffer*.

Kaiser. Title of the Holy Rom. emperors, and until 1918, of the rulers of Austria and Germany. It was first used in 800 for the Emperor Charlemagne. In 1871, the King of Prussia also took the title.

Kakory Mail Dacoity (Conspiracy) Case (August, 1925). A landmark ofTerrorist Movement of India; such nationalists and revolutionaries as Chandra Shekhar Azad, Mahindra Nath Banerji, Ram Prasad Bismil and Ashfaqullah Khan took active part in conspiracy to remove important mail bags from train at Kakori (Uttar Pradesh), most of whom were tried and hanged.

Kalhana (1095-1175). Born at Parihaspura (in Kashmir); a Brahmana historian, who wrote his master-piece, *Rajatarangini* (River of Kings), a history of Kashmir, in 8 volumes in poetic form; is earliest extent Indian history; first 3 books give account of 52 mythological kings who lived before 1184 B.C.; this section is based on much absurd and illogical mythology; history begins after this, exact dates and accounts being given from about A.D. 713; part about his own period (12th century) is valuable as history; apart from this, it is a great piece of literature in best Sanskrit style of *kavya* writing and is one of the last of the great *kavyas* (great romantic romances).

Kaniskha (120-162 A.D.). He was the greatest of Kushan rulers in India. His territories extended upto Yarkand. His capital was Peshwar (Purushapura). Like Ashoka he was a great patron of Buddhism and convened the *Fourth Buddhist Council* at Srinagar. In his days Buddhism was divided into two sects. Hinayana (lesser vehicle) and Mahayana (great Vehicle). Gandhara School of art (Graeco-Buddhist style) rose to its zenith during his reign.

Asvaghosha was a many-sided genius, who adorned the court of Kanishka. He was author of *Buddhacharitra*, his contemporaries were *Nagarjuna*, the great exponent of the Mahayana and *Vasumitra*.

Kannada Historical Research Institute, Dharwar. Private registered; promotes historical research in Karnataka with special reference to its history and records results, organises research library and museum; collects historical material, arranges lectures, exhibitions, conferences, excursions, etc., publishes books and journals; library of 3,000 books.

Kanva Dynasty. Vasudeva Kanva, who was the minister of the last Sunga King, killed his master and occupied the throne around 75 B.C. The Kanva dynasty was the dynasty of four kings, ruled for about 45 years.

Kaunda, Kenneth David. Zambian statesmen, President after independence (1964). In 1960 he founded the United National Independence Party.

Kautilya (Flourished 321-290 B.C.) An astute Brahmana; also known as Chanakya and Vishnugupta; studied at Taxasila where later he met Chandragupta Maurya and probably induced him to overthrow Nanda King, which he did, becoming founder of first Indian empire; Kautilya became his counsellor and Prime Minister; most of what is known of Chandragupta's empire and government is from Kautilya's manual of statecraft, *Arthasastra* (*artha*, economics; *sastra*, treatise) a complete manuscript copy having been discovered in 1905); Chandragupta left organisation of State to Kautilya who administered in a totalitarian manner through a highly centralised bureaucracy; State completely and highly organised and very wealthy but controlled rigidly every aspect of life, public enterprise, economy, politics, private life of people, etc., nothing escaped its eagle eye and talons; everything was owned by it; worked with secret agents, police and spies who infiltrated every walk of life; punishments were ferocious and were imposed even for trivial crimes; in spite of such control and the fear it engendered, Kautilya describes 40 ways of embezzlement and says it was difficult to catch guilty officials; nothing is known about his later years or where and when he died.

Kemal Ataturk Mustapha Kemal. (1881-1938) Turkish Gen. and statesman. B. Thessalonica. The Sultan was overthrown in Nov. 1922 and Kemal was elected 1st Pres. of the Turkish Repub. He became the virtual dictator of his country and shaped its complete redevelopment on W. lines. In politics his aim was the formation of a Balkan Federation.

Kennedy, John Fitzgerald. (1917-63) US statesman, Democratic President (1961-63). His charisma, youthful appearance, effective organisation and political style made him the most popular President this century.

Foreign affairs dominated his administration. They included the Bay of Pigs fiasco; discussions with Khrushchev in Vienna; the building of the Berlin Wall; the launching of the Peace Crops, the purpose of which was to develop assistance to underdeveloped countries, and the Alliance for Progress, and aid programme for Latin America (1961); the Cuban Missiles Crisis; and the conclusion of the Nuclear Test Ban Treaty (1963).

Kenyatta, Jomo (?1891-1978). Kenyan politician. He was a pioneer of African nationalism and a campaigner for African and land reform. He became President of the Kenya African Union (1947) which advocated extreme nationalism and was a screen from Mau Mau terrorist activities. Although Kenyatta eventually denounced these excesses he was distrusted by the UK government and sentenced to imprisonment (1953-61). While still in jail he was elected President of the Kenya Africa National Union (KANU) (1960) and when it came to power (1963) he became PM, playing a prominent part in negotiations towards independence(1963). He was President of the Republic (1964-78).

Khalji. A family of Turkish descent that ruled North india at the turn of the 14th century A.D., carried Muslim arms to the South, and established an efficient army and administration.

Kharavela. This Jain kingdom threw off the yoke of the Mauryas sometime after the death of Ashoka. Kalinga reached the zenith of its glory under him and his empire vanished soon after his period. The period assigned to him is 1st century B.C.

Khilafat Movement. The indian Muslims recented harsh terms imposed by the British government on Turkey after the First World War. They looked upon the head of Turkey as the Khalifat or their religious head. The Muslims under the leadership of Ali brothers. Maulana Mohammed Ali and Shaukat Ali started the movement known as the Khilafat movement to agitate for the preservation of office of Khalifa and better treatment for Turkey. Gandhiji took up the cause of the Khilafat Movement and the Congress adopted it as a part of the non-cooperation movement. The Muslims activity participated in the movement and joined non-cooperation movement in large numbers.

However, later the office of Khalifa was abolished in Turkey itself and Turkey succeeded in securing much better terms. The

Khilafat movement thus petered out.

Khilji Ala-ud-Din (1296-1316). Was a great conqueror and reformer. The Southern India was conquered for the first time by him. His claim to fame is secularisation of administration and various civil, military and economic reforms. He enforced *price control* system.

Khmer Rouge. The Cambodian (now Kampuchean) Communist Party. It seized power following its victory in the civil war (1970-75), and under Pol Pot instituted a harsh, regimented regime, expelled all foreigners, and cut off the country from contact with the rest of the world. Cities and towns were forcibly evacuated and their populations made to take up agricultural work. After the country's invasion by Vietnam in support of an uprising by the Kampuchean National united Front (1978) and the fall of the capital Phnom Penh (1979), the Khmer Rougi went underground and is now waging a Guerrilla war.

Khomeini, Ruholla. (1901-1989) Iranian Muslim leader known as the Ayatollah Khomeini. Exiled since 1964, in 1979 he deposed the Shah of Iran and instituted a fundamentalist Islamic republic.

Khrushchev, Nikita. (1894-1971) Soviet statesman. He became First secretary of the Party (1953-64) following Stalin's death. At the 20th party Congress (1955) he made a remarkable attack on Stalin's 'personality cult' and other misdeeds. He was PM (1958-64) while remaining First Secretary, and undertook a series of overseas visits, talking much about peaceful intentions yet accompanying them with threats, although in 1963 he signed the Nuclear Test Ban Treaty.

He was responsible for instigation the Cuban Missiles Crisis, allowed relations with China to deteriorate and disrupted the economy by encouraging agricultural decentralization and the production of consumer goods at the expense of heavy industrial output. His responsibility for these crises, together with accusations of nepotism, the revival of a personality cult, and authoritarian and unruly handling of state and Party affairs, resulted in his deposition and enforced retirement (1964). He was succeeded as First Secretary by Brezhnev and as PM by Kosygin.

Kibbutz. Israeli collective agricultural settlement, administered and owned by its members and on which children are collectively raised.

The first was established by Jewish settlers in Palestine in 1910.

Kiesinger, Kurt George. (1904-) West German Christian Democrat Chancellor (1966-69). His government was a coalition of the Christian and Social Democrats. It succeeded in arresting the recession which had led to the downfall of Erhard's government and re-established diplomatic relations with Romania (1967) and Yugoslavia (1968) which had been broken off during WWII. Kiesinger was a believer in reconciliation with the Warsaw Pact countries and an advocate of European unity.

Kingdom of Vijaynagar. (1336-1565 A.D.). It was the last great Hindu kingdom of southern India founded by Harihara and Bukka brothers in 1336 A.D. During this dynasty Hinduism (both Vaishnavism and Saivism) were revived. The greatest ruler of this dynasty were Deva Raya II and Krishnadeva Raya; the latter was successful warrior. He was on friendly terms with the Portuguese who imported horses and foreign goods for him. He was a great patron of art and learning.

In 1565, the Deccan Sultanates fought and defeated Ramaraja, the ruler of Vijaynagar in the famous battle Talikota, which destroyed once for all the chances of Hindu supremacy in South. India's Ramaraya was killed. The main reason for the defeat of Ramaraya was the unity among muslim rulers.

King, Martin Luther. (1929-68) Outstanding Amer. negro leader in campaign to end segregation in U.S. B. Atlanta, Georgia. Awarded Nobel Peace Prize 1964, and in April 1968, was assassinated.

Kings, Books of. Two books of the O.T. They give a history of the Jewish kings from the time of Solomon to the end of the monarchy. The author is unknown.

King II Sung, orig. Kim Songju. North Korean Communist marshal and politician. He joined the Party (1931) and organized and led the Korean People's Revolutionary Army against the Japanese (1932-45). He was put in charge of administration by the Soviet army of occupation (1945), quickly established himself, and became PM on the formation of the Democratic People's Republic (1948-72).

King, Martin Luther. (1929-68) US Baptist minister and civil-rights leader. He advocated non-violent confrontation as a weapon of social protest. In Montgomery, Alabama, he organized a boycott of buses by the black American community in protest at racial segregation, which eventually produced a federal court desegregation order (1955). This success encouraged him to extent the campaign, and in many parts of the country peaceful demonstrations were held opposing racial discrimination in matters such as employed, housing and schooling. This agitation contributed towards the passing of several Civil Rights Acts, and in 1964 King was awarded the Nobel Peace Prize. He was assassinated in Memphis, Tennessee, by James Earl Ray.

Kissinger, Henry. US diplomat, *b.* Germany. He was President Nixon's Special Adviser on National Security (1967-73), visiting China and the USSR in efforts to obtain some form of detente and the easing of tension between East and West. For his efforts to secure peace in the Vietnam War he was awarded the Nobel Peace Prize (1973). He was Secretary of State (1973-77), practising a conservative and pragmatic style of diplomacy. He became particularly well-known for his 'shuttle diplomacy' in the Middle East where on several visits he flew from country to country in effort to secure peace between Israel and its Arab neighbours, notably helping to negotiate a ceasefire in the 1973 Arab-Israeli War.

Koh-i-Noor. World famous diamond, was in possession of Mughal Emperors whose crown it adorned; taken away by the Persian invader Nadir Shah in 1739, after his death fell in the hands of Ahmad Shah Abdali, from whose descendant Shah Shuja, it came into the possession of Maharaja Ranjit Singh; from latter's successors it was taken over by British Government; it now adorns the crown of British monarchs.

Korea. The peninsula of NE Asia, now divided into North Korea and South Korea.

Korea was annexed by Japan (1910), and after Japan's defeat at the end of WWII, forces of the USSR and the USA occupied the country. For mutual military convenience the occupiers divided the territory into 2 regions along the 38th parallel of latitude, in accordance with terms agreed at the Yalta Conference. The ultimate objective was a unified democratic country, but it soon became evident that North and South were polarized in their allegiances, the former towards the USSR and the latter towards the USA, and so it has remained since negotiations between the Americans and Russians broke down (1946). In 1950 North Korea invaded the South, marking the start of the Korean War (1950-53).

Korean War. (1950-53). The conflict resulting from the partition of Korea into the Soviet-occupied North and the US-occupied South along the 38th parallel of latitude (1945).

Kosala. Ancient Kingdom establish by the Aryans in the eastern part of North India, reputed empire from which Rama was exiled and over which he eventually ruled.

Kosygin, Aleksei Nikolayevich. (1904-80) Soviet politician. In 1964 he succeeded Kruschev as Chairman of the Council of Ministers, sharing authority with Brezhnev, Secretary of the Communist Party. In 1980 he resigned because of ill health.

Kremlin (Russian, 'Citadel'). The former imperial palace in Moscow, now the administrative HQ of the USSR government. Hence the term is also used for the central government of the USSR.

Krishna Deva Raya. (1509-1529) A scion of the Tuluvas, greatest ruler of Vijayanagara kingdom (1336-1565-1646); versatile personality; military strategist, conquering many invaders, capturing Raichur, Gulbarga, Bidar and Goa; subduing the Ummattur chiefs (within his own kingdom) and Gajapatis of Orissa and taking forts of Svasamudram. Firuzabad, Sagar and Udaigiri (in 1513); also captured Kondavidu and Rajamundry and established himself in Telangana and occupied Bijapur for a while; extended his domain to south Konkan in the west, Vishakhapatnam in the east and to the south of the Peninsula including some islands in the Indian Ocean; capable administrator, statesman; patron of arts and literature, particularly of Tamil and Kannada poetry; gave large sums for advancement of Sanskrit studies and encouraged musicians, scholars, philosophers, religious teachers and saints; himself a noted poet and scholar.

Kronstadt Mutiny (1921). The revolt by the Soviet garrison (consisting largely of peasant recruits) of the Kronstadt naval base on Kotlin Island in the Gulf of Finland.

Although the mutiny was eventually put down by loyal troops

it was not successful since policy changes (*e.g.*, the New Economic Policy) were made in line with the mutineers' demands.

Krupps. German industrial combine founded (1811) for steel manufacture but latter expanding into armaments, mining, ship-building and agricultural and railway machinery. It remained a family concern for 5 generations. It was vitally important to Germany's ability to wage both World Wars, and was notorious for its exploitation of occupied countries and the use of slave labour.

Krushchev, Nikita Sergheyevich. (1894-1971) Russian polit. Son of a coal-miner, he joined the Communist Party in 1918. In 1932 he was apptd. Sec. of the Moscow city committee of the Comm. Party. In March 1939 he was apptd. by Stalin to full membership of the Politburo. After Stalin's *d.* in 1953, he succeeded Malencov as Sec. Gen. of Cen. Comm. Party. In 1954 he began a series of foreign visits, including the 1955 visit to the U.K. He was apptd. Chairman of the Council of Ministers, 1958. In Nov. 1964 he was replaced as P.M. by Mr. Kosygin, and as 1st Sec. of the Communist Party by Mr. Brezhnev.

Kublai Khan. (*c.* 1216-94) Mongol Emperor of China, the grand son of Jenghiz Khan. His great work was the conquest of China. He then became head of a great Mongol Empire with his cap. at Peking. Under him Buddhism became the State religion. He was the patron of Marco Polo.

Ku Klux Klan. US secret society of white Southerners formed after the Civil War to fight Northern domination and black emancipation, Largely a Protestant organization it has directed its hostility towards blacks, Catholics, Communists, Jews and alien minorities. Its symbol is a fiery cross and its members disguise themselves in white masks and robes, their leaders being given fanciful names such as Grand Wizard, Grand Dragon, etc. Murder, lynch law and intimidation were practised but its effectiveness has waned in recent years.

Kumarapala (*d.* 1172 A.D.). Chalukya king of Gujarat 1143-1172 A.D., reputed to have instituted a Jain reformation imposing strict fines on those who killed animal—even fileas— and prohibiting the production and sale of alcoholic beverages.

Kun, Bela (1886-1937). Hungarian Communist dictator. He was captured in WWI by the Russians, who after indoctrination returned him to Hungary as an agitator. He succeeded in overthrowing the liberal government and establishing a regime noted for its cruelty and ruthlessness (1919) although it only survived a few months. The country got invaded by Czechoslovakia and Romania and a counter-revolutionary government established by Horthy, causing Kun to flee to the USSR where he perished in the purges.

Kuomintang. Polit. party in China. Composed of the followers of Sun Yat Sen it stands for a policy of 'China for the Chinese'. Under Chiang Kai-Check it then monopolised the government of the Repub. but attempts to present a united front against the Jap. invasion failed and since the war the Communists have completely taken over the country.

Kuomintang. Chinese nationalist policies movement. Under Sun Yat-sen it helped in the overthrow of the Manchu dynasty (1911). Chiang Kai-shek took over as leader (1925-75) and set out to reunify China by extending the movement's political influences and military domination. Superficially this objective was achieved (1928) and the Kuomintang was China's ruling party until 1949.

Kurd. People of mixed stock inhabiting the region called Kurdistan now divided among Turkey, Iran and Iraq. Kurds are partly nomadic. They are mainly Muslim.

Kushana. An empire established by nomadic peoples (known as Yueh-chih to the Chinese) from central Asia who invaded and conquered northwest India *c.* 1st century A.D. and became patrons of the Buddhists.

L

Labour Party. British and Australian socialist movements.

The British Labour Party was founded in 1900 as the Labour Representation Committee, an amalgam of various socialist bodies. The Committee became the Labour Party (1906).

The Australian Labour Party formed coalition governments with the Liberal Party (1904 and 1908) before being able to form majority governments (1910 and 1914).

Lahore Conspiracy Cases I, II and III. Special tribunals were constituted at Lahore under Defence of India Act, 1914, to try 9 batches of persons for waging war or conspiring to do so against Government in India and abroad (sabotage of railways, bridges, arsenal, etc.; manufacture and collection of arms, public agitation, etc.); at first trial (September 1915) of 61 persons tried; 24 were sentenced to death and others to other forms of punishment; at second (March 1916), of 102 accused, 6 were sentenced to death, 53 to other types of punishment and rest were acquitted; in third (January 1917), of 17 tried, 5 were sentenced to death, 2 to other punishments and rest acquitted; public was denied access to hearing.

Lahore Conspiracy Case (1929). In 1929 two important revolutionaries Bhagat Singh and B.K. Dutt threw a bomb in the Central Legislative Assembly and were arrested. A number of their revolutionary associate members of the Hindustan Republican Socialist Association were also arrested and brutally treated. Bhagat Singh and Rajguru and Sukh Dev were sentenced to death for murdering a superintendent of police at Lahore. Others were sentenced to long periods of imprisonment. The case filled the minds of the people with the heroic deeds of these youngmen.

Lajpat Rai (1865-1928). Born in village in district Ludhiana (Punjab) in Agarwal Family (mother Sikh); did his Law from Lahore and set up practice at Lahore; became interested in politics because his father; withdrew his admiration of Syed Ahmad Khan as he was against Indian National Congress; joined INC (1888) and became a fighter against British atrocities against nationalists; toured country to educate people about their economic exploitation and to urge them to rise to free country from alien rule; joined the Arya Samaj being interested in educational and social reform; once sent Rs. 24,000 to Indians in South Africa for their *Satyagraha* activities; went to England (1905) to inform people about conditions in India and enlisted support of Labour Party and democratic and socialistic opinion in favour of India's struggle for freedom; organised a massive agrarian movement in Punjab which led to his deportation to Burma (1907); on release went on with work of arousing people; being harassed by police on account of his political activities, went to Europe and United Kingdom to inform public about India's right to freedom; returned (1920) but went back to Europe in 1924, 1926 and 1927; though not entirely in favour of a passive resistance movement against British, he acted in concert with Gandhi's ideas of complete non-co-operation and independence; on October 30, 1928, was injured in a police lathi-charge when demonstration against the Simon Commission and died of his injuries on 17th of following month; about the police assault he said that every blow aimed at him was a nail in the coffin of British imperialism in India.

Lakshmi Bai, Rani of Jhansi (1835-1858). Born at Varanasi and given name of Manikarnika; at mother's death when a child, her father (Moropant Tambe) shifted to Bithur where she grew up in the last Peshwa, Baji Rao's household; became an expert rider and accomplished in swordsmanship and use of arms; developed into a generous, intelligent woman with an outstanding personality; married Gangadhar Rao, Maharaja of Jhansi (1852); on death of only child, a son, a few days after birth, they adopted validly, under Hindu law, Damodar Rao, a five year old boy; when Gangadhar died in 1853, she became son's regent and started carrying out her administrative duties competently; British Government refused to recognise Damodar as legal heir and in 1854 Dalhousie (Governor-General) annexed kingdom under Doctrine of Lapse; when information was conveyed to her by (Major) Ellis, she uttered the famous words, "*Jhansi nahin denge*" (we will not give up Jhansi); was forced to vacate fort and take up residence in city palace and accept pension of Rs. 60,000 per annum out of which government deducted certain debts left by Gangadhar Rao, also acquired some villages assigned for family deity and 6 lakh rupees held in trust by them for Damodar Rao; she spent a large sum in taking her case to the Court of Directors (in England) but to no purpose; freedom struggle broke out in Jhansi on July 5, 1857 but she did not join it till February 1858, after she had defeated the Raja of Orcha who had taken some of her territory and beseiged Jhansi and when the British did not assist her and she became apprehensive that they would displace her eventually; when British troops marched on Jhansi on March 15 to invest it and for 17 days the besieging battalions and cavalry kept on pounding the fort; she put up a spirited resistance and returned fire, encouraging her soldiers in person; but on April 2, British captured her palace, the Rani making a strong resistance, placing herself at head of her 1,500 Pathan soldiers (*Vilaitis*) and fighting with a sword in each hand and holding her horse's reins in her mouth; being in imminent danger of being shot down, she returned to the fort but as British took it, she, with her son tied to her back, let herself down from a window and, with her father and some of her faithful *Vilaities*, broke through the Brither cordon and proceeded to Kalpi; as Hugh Rose was in hot pursuit, she went on to Gwalior to the fort there and personally supervised some battles that were fought there remaining constantly in the saddle escorted by her picked *sowars* and a woman attendant (who was always her companion) but in one of these frays she died, mortally wounded; there are a number of versions about the manner of her death but all acclaim her valiant and untiring resistance; when Hugeh Rose was told of death he said, "The Rani of Jhansi was the bravest and best military leader of the rebels"; she was a great patriot who lived and died for her country and an illustrious figure in history; she lived a life of piety and had a high moral character; was held in great esteem and affection by her people; had great administrative ability and attended to military and other matters of State herself; was a capable ruler; trained a large force of men and women in military tractics and her valour was unsurpassed; after Independence, Government of U.P. erected a memorial to her at the base of the fort at Jhansi, in form of a bronze statue and on May 10, 1957, presented to Damodar Rao's son, Lakshman Rao Jhansiwala (who died in 1959) a sanad and a monetary award in memory of the Rani.(Adopted from India edited by Chopra, P.N.).

Lalitaditya (733-769 A.D.). He was the most renowned of the kings of Kashmir. He defeated, Yasovarman, king of Kanauj in 740 A.D. He built the famous *Martanda temple* of the Sun.

Lancaster, House of. Family that provided kings of Eng. from 1399 to 1461. Its founder was Edmund, a son of Henry III. Henry, son of John of Gaunt claimed the throne, and in 1399 landed in Eng. and was crowned Henry IV, Richard II being deposed. He, his son Henry V, and his grandson Henry VI were kings in turn, Richard, Duke of York, claimed the crown in opposition to Henry VI, and the Wars of the Roses began. Henry VI was deposed 1461, and murdered, 1471. His son had already been killed and the house of Lancaster became extinct in the male line.

Later Vedic Period or the Epic Age. The Aryans had settled in the valleys of the Ganga and the Yamuna. Two important epics the *Ramayana* and the *Mahabharata* reflect social, religious, economic and political condition of India in the later Vedic Period.

(*a*) *Political Condition:* (*i*) The political condition of the Aryans was more developed than that in the early Vedic period. The tiny tribal settlements of the Vedic period were replaced by strong kingdoms. The *Ramayana* and the *Mahabharata* mention such kingdoms *e.g.* Kurus, Panchalas, Koshala (Oudh), Videha (North Bihar), Kashi, Matsya, etc. There were small republics but there were no big empires. (*ii*) The power of the kings increased immensely and kingship became hereditary. Instead of *Rajan*, they came to be called *Samrat*. The importance of the *Sabha* and the *Samitri* declined. (*iii*) The chief source of government income was the land revenue which was *one-sixth* of the produce. (*iv*) A regular army was maintained. It consisted of the four arms : *Cavalry, Infantry, Chariots* and *Elephants*.

(*b*) *Economic life* : In addition to agriculture and cattle rearing, trade and industry had also made a great progress. Many crafts were practised. The marchants were organized. They had contacts with sumerions.

(*c*) *Social Condition:* (*i*) There was growth of big cities like Ayodhya, Indraprastha and Mathura. (*ii*) The caste system became more defined and rigid. (*iii*) People were mostly vegetarian. The rich were addicted to gambling and drinking. (*iv*) Women enjoyed some freedom and received Vedic education. But the status of women was much higher in the Rig-Vedic period. It had deteriorated. Women came to depend more and more on their husband. The custom of *sati* started in the Punjab. (*v*) Education was free and universal. There were several *ashrams* in the forests. The *Brahmins* lived with their students and taught them.

(*d*) *Religious Conditions* : The Vedic religion had undergone a great change. In the Epic or later Vedic period the religion came very near modern Hinduism. It is called *Brahmanical Hinduism*. The *idol worship* was started during this period.

(*e*) *Caste System* : At the outset, Hindu society was divided into various groups or families. Such a group was called caste. In the beginning, this division was based on occupation. Later the caste system became hereditary and rigid. The Aryans were split up into four groups according to occupation—(*i*) *Brahmins* or the priestly class, (*ii*) *Kshatriyas* or military class, (*iii*) *Vaishyas* or trading class or the farmers and artisans; and (*iv*) *Sudras* or the labour-class.

Lausanne, Treaty of. The final peace settlement (1923) between Turkey and the Allies after WWI, following the refusal of the Turkish Republic to consider the Treaty of Serves binding.

Turkey surrendered all claim to former territories of the Ottoman Empire occupied by non-Turks. Greeks were confirmed in possession of all Aegean Islands, but they surrendered the Turkish port of Izmir (Smyrna). Italy annexed the islands of the Dodecanese, and the UK annexed Cyprus. The Bosphorus and Dardanelles were demilitarized, and Turkey recovered E Thrace. Following the territorial changes dictated by the treaty, considerable exchanges of population occurred.

Laval, Pierre (1883-1945). French statesman. A socialist until 1920, he moved further and further to the right. He was PM (1931-32 and 1935-36) and Foreign Minister (1934-36), But public indignation over the Hoare-Level Pact forced him to resign. He subsequently supported the ideas of Petain, and joined his Vichy Government (1940), later becoming PM (1942-44). He avoided any military commitment to the Nazis, and in trying to convene a National Assembly in 1944 he was arrested by the Germans. Laval fled to Spain but returned to France in 1945 to be tried for treason, and was shot.

Law, Andrew Bonar. (1858-1923), British Conservative statesman, PM (1922-23). He became leader of the Conservative Party in 1911. In the WWI coalition government, Law was Chancellor of the Exchequer (1916-18). Law's brief premiership set the fashion for tranquillity and 'safety first' which was to make British Conservatism throughout the interwar period.

Lawrence, Thomas Edward. (1888-1935). British soldier. He became known as 'Lawrence of Arabian' because of his leadership of the Arabs in the revolt (1917-18) against the Ottoman Empire in WWI. During the revolt Lawrence led raids on the Hezaj railway, took part in the capture of Aqaba and Damascus and maintained close Arab liaison with General Allenby's Palestinian army. He was trusted implicitly by the Arabs, opposed the Declaration, and supported the Arab cause at the Paris Peace Conference.

League of Nations. International organisation. It came into existence Jan. 10, 1920, as part of the treaty that followed World War I, and was finally wound up in 1945. Its headquarters were at Geneva. It had over 50 members, including all the leading countries of the world except the U.S.A., Russia. Mexico and Brazil. The Covenant of the League contained fundamental clauses on the prevention and settlement of disputes. 2 depts. are now parts of UNO; the permanent Court of International Justice at The Hague; and the International Labour Office at Geneva. The failure of the League to hold its members together in action against aggressor nations (*e.g.* Japan in Manchuria and Italy in Abyssinia) coupled with the withdrawal of these nations from membership, caused its abandonment.

Lebensraum. (Ger, 'living space'), term coined by the Nazis for the non-German-speaking territories to the E of Germany which they thought the German people should settle. Hitler attempted to implement this policy in his invasions of Poland (1939) and the USSR (1941). These territorial objectives were in addition to Hitler's claims to countries already settled by German.

Lee Kuan Yew. First Prime Minister of Singapore, from 1959. In 1965 he withdrew the coountry from the Federation of Malaysia, of which it had been a member since 1963.

Lend-Lease Act. (1941). US legislature authorizing the lease, loan, transfer or exchange of equipment required by any state recognized as being of vital importance to the defence and security of the USA. Practically, this meant the immediate release of vast qualities of war materials to the UK, and later to China and the USSR, and placed US industry on a war footing even before the country entered WWII. Land-Lease ended (1945) after some $ 50 billion worth of aid had been granted.

Lenin. (1870-1924) Name taken by the Bolshevist leader Vladimir Ilyich Ulyanov. Exiled to Siberia while a student. Lived in Paris, London, Switzerland, becoming a leader of internat. socialism. In 1917 he returned to Russia and overthrew Kerensky. Council of People's Commissars was set up with L. as Pres. to put Marxist theory into Practice. Peace was singed with Germany and the system firmly estabd. He survived an attempted asassination in 1918 but became a complete invalid after 1922. He is buried in a mausoleum in Red Sq., Moscow.

Leningrad, Siege of (1941-44). The heroic defence of the USSR's second city during WWII when Finish and German armies encircled and practically cut it off from the rest of the country. About 1- ½ million civilians and troops perished from cold and hunger even though a counter-offensive partially relieved the city (1943). The complete lifting of the siege occurred after the Germans had been forced to retreat by massive Soviet counter-attacks.

Leonidas. King of Sparta, leader of the small band of Spartans who defended the Pass of Thermopylae against the Persians. He was killed in the pass in 480, with *c.* 1,000 followers.

Leopold I (1790-1865) King of the Belgians. Son of the Duke of Saxe-Coburg-Gotha, he became a soldier and fought against Napoleon. In 1816 he mar. Charlotte, only child of George IV. In 1831 he was chosen the 1st King of the Belgians. He reigned for 34 years and did much to make Belgium peaceful and prosperous. He was on friendly terms with Queen Victoria.

Leopold II (1855-1909) King of the Belgians. The elder son of Leopold I, *b.* in Brussels, he served in the army. He became king in 1865 and ruled, on the whole, successfully, although his management of the Congo free State was not universally approved. Succeeded by his nephew.

Leopold III. King of the Belgians. Son of King Albert (*q.v*), he mar. Princess Astrid of Sweden 1926 (*d.* 1935), and succeeded to throne 1934; as C-in-C-Belgian Armed Forces, May, 1940, he capitulated to the Germans. Throne held by brother, Prince Charles acting as Regent, until Mar. 1950, when Leopold returned to Belgium. Forced by Government to abdicate in favour of his son Baudouin, 1951.

Liberalism. A loose term for political views favouring progress, reform and individual freedom.

Liberal Party. British, Australian and Canadian political parties.

The British Liberal Party is the succesor of the 18th and 19th-cent. Whig Party and, until it was overtaken by the Labour Party (1922), was one of the two major political parties, a position it has never able to regain.

The Australian Liberal Party was founded (1944) by Menzies out of the United Australia Party which evolved (1931) from the Nationalist Party established in 1917.

The Canadian Liberal Party had held power for much of this century (1896-1911, 1935-57, 1963-79, and 1980-84). In coalition with the Progressive Party it was also in office from 1921 to 1930. Its policies are in line in many ways with those of the British Party. It split into two factions due to policy disagreements in the period from 1911 through WWI.

Lie, Trygve (1896-1968). Norwegian socialist politician, first Secretary-General of the UN (1946-53). His period as Secretary-General was notable for his unsuccessful advocacy of the admission of China to the UN and his organization of UN forces to stem North Korea's attack on South Korea (1950-53).

Lin Biao or Lin Piao. (1908-71), Chinese Communist soldier, politician. He was appointed Minister of Defence (1959), setting himself the task of politicizing the army, ind. the unusual step of abolishing ranks. During the Cultural Revolution he emerged as Mao Zedong's principal supporter and was designated his successor (1969). He disappreared in unusual circumstances, supposedly dying in an air crash while fleeing to the USSR after organizing an unsuccessful coup against Mao Zedong in Peking.

Lincoln, Abraham. (1809-65) 16th Pres. of the U.S.A. *b.* in a log cabin in Kentucky. His mother *d.* when he was a boy. He was known as a man unusual strength and was popular as a story teller. He earned a living on the land, then became a clerk at New Salem, Illinois, and went on a campaign against the Indians in 1832. He qualified as a lawyer in 1836, and began to practise at Springfield in 1837. In 1834 he was elected to the legislature of Illinois, where he became leader of his party. In 1847 he was elected to the House of Representative at Washington. The Republican party was formed to prevent any extension of the slave holding area ; Lincoln soon became its leader in Illinois and continued a series of debates with Stephen A. Douglas, begun in 1839-40. He was nominated for the presidency and in 1860 was elected. In 1861 the S. States seceded and the Civil War began, the N. States being under Lincoln's direction. In 1863 he announced the emancipation of the slaves. In 1864 he was again elected Pres. In April, 1865, Lee surrendered and the N. was finally victorious. The union was saved and Lincoln's aim in going to war was achieved. Only 5 days later he was shot by J. Wilkes Booth, when at the theatre.

Little Entente (1921. An alliance formed under French patronage by Czechoslovakia, Romania and Yugoslavia to resist any attempt by Hungary to recover territory. In the same year France itself concluded an alliance of mutual guarantee with Poland. The alliances were intended to maintain the status quo in Central Europe and to prevent a restoration of the Austro-Hungarian Empire or any change in the frontiers. In 1933 the Little Entente was converted into an international community with a Permanent Council and Secretariat. It was dissolved in 1939.

Liu Shaoqui or Liu Shao-chi. (1898-1974), Chinese Communist politician. The Party's principal theoretician, he became Chairman of the People's Republic and Head of State (1959), but during the Cultural Revolution he was deposed and denounced for opposing Mao Zedong's belief in the importance of the peasantry over industrial workers, for 'taking the capitalist road', and being an advocate of 'Soviet revisionism'.

Livy. (59 B.C.-A.D. 17) Rom. historian, *b.* in Padua. His *History of Rome* was in 142 books, and the 35 books extant cover the period from the founding of the city (753 B.C.) until 9 B.C.

Lloyd George, David. Earl of Dwyfor. (1863-1945), British Liberal statesman, PM of coalition government (1916-22).

As PM from 1916 he proved an energetic was leader. He modified the harsher proposals of the Treaty of Versailles, but fell from power following his handling of the Chanak Crisis.

Locarno, Treaties of (1925). The agreements between various groups of nations in an attempt to settle problems stemming from WWI.

The principal Treaty was signed by Belgium, France and Germany, agreeing to the maintenance of their existing frontiers, settlement of disputes by arbitration without resort to force, and acceptance of the demilitarization of the Rhineland. This treaty was guaranteed by Italy and the UK, but neither they nor Belgium and France took action, other than by formal protest, when Germany occupied the Rhineland in 1936.

The other Treaties concerned France, which agreed mutual security gurantees with Czechoslovakia and Poland; and Germany, which concluded agreements to settle disputes by arbitration with Belgium, Czechoslovakia, France and Poland.

Lodhi. A dynasty of Afghan, chief of whom was Sikandar (ruled 1849-1517 A.D.), who ruled over the remnants of the Delhi Sultanate 1451-1526.

Lombards. People of Europe. Their first home was in Germany but *c.* 470, they conquered much of Italy including the district still called Lombardy. They formed an indep. kingdom, their kings wearing the famous iron crown.

Lome Conventions (1975 and 1979). The trade agreements, the first of which permitted 46 developing countries (known as the African, Caribbean and Pacific States) free access for their exports into the EEC. Provision was also made for aid and investment to be supplied by the EEC. The second Convention (1979) provided for $ 3.6 billion aid from the EEC to developing countries in the period 1980-85.

London, Treaty of (1915). The Secret agreement between Britain, France, Russia and Italy, guaranteeing. Italy territorial gains if it entered WWI on the Allied side within a month of signing, which it duly did.

The Treaty's terms were public by the USSR in 1918 when the Bolsheviks disclaimed all pre-revolutionary international commitments, and the revelation angered the USA to the extent that it rejected them as binding on the grounds that they contravened the principle of each people's right to self-determination—the territories involved incl. many non-Italian-speaking peoples.

At the Paris Peace Conference (1919), Britain and France refused to honour the Treaty, and Italy received considerably less territory than she had been promised. This caused much resentment in Italy and was a factor in the rise of Italian Fascism.

Long March (1934-35) An epic migration of Chinese Communists in the course of the civil war with the Kuomintang. In 1931 the Communists had established a Chinese Soviet Republic in Jiangxi, but the successes of Chiang Kai-shek's armies forced the Communists to evacuate and march 8,000 miles, heading NW for a year to Yanan. Of the 100,000 who set out, less than half survived, but they regrouped in stronger positions against the Kuomintang until 1937, when a truce was declared in order to fight the common enemy, Japan. Mao Zedong establish himself as the Communist leader during the march.

Lord Canning (Viceroy of India, 1858-62). Queen Victoria's proclamation of 1858 led to the transfer of Government from the East India Company to the British Crown. Load Canning's work was that of conciliation, settlement, reconstruction and reorganisation.

Lord Cornwallis (Governor Gen. of India, 1786-1793). He introduced many administrative, judicial and revenue reforms. The Parmanent Settlement of Bengal was introduced by him in 1793. It fixed permanent revenue of land and clearly defined the rights of the various classes of tenants. It also gave greater powers to zamindars to collect the rent from their tenants. This reform gave a temporary impetus to agriculture and investment of capital in land.

Lord Curzon (Viceroy of India, 1899-1905). He was responsible for the new policy of administration, of the North Western Frontier Province. In 1905 he passed the Punjab Land Alienation Act, forbidding transfer of land from agriculturists to non-agriculturists by sale or mortgage. In the same year, Bengal was partitioned. It evokes strong criticism from the people.

Lord Rippon (Viceroy of India). He repeated the Vernacular Press Act, passed the Local Self Government and Factories Acts. He improved the primary and secondary education. He also passed the famous Labert Bill, which sought to remove judicial disqualifications based on racial distinction.

Lord William Bentick (Governor Gen. of India, 1828-35). He was greatly responsible for the abolition of *Sati* and Infanticide (1829).

Luftwaffe. The German air force. Commanded in WWII by Goering, it was defeated by the RAF in the Battle of Britain, and was then used for the air-raids of the Blitz.

Ludendroff, Erich Von. (1865-1937). German general and politician. He achieved prominence in WWI when he captured Liege and was successful in the Battle of Tannenberg and the Masurian Lakes (1914), victories on which he subsequently built his political power, claiming that his military responsibilities gave him a legitimate interest in any policy which had a bearing on the prosecution of the War. His military prestige made him something of a national hero and he was able to dictate government policy by threatening to resign from his military command. His power collapsed with the 1918 Allied successes and he resigned and fled to Sweden before Germany capitulated.

Ludendorff was a nationalist and racist, and as such took part in the Munich Putsch (1923). He became a Reichstag National Socialist member (1924-28), and unsuccessfully stood as Nazi Presidential candidate (1925). He remained on the fringes of extremist politics, even founding his own right-wing anti-Semitic movement, the Tannenbergerbund.

Lusitania. British liner torpedoed and sunk without warning by a U-boat off Ireland in 1915, with the loss of 1200 lives of whom over 100 were US citizens. The sinking caused wide-spread anger and resentment in the USA with calls for declaration of war on Germany, which maintained that the vessel's cargo incl. war material. The incident contributed to the entry of the USA into WWI in 1917.

Luthuli, Albert John. (1898-1967), South African political leader, president of the african National Congress (1952-67). Openly opposed apartheid, advocating nonviolent resistance. Kept under restriction after (1952; arrested for treason (1956) but acquitted (1959). Awarded Nobel Peace Prize (1960).

Lusemburg, Rosa (1871-1919). Polish-born German revolutionary. A Marxist, she founded the Spartacus League (1916) with Karl Liebknecht. Arrested and killed after leading the Sparticist Rising.

M

McCarthyism. A term used to describe the practice of accusing people of being associated with Communist-oriented organizations having little evidence to substantiate the claim, and named after Joseph McCarthy (1908-67), Republican Senator for Wisconsin.

At the height of the Cold War in 1950, McCarthy alleged that the US State Department was having on its staff 205 employees known to be Communist sympathizers and 57 who were Party members. This revelation got followed by a campaign to discredit prominent Democrats, incl. such respected figures as Dean Acheson and George Marshall. On becoming Chairman of the Permanent Sub-committee on Investigation (1953) his attacks got intensified, involving Robert stevens, Secretary of the Army, and many intellectuals and officials. His activities gave rise to the establishment of 'black lists', and many people's careers were ruined. Finally, after his activities were condemned by the Senate (1954), McCarthy attacked President Eisenhower and this completed the discrediting of his campaign.

Macbeth. (*d. c.* 1057) King of the Scots. He became king in 1040, by murdering Duncan.He was killed during a battle with Duncan's son. Malcolm. The story as told by Holinshed in his *Chonicle* served as the basis of Shakespeare's tragedy.

MacDonald, Ramsay (1866-1937). British Labour Statesman. PM (1924 and 1929-35).

He was the first Labour PM and Foreign Minister (1924) but his government collapsed over the Zinoviev Letter. He became PM again in 1929, but his desire for a 'responsible party of government' led to the 1931 Cabinet split over his plan to cut unemployment benefit. This in turn led to his decision to form a National Government and to campaign against the Labour Party, for which he was expelled from the Party during the pre 1935 election campaign. He served in Baldwin's government (1935-37).

MacMahon Line. Boundary Drawn by Sir Henry MacMahon between India and Tibet now in possession of China along the North-East Frontier of India.

Macmillan, Harold, 1st Earl of Stockton (1894-1986). British Conservative statesman, PM (1957-63). He was successively (1951-57) Minister of Housing and Local Government, Minister of Defence, Foreign Secretary, and Chancellor of the Exchequer, before becoming PM.

Magadha Empire. From 6th century B.C. to 4th century B.C. the political scene in India is vague from the historical point of view. Magadha was the most powerful kingdom in North India. Its capital was Pataliputra. Notable ruler were *Bimbisara* and*Ajatsatru*. They were followed by weak successors till the foundation of the *Nanda dynasty*. The tyranny of the Nanda rulers could not win popularity. They were finally overthrown by Chandragupta Maurya. *The greatest contribution of the Nandas was that they tried to give political unity to the country.*

Magasthenes. Greek Ambassador to the court of Chandragupta Maurya, at Pataliputra in about B.C. 222 travelled in most parts of the north India and wrote a book '*Indica*'; original work lost but fragments by Arrian and Diochoras; complied and edited by Morindh; throws light on Mauryan times.

Maginot Time. The series of French fortifications built (1929-34) from Longwy (on the Luxembourg border) to the Swiss frontier and named after the Minister of War, Andre Maginot (1877-1932). Belgian opposition prevented the Line being continued along the Franco-Belgian frontier to the North Sea, and it was this weakness that Germany exploited in WWII by circumnavigating the Line and advancing into France from Belgium (1940). The Line was practically intact when France capitulated.

Magna Carta. The year 1215 is known as the first politico-constitutional struggle in English history. King John II (1199-1215), the youngest son of Henry, was cruel, mean, licentious, and weak of will. The feudal barous, supported by the clergy (Archbishop Lengton) and the public opinion, rose against King John II to enforce their rights under their feudal contract with the King, though the struggle did not aim at destroying the monarchy or the royal administration. The barons ultimately compelled King John to redress their grievances by singing the Great Charter in 1215 at Runnymede.

Magna Carta was essentially a feudal document, but with national implications in its reforms. The Charter contained 63 clauses guaranteeing the freedom of the barons, the Church and the common people. The most significant provisions of the great Charter are :

(1) Chapter 12 : No scutage or aid (except for the traditional feudal three) to be levied without the Great Council;

(2) Chapter 14 : Definition of the Great Council and its powers;

(3) Chapter 39 : No free man shall be arrested and imprisoned, or dispossessed, or outlawed, or banished or in any way molested; nor will be set forth against him, nor send against him, unless by the lawful judgement of his peers and by the law of the land.

(4) Chapter 40 : To none will he sell, or deny right or justice.

Even these clauses were feudal and specific in background, but centuries of experience transformed them into a generalised formula of constitutional procedure, making them the basis of the modern English Constitution. At that time their chief significance lay in the assertion of the supremacy of law over the king. Careful provisions were made the enforcement of the Charter by the barons, even by force of arms. The charter was repeatedly reissued barons, even by force of arms. The charter was repeatedly reissued by succeeding rulers. Magna Carta was hailed by Elder Pitt as the "Bible of the English Constitution". It laid the foundation of the rights and liberties of the English people.

Makarios III (1913-77). The orig. Mikhail Christodoulou Mouskos, Cypriot archbishop and politician. As head of the Cypriot Orthodox Church from 1950, he became the political and spiritual leader of the Greek Cypriots, leading the movement for union with Greece (Enosis). The British arrested him and deported him to the Seychelles (1956-57) believing he was involved with the EOKA terrorist organization.

Makarios eventually renounced Enosis in favour of British

proposal for Cypriot independence, when he realized that the opposition to Enosis by Turkish Cypriots could lead to the partition of the island. On independence (1960), Makarios was elected President, but independence failed to stop intercommunal violence (*See* Cyprus). In 1974 Makarios was overthrown by a pro-Enosis coup backed by Greece, which led to the invasion and occupation of N Cyprus by Turkey. Makarious resumed the presidency, but was left in control of only about 60% of the island.

Mahatma Gandhi (1869-1948). He was leader of the Satyagraha Movement is South Africa. He had started a non-Cooperation and Civil Disobedience Movements. He was preacher of truth and non-violence. He was father of Indian Nation. He won freedom for India. He was killed on 30th Jan. 1948 by Nathu Ram Ghodse.

Mahdi, El. The Moslem Messiah. Best known was Mohammed Ali of Dongola (1843-85), who successfully opposed Egyptian rule in the E. Sudan, defeated an Egyptian Army led by Hicks Pasha, 1883 and in 1885 captured Khartoum, where General Gordon was killed.

Mahmud Ghazni (997-1030 A.D.). He was the son of Subuktgin. He was a great conqueror and warrior of his time. His greatest ambition was to become the master of whole of Asia and to build an Asian empire. India's immense wealth attracted him and he carried 17 invasions to the country between 1000 to 1026 A.D. to *plunder the wealth* of India to finance his expeditions of Asia. His court poet was *Firdausi*, who wrote *Shahnama* in his honour. *Al Beruni*, the historian, who had accompanied the king to India during his expeditions, has given a reliable description of the invasions and Indian conditions.

Mandates or Mandated Territories. The former German colonies and non-Turkish areas of the Ottoman Empire ceded to the Allies after WWI but remaining the ultimate responsibility of the League of Nations. The UN took over responsibility from the League (1946) and mandates were renamed 'trust territories'.

Mandate territories incl. such divergent areas as the Cameroons, Iraq, Lebanon, New Guinea, Palestine, Samoa, South West Africa, Syria, Tanganyika, Togoland and Trans-jordan. The Administering countries incl. Australia, Belgium, France, New Zealand, South Africa and the UK.

Mannerheim. *Carl Gustav Emil, Freiherr Von* (1867-1951). Finnish soldier and statesman. After Finland gained independence (1917) there was civil war between the Bolsheviks and the Whites led by Mannerheim. The Bolsheviks were defeated and Mannerheim became supreme commander and regent but was defeated in the 1919 presidential election. He was responsible for the construction of the system of fortification known as the 'Mannerheim Line' close to the Russian frontier near Leningrad, and when the Russians attacked Finland at the beginning of WWII was appointed C-in-C and allied the country with Germany. He was elected President (1944-46) and made peace with the Russians (1944), joining them in the fight against Germany (1945).

Mansabdar. The holder of any of a class of ranks within the Mughul empire. Each *mansabdar* was assigned a certain rank on the basis of (*a*) his personal status and pay, (*b*) the number of horsemen he was to maintain and their pay.

Maoism. Marxism-Leninism as interpreted by Mao Zedong based on the revolutionary potential of the peasantry and guerrilla warfare.

Mao Tse-Tung. (1893-1976) Chinese communist leader. B. Human, in 1918 went to Peking Univ. He helped to form the Communist Party in Shanghai, 1921, and took part in the Nationalist-Communist March. 1926, and in the ill-fated Nanchang rising, 1927, when he set up the first Chinese Soviet Republic. He gained full control of the Party in 1935. A truce was brought about in 1936 which lasted during the course of the Jap. War but in 1946 civil war was renewed and the Communists under Mao won the whole Chinese mainland. In 1959 resigned his gov. though not his party chairmanship. He initiated the Cultural Revolution (*q.v.*) in 1966.

Maquis. French underground resistance movement which fought against the German occupying forces in WWII.

Marathas (1649-1708). The rise of the Marathas is an important factor in the Indian political life. Shivaji (1627-1680) was the founder of the Mahratha Kingdom. He considered it has mission to liberate India from Muslim rule. At a very early age he conquered the forts of Torna, Rajgarh, Purandhar, etc. Soon he was powerful enough to begin a campaign against Mughal rulers. Shivaji was a brave general and he was also an efficient administrator. The Maratha method of warfare was *guerrilla warfare*.

Marathon. Plain of Greece, 25 m. N.E. of Athens. It is famous for the battle fought there in 409 B.C. The Persians invaded Greece and encamped on a plain near the sea. There they were attacked by a Gk. army chiefly composed of Athenians, directed by Miltiades. The Gk. victory was conveyed to Athens by Pheidippides an Olympic champion runner, who fell dead as he entered the city.

March on Rome (1922). A Fascist-inspired legend of the way in which Mussolini came to power in Italy. Throughout 1922 there was a danger of civil war in Italy, with the Fascists seizing control of several cities. Mussolini demanded a Fascist government and concentrated his supporters on the approaches to the capital. King Victor Emmanuel III gave way before the Fascist threat, dismissed the PM, and invited Mussolini to return from Milan to Rome to form a government.

Marcus Aurelius. (121-180). Rom, emperor and Stoic philosopher. He became co-emperor in 161 and sole emperor in 169. He re-estabd. discipline, ameliorated the conditions of slaves, reformed the civil laws and carried out long and successful wars against the barbarians. His *Meditations* show him to have been, at a time of universal corruption, self-denying, just and unaffected.

Margaret. (*c*. 1045-93) Saint and Queen of Scot. In 1067 she was mar. at Dunfermline to Malcolm III. In 1093 her husband was killed, and the same year the queen *d*. leaving 3 sons, Edgar, Alexander I and David I, who all became kings, she was canonised 1250.

Margaret. (1283-90) Queen of Scot. called the Maid of Norway. She was the daughter of Eric, King of Norway, and a grand-daughter of Alexander III of Scot. In 1290 on the *d*. of Alexander she was sent for to become Queen, but, on her way to Scot., *d*. at the Orkney Is. The appearance of 13 claimants to the throne led to the intervention of Edward I of Eng. and to the War of Indep.

Margaret of Anjou. (1430-1482) Queen of Henry VI, whom she mar. in 1445. Her politics helped to rouse discontent ending in a quarrel for the throne, claimed by Richard, Duke of York. In 1455 began the Wars of the Roses, and Margaret actively supported the claims of her husband and young son. After Tawton (1461), she went to Fr. for help, but defeat at Tewkesbury (1471) ended Lancastrian hopes.

Margrethe II. Queen of Denmark. She succeeded her father, Frederick

IX, in 1972, the Salic Law having been revoked in 1953.

Maria Theresa. (1717-80) Empress of Austria. Daughter of Charles VI. As her father had no sons, he named her as his successor and persuaded the powers to agree to this. When he *d.* a Bavarian prince was elected emperor, and Frederick the Great invaded Silesia. The result was a European war which lasted until 1748, and then the Seven Years' War, 1756-63. Maria Theresa lost Silesia, but in 1748 she secured the election of her husband, Francis, Duke of Lorraine, as Holy Rom. Emperor. Her large family included the Emperor Leopold II and Marie Antoinette.

Marie Antoinette. (1755-93). Queen of Louis XVI of Fr. A daughter of Maria Theresa and Francis I. In 1770, she mar. the Dauphin, who in 1774 became King of Fr. Her frivolity made her most unpopular. In 1792, with Louis, she was arrested. At her trail in Oct. 1793, she defended herself with dignity and spirit, but sentence of *d.* was passed Oct. 16, 1793 and she was guillotined.

Marie De Medici. (1573-1642) Queen of Fr., wife of Henry IV, B. Florence and mar. Henry in 1600. After the murder of her husband in 1610, she was made Regent for her son, Louis XIII and was at war with him, 1617-20.

Marie Louise. (1791-1847) Empress of the Fr.; daughter of the Emperor Francis II. In 1810 she became the 2nd wife of Napoleon. In 1814 she returned to Austria. She had a son by Napoleon, and several children by her lover, Count von Neipperg, whom she mar. in 1822.

Marne, Battle of the. Two engagements fought at the beginning and end of WWI. The first battle (1914) halted Germany's advance into France. The enemy came within a few miles of Paris and the French had to withdraw troops from Lorraine and rush them by train and taxi to the River Marne, such was the extremity in which they were placed. This desperate move was successful and the French supported by the British, were able to force the germans back behind the Aisne to positions they were to hold until the second battle (1918). This was the last German offensive of the war and brought them again within striking distance of Paris, but French counter-attacks drove them back, the strategic initiative passed to the Allies, and within 4 months the War was over.

Marshall Plan. (1947). The Proposals drawn up by the US Secretary of State, George Marshall (1880-1959), offering US economic and financial help wherever it was needed to fight the hunger, poverty, desperation and chaos that followed WWII. The Plan led to the establishment of the European Recovery Programme by which 16 W. European countries (but not the USSR or other Communist states) accepted US aid. $ 13 billion flowed into W. Europe, fostering the recovery of agriculture and industry. The Russians saw the programm as an attempt at political indoctrination by the USA, rather than as an economic necessity.

Mary. (1867-1953) (Queen of George V. Only daughter of the Duke and Duchess of Teck. In 1891 she was betrothed to Albert Victor, Duke of Clarence. He died early early in 1892 and in May, 1893, the princess was betrothed to George, Duke of York. Only July 6, 1893, they were mar. in London. In 1910 George became king. When the king *d.* in 1935 queen Mary retired top live in Marlborough House.

Mary I. (1516-58) Queen of Eng. Daughter of Henry VIII and Catherine of Aragon. In July, 1553, her half-brother, Edward VI, *d.* The plan to make Lady Jane Grey his successor failed and Mary was proclaimed queen. In 1554 she mar. Philip II, King of Spain. Mary's short reign was marked by the restoration of the R.C. religion in Eng. and the persecution of the Protestants. She was succeeded by her half-sister Elizabeth.

Mary II (1662-94). Queen of Eng., daughter of James II, and his 1st wife, Anne Hyde. In 1677 she mar. William, prince of Orange. In 1688 William was invited to take the Brit. throne, and after James II had fled, he and his wife became joint rulers of Gt. Brit. She had no children.

Marxism. A political theory and doctrine based on the writings of Karl Marx (1818-83).

Many of the specific points that Marx advocated—such as the nationalization of industry and transport, a state bank, a graded income-tax systems, universal state education, and the abolition of child labour—have been established in various degrees in many democracies without the tight and often repressive controls of many Communist countries. However, the redistribution of land and the abolition of private property, which Marx also advocated, have by and large only taken place in Communist states.

Massacre of Jallianwala Bagh. On 13th April 1919, the day of Baisakhi, there occurred, at Amritsar, terrible massacre of Jallianwala Bagh. Here, near sunset, General Dyer fired on an unrmed and peaceful people assembled in a protest meeting. Hundreds of people were killed and thousands wounded. After this the Government declared Martial Law in some districts of the Punjab like Lahore, Amritsar and Gujranwala, and many atrocities were perpetrated.

Matsya-Nyaya. A doctrine that, in periods of anarchy, big fish eat up little fish (*i.e.* the strong dominate or destroy the weak). This doctrine was used to justify a powerful kingship.

Mau Mau. Kenyan secret terrorist society based in Kikuyu tribal area. It considered itself to be a national liberation movement, and was committed to the expulsion form the country of white settlers. The organization was operative 1952-59, but its worst excesses—also committed against Africans who opposed them—were committed in 1952-54. Some 11,000 Mau Mau members were killed against about 2,000 settlers and loyal Africans. After it was eliminated rapid constitutional change took place leading to independence (1963).

Maurya, Chandragupta. Founder of Maurya dynasty; established his rule by throwing Nanda dynasty with the help of Brahman named Chanakya or Kautilya sometime in 322 B.C.; conquered whole of northern India; defeated Greek General Seleucos, thus extending his kingdom of Hindukush mountains; one of the greatest emperors of India; ruled vast empire for 26 years (322 B.C. to 298 B.C.).

Mauryan Dynasty (321 B.C. — 184 B.C.). *Chandragupta Maurya* (322 B.C. — 298 B.C.). He was the founder of Maurya dynasty. He defeated Seleukos, the General of Alexander in 305 B.C. He founded an excellent system of Government and military organisation.

Magesthenes was the ambassador of Seleukos in the court of Chandragupta Maurya. He was in Pataliputra for 5 years from 302 B.C. His account of India, *Indica*, which exists today only in parts, throws light and the political and social conditions of that age.

Kautilya (Chanakya) was the Prime Minister of Chandragupta and an authority on Political Science in 4th century B.C. Wr. of Arthshastra *i.e.*, 'Statescraft'.

Bindusara (298 B.C. — 273 B.C.). He was the son of Chandra- gupta Maurya. His empire extended the whole of northern India and parts of Deccan. His reign ended in 273 B.C.

Ashoka (273 B.C. — 232 B.C.). He was one of the best and ablest rulers in the world history. He had embraced Buddhism after the bloody war of Kalinga (261 B.C.), for he was greatly moved by the loss of human life in this war. The rest of the life he devoted towards the propagation of Buddhism far and wide. His inscriptions on rocks and pillars (in Prakrit language) are a source of great historical interest.

Maximilian I. (1459-1519) Holy Rom. Emperor. Son of Frederick III. He became Emperor in 1493. *March* of his reign was occupied with warfare against the Fr. in Italy and the Turks in the valley of the Danube. By the mar. of his son Philip to Juana, heiress of Ferdinand and Isabella of Spain, he brought about the succession of the Habsburgs to the vast Spanish dominions, while the mar. of his grandson Ferdinand to Anna of Hungary brought Hungary and Bohemia.

Meerut Conspiracy Case. (1929). In 1929, about 32 labour leaders including three Britishers were arrested and tried at Meerut for conspiracy to overthrow the government. Many of these were sentenced to long imprisonment. The case came to be known as Meerut Conspiracy Case.

Meir, Golda. (1898-1978) Israeli political leader, born in Russia. She was a founder member of the Israeli Labour Party. Her premiership (1969-74) ended with her resignation after the fourth Arab-Israeli war.

Mendcs-France, Pierre. (1907-82). French Radical Socialist statesman. He represented France at the Bretton Woods Conference, on the IMF and at the World Bank. He was PM of a coalition government (1954-55) which ended the Indo-China War, but which was dissolved due to internal differences over Algeria.

Menzies, Sir Robert (1894-1978). Australian Liberal statesman. He entered the Federal Parliament as a United Australian Party (UAP) member (1934), serving as Attorney-General (1935-39) and PM (1939-41 and 1949-66). He reorganized the UAP into the broader-based Liberal Party (1943-45), which became the official Opposition and which he led (1943-49). He was an advocate of close links with the UK and of Commonwealth interests.

Mercenary. A person who is hired to fight for a foreign army.

Mesopotamian Civilisation. *Mesopotamia* means the 'land between the river'. It is watered by the Tigris and Euphrates rivers. Its southern region was called Sumer and was the heart of Mesopotamia. The regions to the north-east of Sumer were called Babylonia and Akkad. The high-land in the north was Assyria. Mesopotamia is a flat plain sloping to the south. The Tigris and Euphrates which rise in the snow-capped mountains of the north brought a perennial supply of water and fertile soil to the plain. The Mesopotamians devised ways and means of a perennial irrigation system.

By about 3000 B.C., the Sumerian civilisation had reached a high level of achievement. The most important cities of this civilisation were Erech, Eridu, Lagash and Ur. Erech was the capital of a small state, and the pattern of their cultures was similar. They were always fighting among themselves. By about 2600 B.C., the kings of Ur had become powerful and their influence spread to other regions also. About 2500 B.C. a strong king combined Sumer and Akkad into one kingdom with its capital at Agade. Hammurabi, the greatest Babylonian ruler, united the whole of what is now called Iraq into a single kingdom. By 1600 B.C. this kingdom was destroyed by the Hittites who came from Asia Minor, now Turkey. The Hittites were the first to make regular use of horse for war chariots and make iron implements.

In Sumerian and Babylonian society, the king was regarded as God's represented on earth, and the priests occupied the next place of importance. The king's officers and scribes came next in the social scale. Merchants, landowners, craftsmen and shopkeepers formed the middle class. The lowest in the social hierarchy were the slaves, most of whom were prisoners of war.

Agriculture was the main occupation of most Mesopotamians. They used called to draw the plough. They wore clothes made of sheep-skin. The cloth industry was in the hands of a special class of workers—spinners, weavers and dyers. Metal workers had developed a very high level of technical knowledge and skill. The potter's wheel was perhaps first used in Mesopotamia. The Mesopotamians also seem to have been the first make glassware. The prosperity of the people depended largely on foreign trade. For transportation on land, the Mesopotamians had wheeled cars. The discovery of the articles of the Indus civilisation at Ur and of Mesopotamian articles at Mohenjodaro and Harappa shows that there was extensive trading between the two civilisations.

The Sumerians were the first to evolve a proper system of writing. This system is called *cuneiform*. There was considerable growth in knowledge. The people in Mesopotamia counted by sixties as we count by tens. Ours is the decimal system; their system was *sexagesimal*. This system is no longer in use but we still use it as the basis of division of time into minutes and seconds. In geometry, the Mesopotamians had discovered what was later called the *Pythagoras' theorem* and made astonishing progress in astronomy. They could calculate the length of the day and the night, and the rising and setting of the sun and the moon. They divided the whole day into 24 hours and the sky into twelve parts, each assigned a name. This has come down to us as the twelves signs of the *zodiac*. Another remarkable achievement of the Mesopotamians was the invention of calendar.

By 750 B.C. with the conquest of Babylon and the fall of Damascus there came into existence what may be called the Assyrian empire. Senna-cherib was great Assyrian conqueror and builder. He made Nineveh the finest city in western Asia—a city of vast palace and imposing temples. The Medes, the Chaldeans and the Iranians destroyed Nineveh in the seventh and sixth century B.C. It was now the turn of the Iranians, the Indo-Europeans from Central Asia, to build up an empire. This empire was conquered first by Alexander, fourth century B.C., and later by the Arabs.

Metal Age. The stone age in India, as in other countries, was followed by what may be called the Metal Age, i.e., the age when the use of metals superseded that of stone in making tools and implements. In northern India, the metals first used was copper and after that iron. In southern India, the use of stone was immediately followed that by that of iron, though it was introduced much later than in the north.

Michael. King of Rumania, son of Carol II. He was recognised as heir apparent when Carol renounced his rights in 1925. Carol returned and was recognised as king in 1930. In 1940 Carol once more left Rumania and Michael became king. The Communist forced him to abdicate, 1947.

Mihir Bhoja. (836-885 A.D.). He was the greatest of *Pratihara* (*Parihara*) emperor, who ruled from Kanauj. He was defeated by Dhruva, the Rashtrakuta king.

Minto-Morley Reforms of India Councils Act, 1909. Lord Minto passed drastic laws to supports revolutionary activities of the extremists. But at the same time he wanted to conciliate the moderate section of Indians. So, in collaboration with Lord Morley, the then Secretary of State for India, he introduced some political reforms in the country, the *Minto-Morley Reforms*. These provided for (*a*) increase of members of Imperial Legislative Council from 21 to 60; (*b*) increase of members of Provincial Legislatures; and (*c*) introduction of communal representation for Muslims.

Mithridates. VI Eupator (*c.* 131-63 B.C.) King of Pontus and great soldier known as Mithridates the Great. His conflict with the Rom. repub. resulted in the *1st Mithridatic War* (88-84 B.C.). In 88 B.C. M. conquered virtually the whole of Asia Minor. In 85 B.C. Fimbria's victorious attack in Asia Minor coincided with the destruction of M's army in Greece. The *2nd Mithridatic War* (83-81 B.C.) was between M. and the Roman L. Murena. Murena was defeated and was superseded by A. Gabrinius, who made peace with M. The Roman decision to annex Bithynia led to the *3rd Mithridatic War* (74-63 B.C.). Lucullus was sent against M. In 66 B.C. Lucullus was sent against M. In 66 B.C. Lucullus was superseded by Pompey who quickly drove M.E. to the Crimea, the last of his proves.

Mitterand, Francois. French statesman. As leader of the Socialist Party, he became the first socialist of 35 years to be elected President in 1981.

Mohammad Ghori (1186-1206). In 1185 he occupied Lahore. In 1191, he was defeated by Prithvi Raj, the ruler of Delhi and Ajmer in the battle of Tarain. However, he defeated Prithvi Raj at Thanesar in 1192 and laid the foundations of Muslim rule in India.

Mohammed Bin Qasim. He was the first Arab Commander to conquer a portion of India *i.e.*, Sind in 712 A.D.

Mohd. Tughlaq (1325-1351). He was a great scholar and writer. However, some of his novel administrative experiments (such as shifting capital to Devgiri, new coinage etc.) made him unpopular. He is sometimes called the Wisest Fool of the Muslim period.

Mohenjo-Daro. A major city and excavation site of the Harappa civilization located on the Indus River about 250 miles north of the Persian Gulf.

Mongols. Yellow-skinned race from the plains E. of L. Baikal. In the 12th cent. Genghis Khan (1162-1227) made himself master of the whole of C. Asia. In 1234, a Mongol emperor seized the thrown of China and one of his descendants was Kublai Khan (1216-94). Another branch pushed W. as far as Moravia and Hungary and founded the empire over which Tamerlane (1336-1405) held sway. A 3rd was that from which came Baber (1483-1530) founder of the Mogul empire of India.

Monroe Doctrine. Principle of US foreign policy expounded (1823) by President James Monroe (1758-1831), which stated that 'the American continents are henceforth not to be considered as subjects for future colonization by any European power'.

In 1904, President Theodore Roosevelt extended the principle to justify any future US intervention to stop European interference in the Americans (the 'Roosevelt Corollary'). Eventually this unilateral US policy was adopted by all the republic of the Whemisphere, acting on the theory that aggression against one would be considered an attack against all.

Since WWII Communist penetration of the area has given added significance to the Doctrine, and the USA has supplied vast amounts of economic and military aid to its neighbours to counter what it sees as the Communist threat. In particular, the actions of the USA over Cuba, such as the Bay of Pigs and the Cuban Missiles Crisis, have been examples of the Doctrine in action.

Montenegro (Serbo-Croat, *Crna Gora*). The federal republic of SW Yugoslavia. As a kingdom it fought against Turkey in the Balkan Wars and joined Serbia against the German alliance (1914). In 1918 it became part of a newly constituted Yugoslavia.

Montezuma. Name of 2 Aztec emperors, Montezuma II (*c*. 1466-1520) greatly enlarged his empire. In 1519 the Spaniards, under Cortes, made the emperor a virtual prisoner. In 1520 Montezuma tried to prevent the Mexicans from attacking the Sp. but was killed.

Montgomery, Viscount of Alamein, Bernard Law. (1887-1976). Brit. Field Marshal. Served in World War I. As a Maj.-Gen. he took part in the Dunkirk evacuation. In 1942 he took command of the 8th Army in Libya, won the battle of El Alamein, drove Rommel from N. Africa. Commanded Allied armies at D. Day and later, under Eisenhower, took part in the liberation of N. Europe. He was in charge of the Brit. occupation army till 1946, when he became C.I.G.S. Created Field Marshal in 1944. On creation of N.A.T.O. he became Deputy Supreme Commander, Europe, 1951-58.

Mountbatten, Lord Louis Earl Mountbatten of Burma. (1900-1979). P.C. Gov. -Gen. of India. 1947-48, last viceroy of India. He was the youngest son of Admiral of the Fleet 1st Marquess of Milford Haven and Princess Victoria. Their name was changed from Battenberg to Mountbatten in 1917. Entered the Navy in 1913. He was Chief of Combined Operations (1942-43). From 1943-46 he was Supreme Allied Commander in S.E. Asia. Victory of India. Mar.-Aug. 1947. He Submitted a plan for the partition of India which was accepted both by the Brit. Government and Indian leaders. First Sea Lord and Chief of Naval Staff (1955-59). Promoted Admiral of the Fleet. Oct. 1956. Chief of Defence Staff (1964-69). He was murdered by the I.R.A.

Mubarak, Hosni (1929-). Egyptian statesman. He succeeded Sadat as President in 1981 and has continued his moderate, pro-Western policies.

Mugabe, Robert. (1924-) Zimbabwean political leader, first Prime Minister of the independent Zimbabwe. He was co-founder of the Zimbabwe African National Union in 1963 and with Nkomo, led the Patriotic Front's guerrilla campaign for majority rule. This was achieved by the elections of 1980, after which Mugabe became Prime Minister.

Mughal. A central Asian dynasty founder by Babur in 1526 A.D., that at its height controlled North India, parts of Afghanistan, and much of the Deccan. Although Mughal rule officially ended in 1857, its power had rapidly diminished after the death of Aurangzeb in 1707. Much of the Mughal period witnessed Hindu-Muslim syntheses in art, architecture and even religion.

Mukherjee, Shyama Prasad. Born in Calcutta in 1901; so of Asutosh Mukhopadhyay, great educationist; Vice-Chancellor, Calcutta University at 33; joined politics in 1937; elected to Bengal Legislative

Assembly in 1937; returned unopposed in 1946; joined Hindu Mahasabha in 1939 and its President 1940 to 1944; Finance Minister, Bengal 1941-42; resigned in protest; Union Minister for Industries and Supplies for sometime; Jana Sangh; led agitation for full integration of the State of Jammu and Kashmir with India, passed away while under detention in Srinagar in 1953.

Mulk Raj Anand (b. 1905). Writer and art critic of world fame; author of many books including *Coolie, Untouchable, The Village, Two Leaves and a Bud.*

Multiracial. This term means comprising people of many races.

Mummy. Dead body prepared for burial in ancient Egypt. To postpone natural decay it was at first soaked in crude natron. From the 21st dynasty onwards, brain and entrails were removed, the body-cavities repacked, the whole enswathed in smeared linen bandages and enclosed in a mummy-case. It ceased *c.* A.D.700.

Munich Agreement. (1938).The settlement agreed Hitler, Daladier, Chamberlain and Mussolini on behalf of Germany, France, Britain and Italy.

The Agreement compelled Czechoslovakia to cede the Sudetenland to Germany, and smaller amounts of territory to Hungary and Poland. In return the signatories to the Agreement guaranteed Czechoslovakia's revised frontiers. France had previous treaty obligations with Czechoslovakia, but these were ignored at Munich in the hope that the Agreement would put an end to Hitler's territorial demands.

In 1939 Germany occupied the remainder of Czechoslovakia, ignoring the territorial guarantees made at Munich, and appeasement was shown to have failed.

Murat, Joachim (1767-1815). King of Naples. He distinguished himself as cavalry general under Napoleon who made him King of Naples in 1808. Murat abandoned Napoleon in 1814, to ally himself with Austria and Eng. but was himself abandoned later by his allies. He was captured and shot.

Muslim League. The Muslims in India were growing suspicious of Hindu majority. Moreover, the English wanted to drive a wedge between the two. So in 1906 was formed the Muslim League, under the leadership of a Muslim religions leader, Syed Ahmed Khan, to promote among the Muslim feelings of loyalty to the British and to provided and advance the political rights and interests of the Muslims of India. Later on, for many years Mr. M.A. Jinnah was its President. Ultimately it led to the formation of Pakistan.

Mussolini Benito. (1883-1945). Italian dictator and founder of Fascism (1919).

In his early years he was a revolutionary socialist but after serving in WWI decided to promote his nationalist ambitions by establishing Fascism, the system that was to become synonymous with his name. His socialism withered as he developed the movement into an anti-Communist, conservative, middle-class organisation.

In the aftermath WWI the country was practically in a state of civil war and King Victor Emmanuel III appointed Mussolini as PM in an effort to subdue the rioting that was prevalent in the major cities and to prevent a Communist insurrection. Mussolini assumed the title *Duce* (Leader) and headed a Fascist and nationalist coalition.

Mussolini assumed dictatorial powers in 1925, curtailing civil liberties, intensifying attacks on the oppositions and creating all-party state which ruled by decree with the aid of the secret police. His sense of grandeur and desire for military glory promoted the conquest of Abyssinia (see Ethoiopia) and albania, support for Franco in the Spanish Civil War, the Axis ties with Germany and Japan, and entry into WWII (1940).

The disasters of WWII caused his followers to desert him and he resigned (1943), was arrested, rescued by German paratroopers and placed at the head of a puppet regime in German occupied N Italy where he arranged the execution of some of his principal opponents, including his son-in-law Ciano. He himself was executed by partisans after being captured beside lake Como (1945).

Mutiny of 1857. The Revolt of 1857 (also called the first war of Indian Independence) rose out of a combination of political, economic and socio-religious caused. It took place when Lord Canning was the Governor-General. The Mutiny was mainly a rebellion of the army. The immediate cause was a rumour that cow and pig fat was being used to grease cartidges, and this enraged both Hindu and Muslim feelings. Political causes included the resentment of Indian rulers about the Doctrine of Lapse, the abolition of titles and pensions. Socio-religious and economic caused included the mistreatment of Indians, refusal to give even talented Indians good jobs, the bad condition of peasants because of high revenues, taking over of rent free estates, discontent among landlords of Oudh. The Indians felt alarm at the spread of Christianity, resented the reforms which they felt were interference in their religion,and felt the English to be usurpers. Military caused included discontent among the Indian soldiers because of low pay, bad treatment, being debarred from higher posts, being ordered not to use caste marks, requirement to serve farther and farther away from home without extra allowance, boldness arising from the English defeat in the first Afghan War shattering their seeming invincibility. The decisive outbreak was at Meerut. Its main leaders were Rani of Jhansi, Tantia Topi, and Nana Saheb. Rani of Jhansi was the ablest and most courageous of leaders. She was killed while fighting in June 1858.

The Mutiny failed because it was a premature rising, a localized affair, not a national movement, and not well planned, leaders were inexperienced, poor resources, British control over communications and the sea, and lack of a definite programme.

Results of the Mutiny include transfer of power to the Crown, revocation of the Doctrine of Lapse, re-organisation of the army with proportion of British soldiers increased, religious liberty, growth of national feeling which was soon to lead to the movement for independence.

N

Nadir Shah (P). (1688-1747 A.D.) Ruler of Persia (1736-1747) who defeated the Mughal army at Karnal in 1739 and sacked Delhi, carrying away rich spoils including the Peacock Throne.

Nagarjunakonda. A site of pre-historic importance in district Guntur (Andhra Pradesh) on the Krisna, of the latter half of the 3rd millennium B.C. (when Harappa culture flourished in north India) where a Pastoral people lived, made use of polished stone axes, adzes and other tools, small blades, awls, etc.,of jasper, chalcedony and chert and tools of bones of cattle; Excavated in the twenties of this century, this region yield up pottery, some with sophisticated shapes (such as spouted vessels, strainers and cups with three legs); In the latter period of this particular culture, black on red pottery, with painting in elite on the inside of the articles, was also made came to light Buddhist structures—a *stupa, 2 chaityas* (chapels), 20 *vihars* (monasteries), a Brahmanical temple and many secular structures including and amphitheatre, established during Iksvaku times (3rd and 4th centuries) and sculptures in the Amaravati style. As the site was to be submerged in the fifties to make a dam on the river, the valley was excavated thoroughly and it was revealed that the site had been in continuous occupation from early stone and neolithic times till after the period of the Iksvakus. To preserve some of the outstanding specimens of sculpture, they were removed to museums. The place became known as the hill of Nagarjuna in the 3rd century A.D. probably in honour of the famous Buddhist philosopher (2nd century A.D.) who founded the *Mahayana Madhyamik* school of Buddhism. (Government of Andhra Pradesh, District Gazetteer of Guntur.

Nagasaki. The Japanese port on the island of Kyushu destroyed (1945) by the USA by means of an atomic bomb, the second wartime use of a nuclear weapon. This event and the earlier devastation of Hiroshima brought about Japan's unconditional surrender to the allies.

Nassau Agreement. (1962). The settlement reached at Nassau in the Bahamas, whereby the USA agreed to supply the UK with Polaris missiles for its nuclear submarines. The outcome of this meeting between Kennedy and Macmillan displeased DE Gaulle, who regarded Anglo-American nuclear collaboration an indication that the UK was not sufficiently orientated towards Europe to merit admission to the EEC, and accordingly he vetoed the British application (1963).

Nasser, Gamal Abdel. (1918-70). Egyptian soldier and politician. After the first Arab-Israeli War he and other officers saw a need for radical change and in 1952 mounted a coup d'etat. After some political intrigue, Nasser became PM (1954) and President (1956) with virtually dictatorial powers.

His social economic policies were dominated by the need to improve agriculture, establish industries, and introduce improve social welfare schemes. In 1956 he nationalized the Suez Canal, so precipitating the Suez Crisis. Nasser united Syria and Egypt as the United Arab Republic (1958-61), and he concentrated on cementing relations with the USSR in order to receive aid. His offer to resign after the Egyptian defeat in the 1967 Arab-Israeli War was not accepted, and he remained in office until his death.

Nationalization. The subjection of an industry or resource to state control or ownership, a policy espoused by Communist and socialist doctrine.

National Socialism (Nazism). The extreme rightwing political ideology similar to Italian Fascism, and adopted by the National Socialist German Workers, Party (NSDAP), successor of the German Workers, Party of which Hitler was a founder member (1919). Hitler soon gained control of the German Workers' Party renamed it the NSDAP (1920). Membership grew rapidly and by the time Hitler achieved power it was some 2 million strong, its representation in the Reichstag rising from 12 (1928) to 288 (1933).

The Nazi doctrine incl. the principle of the individual being subservient to the state and the state being subservient to the Party, which in turn was controlled by a single leader—Hitler himself. It also incl. the conviction of Aryan superiority, the Germans being considered the 'master race'; the pursuance of a policy of anti-

Communism, Anti-Semitism and racialism; the building up of armed forces; and a determination to regain territory lost at the Treaty of Versailles and to create a German empire in E Europe.

These were Hitler's own beliefs which he successfully imposed on the Party by demagogy, aided by the malaise and frustration which had befallen the country following the German defeat in WWI and the unemployment resulting from the Depression. After WWII the Party was dissolved and its re-establishment became an offence.

Nation-State. The independent sovereign nation inhabited by people of that state only, as opposed to several nationalities. The term does not necessarily imply a racist policy, but indicates opposition to foreign domination.

NATO. North Atlantic Treaty Organization.

Naval Mutiny. (Feb. 19, 1946). On February 19, 1946 some units of the Royal Indian Navy mutinied in Bombay harbour. The wave spread to Cochin and Karachi harbours also. The Mutiny, though short lived, made it clear that the army could not be relied on by the British Government.

Nazi-Soviet Pact (1939). It is also known as the Hitler-Stalin Pact or Non-aggression Pact, treaty signed in Moscow by Ribbentrop and Molotov on behalf of Germany and the USSR.

The published section of the treaty covered a 10 years non-aggression period, and agreement by each party to remain neutral should the other be involved in war. Secret clauses defined spheres of influence in the Baltic States, Finland and Poland. In 1939 Germany invaded W Poland, so precipitating WWII, and 2 weeks later the USSR invaded E Poland, and the country was formally divided between the 2 occupying nations. The Pact was nullified by the German attack on the USSR in 1941.

Nehru, Jawaharlal. (1889-1964). Indian Congress Party statesman, PM (1947-64). He was became a leader of the nationalist movement and follower of Mahatma Gandhi in the 1920s. For this he was imprisoned several times between 1921 and 1945; his imprisonment during WWII was largely due to his opposition to Indian aid to the UK unless immediate independence was granted. When independence was achieved he became PM and Foreign Minister.

Domestically Nehru attempted to solve the poverty problem by adopting a series of Five-Year Plans, accompanied by efforts to secularized the nation and, by equality of educational opportunities, to eliminate restrictions imposed by Hindu religious and social customs, he himself being an agnostic. He committed the country to a process of industrialization and to a reorganization of its states on a linguistic basis, but a population explosion nullified efforts at economic reform.

His foreign policy was one of non-alignment and he became a leader of uncommitted Afro-Asia nations. He cultivated relationships with China and the USSR while maintaining firm Commonwealth connections. He was an anti-colonialist and an opponent of the use of force, although he did not shrink from using it when India annexed Goa from Portugal (1961). However, although unwilling to compromise, he displayed commendable restraint in dealing with Pakistan over the intractable problem of Kashmir.

Neolithic Age. The palaeolithic men were followed by others called neolothic men of the new stone age. They were so called, because their stone implements were of a newer and more improved kind, being more serviceable than used by their predecessors. Although still ignorant of the use of metals except gold, these men were far more civilized than their palaeolithic forerunners. They cultivated the land ,used pottery, kept domestic animals and buried their dead. Traces of these men have been discovery in most of the states throughout India.

NEP. New Economic Policy.

Neuilly, Treaty of (1919). The post-WWI peace settlement between Bulgaria and the Allies, arising out of the Paris Peace Conference. The Treaty restricted the Bulgarian army to 20,000; made the country liable for Reparations; and compelled it to cede territory to Greece and Yugoslavia, the loss of W Thrace to greece depriving Bulgaria of access to the Aegean Sea.

Neutrality. Refers to the state of being impartial or neutral, esp. in a dispute, war, etc., thereby not getting involved in hostilities, or in diplomatic or political exchanges.

New Deal. Refers to the economic and social programme which were launched to help the USA recover from the Depression. 'A new deal for the American people' was the phrase used by Franklin Roosevelt in his Presidential nomination acceptance speech (1932).

There were 2 programmes (1933-35 and 1935-39).

New Economic Policy (NEP). Refers to a modification in Communist practice instituted in the USSR by Lenin in 1921, following peasant disturbances and riots in Petrograd (now Leningrad) and Kornstadt. The NEP allowed some freedom of internal trade, re-introducing limited private commerce and re-established state banks. It was formally abolished by the Bolshevik Party Congress (1929), which gave full support to the first of the Five-Year Plans.

Nicaragua. A republic of Central America.

From the 1930s the government was dominated by the Somoza family, whose corrupt and dictatorial rule was finally ended in 1979 after a civil war with the Sandanista National Liberation Front. The Sandanista government has subsequently pursued socialist policies. The US government has alleged that the Sandanistas have been arming the rebels in the neighbouring El Salvador, and has supported the army of right wing 'Contra' rebels that is attempting to oust the Sandanistas.

Nicholas II. (1868-1918) Tsar of Russia (1894-1917). His reign was marked by the Russo-Japanese War, alliance with Britain and France against the Central Powers in WWI, bad harvests, and the Russian Revolutions of 1905 and 1917.

He was against badly needed political reforms and was unduly influenced in his choice of minister by the unscrupulous Rasputin. He was forced to abdicate (1917), and was exceuted in 1918.

Nigeria. Commonwealth republic of W Africa. Formerly a British colony, Nigeria achieved independence (1960) and was declared a republic in 1963. A federal structure of 12 states was created in 1967, and new states were added in 1976. Its recent history has been one of regional and tribal rivalry, of civil war and a succession of military coups. In spite of its great natural wealth, incl, oil, the country has never exploited its economic potential to the full.

Nixon, Richard. US Republican statesman, Vice-President (1953-60), and President (1969-74). Domestically he introduced his 'new economic policy' (1971), designed to reduce unemployment, stimulate the economy, contain inflation, and correct the balance of Payments deficit.

Nixon became the first US President to resign from office when he was in danger of impeachment for his involvement in the Watergate Affair.

Nkomo, Joshua. Zimbabwean nationalist leader. He founded the Zimbabwe African People's Union (ZAPU) in 1961, which was banned in 1962. Nkomo spent 10 years in detention as a political prisoner and then joined Mugabe as joint-leader of the Patriotic Front, promoting guerrilla activities to achieve independence and black majority rule. With Ian Smith and Mugabe, he participated in the London talks (1979) which eventually led to independence (1980). Nkomo lost the ensuring election to Mugabe, in whose government he served until his dismissal in 1982.

Nkrumah, Kwame. (1909-72). Ghanian politician. In 1949 he founded the Convention People's Party with the slogan 'self-government now'. When Ghana gained independence (1957) he became PM after the Party's election victory. In foreign affairs he pursued a non-aligned policy in the Cold War but was pro-Arab, Pan-African, and opposed to South Africa. Domestically, his drastic economic reforms, interference with the judiciary and the introduction of a 1-party state aroused considerable opposition. He was overthrown by a military coup and went into exile (1966).

Nobel, Dr. Alfred (1833-96). Inventor of dynamite. Swedish Engineer and Chemist, amassed huge wealth from the manufacture of explosives, out of which six prizes are given annually for outstanding work in Physics, Chemistry, Medicine, Literature, peace and Economics.

Non-Aligned Movement. The grouping of nations established at the Belgrade Conference (1961) and consisting for the most part of African and Asian states. The Movement has been pledge to fostering and maintaining foreign policies independent of the East and West superpower blocs, and to use its good offices to mitigate antagonism between the USSR and the USA and their respective allies. India may be regarded as the principal members of the

Movement, which holds regular meetings in the capitals of the associated states.

Nonviolence. (*a*) Refers to the passive resistance or peaceful demonstration for political attainments, (*b*) Refraining from violence on moral grounds to achieve objectives; pacifism.

Normandy Landings (1944). The start of the Allied invasion of Europe in WWII when British, Canadian and US troops stormed the French beaches between the River Orne and St. Marcouf after being transported from S England by an armada of ships, heavily protected by air and naval forces. D-Day was 6 June and the operation was code-named 'Overlord'. After heavy fighting, breaches were made in the German positions and the drive across W Europe commenced, rolling, back the enemy, freeing occupied territory, and finally advancing into Germany itself.

North African Campaigns or Desert Campaigns. (1940-43). The series of defensive and offensive operations in WWII, in which Allied forces fought those of Germany and Italy in efforts to control the S coast of the Mediterranean. The Axis objective was to capture Alexandria, Cairo and the Suez Canal, and ultimately to advance into the Middle East and secure the oilfields. The Allied purpose was to wage a campaign which would secure the area from Egypt through Libya to Tunisia as a springboard for the invasion of S Europe, and which would also relieve pressure on Malta.

North Atlantic Treaty Organization (NATO). The military alliance established by the North Atlantic Treaty (1949). The original members were Belgium, Canada, Denmark, France, Iceland, Italy, Luxembourg, the Netherlands, Norway, Portugal, the UK and the USA. Greece and Turkey joined in 1952, West Germany in 1954, and Spain in 1982. France withdrew from the integrated military command (1966).

Northern Ireland. The part of the UK consisting of the northern 6 countries of Ireland, and forming part of the old province of Ulster.

The Protestant majority in Northern Ireland results from the fact that the area was heavily settled by Scottish and English Protestants in the early 17th cent. Northern Ireland achieved its own parliament (meeting at Stormont Castle) in (1920, which was dominated throughout its existence by the Ulster Unionist Party, representing Protestant interests.

Novotny, Antonin (1904-75). Czechoslovak Communist politician. He became First Secretary of the Party (1953-68) and President of the Republic (1957-68). He was a hard-line Stalinist and as such progressively became more unpopular as the liberalization processes demanded by intellectuals and students spread through the civilian population and armed forces, eventually enforcing his retirement.

Nuclear Test Ban Treaty (1963). The agreement between the UK, the USA and USSR whereby nuclear testing in the atmosphere, outer space or under water or prohibited. Many other nations have since subscribed to the Treaty, notable abstainers being China, France, India and South Africa.

Nuclear Warfare. The potential form of conflict employing either atomic weapons (based on the fission of a heavy atomic nucleus), or hydrogen weapons (based of the fusion of two light nuclei). The theory behind the possession of such horrific weapons has been that they act as a deterrent, no nation daring to use them for fear of retaliation.

Nuremberg Rallies. The annual convention of the Nazi Party held in the 1930s in Nuremberg, Bavaria. They were characterized by vast open air gatherings, impressive marches, torchlight processions, and oratorial performances by Party leaders designed to disseminate propaganda and rouse the assembled multitude to a state bordering on hysteria.

Nyerere, Julius. Tanzanian politician. He became President of the Tanganyika African National Union after completely reorganizing it (1954-55). He entered the Legislative Council (1958) and became chief minister (1960) after the Union's electoral successes. He was PM (1961) before resigning to establish the Union as a Christian Socialist movement. He became President of Tanzanyika on independence (1962) and President on Tanzania when Tanganyika and Zanzibar merged (1964), retiring in 1985. Nyerere adopted a non-aligned policy in foreign affairs for his 1-party state but was an ardent exponent of Pan-Africanism and made his country a leading member of the Organization of African unity.

O

O.A.S. Organisation of American States. Grouping of American countries with the aim of promoting peace and economic development. The organisation was founded in 1948. Cuba was expelled in 1962.

O.A.U. Organisation of African Unity. Grouping of African states with the aim of promoting African solidarity and coordinating policy. The organisation was founded in 1963 and now has over 40 member states.

October 1917 Revolution. It arose from continued opposition to the War, and the determination of Lenin and the Bolsheviks to seize power. Lenin had little difficulty in winning over the masses, already short of food and dreading what another severe winter might entail. Lenin's promises of peace, land and bread met with popular support, and his well-organized revolutionaries overthrew the provisional government in Petrograd and quickly established Bolshevik authority.

Private trading was abolished, factories were handed over to workers' control, property of counter-revolutionaries and the Church was confiscated, a cease-fire was arranged with the Germans, an Bolshevik administrations established in all the principal cities, with a Council of People's Commissars as the country's executive authority. However, counter-revolutionary ('White') forces continued to fight the Bolsheviks, and a civil war followed until the Bolshevik victory in 1920. In 1923 the Union of Soviet Socialist Republics was established.

Obote, Milton. Ugandan politician. He played a prominent part in the independence negotiations with the UK and was PM (1962-66). The first President of Uganda, the Kabaka (Prince) of Buganda, opposed Obote's desire to establish a 1-party state, so. Obote deposed him in a coup. Obote assumed the presidency but was overthrown himself by Amin (1971). He sought refuge in Tanzania and regained the Presidency (1980) following Amin's downfall. He was deposed again in 1985.

Oder-Neisse Line. The post-WWII frontier between East Germany and Poland agreed at the Potsdam Conference (1945). The line follows the course of the River Oder S to its confluence with the River Neisse, and then along the Neisse to the Czechoslovak border.

OECD. Organization for Economic Cooperation and Development.

Oedipus. In Gk. legend, son of Laius, King of Thebes, and Jocasta. Unwittingly he slew his father and wedded his own mother. The gods demanded the discovery of the king's slayer, and the investigation led Jocasta to hang herself and Oedipus to blind himself.

O.E.E.C. Organisation for European Economic Co-operation set up in 1948 by Aust., Belg., Denmark, Eire, Fr., Greece, Iceland, Italy, Luxembourg, the Netherlands, Norway, Portugal, Sweden, Switzerland, Turkey, U.K. and the U.S.A. A conference in 1957 paved the way for a free trade area in Europe. See Common Market.

OFFA. (*d.* 796) King of Mercia. Of royal blood, he elected a rival and obtained the crown, 757. He restored Mercia's prosperity, and secured virtual control of Britain. South of the Humber. Offa's Dyke. Ancient earthwork forming a boundary between Mercia and the Welsh. Built by King Offa, *c.* 779.

Oil Crisis. The problem arising in the late 1960s and early 1970s which was caused by a rise in demand and the simultaneous political action by Arab oil-producing nations against Israel and those countries they considered to be aiding or sympathizing with Israel.

The Arab oil-producers imposed price increases of some 70%, and this increased inflation and imposed balance of payments difficulties for the consumer nations of the West. The situation was further aggravated by supplies being cut or interrupted by about 15% owing to the Arab-Israeli Wars, and the closing of the Suez Canal, which obliged tankers to make the long detour around the Cape of good Hope. The attitude of the Arab producers was criticized by non-Arab members of the Organization of Petroleum Exporting Countries and the crisis gradually faded.

Olav V. King of Norway. He succeeded his father, Haakon VII, in 1957.

Omar Khayyam (1050-1123). Great poet of persia. His work *Rubaiyat* has won universal fame.

O.P.E.C. Organisation of Petroleum Exporting Countries. Grouping of countries exporting large quantities of crude oil, formed to co-ordinate their policies on petroleum. The organisation was founded in 1960. Its member include Saudi Arabia, Libya, Iran and Algeria.

Orange Order. The largest Protestant organization in Northern Ireland, founded in 1795. It was named after William II (William of Orange; reigned (1988-1702) who defeated the Catholic ex-King James II reigned (1685-88) at the Battle of the Boyne (1960). The Order was vehemently opposed to Home Rule and wishes Ulster to remain part of the UK.

Organization for Economic Cooperation and Development (OECD). The international agency with HQ in Paris which replaced the Organization for European Economic Cooperation (1961) when Canada and the USA joined the 18 W European members. Japan joined in 1964, and Finland in 1968, and Australia, New Zealand and Yugoslavia are associate members. The Organization comprises the West's leading industrial states, its objectives being to contribute to the expansion of world trade, provide aid for developing countries, achieve financial stability, and promote economic growth.

Organization for European Economic Cooperation (OEEC). The international agency established (1948) with HQ in Paris. Its members were Australia, Belgium, France, Greece, Iceland, Ireland, Italy, Luxembourg, the Netherlands, Norway, Portugal, Sweden, Switzerland, Turkey and the UK. West Germany joined in 1955 and Spain in 1959. Canada and the USA were associate members, and Yugoslavia was permitted limited participation. Its objective was to attack collectively the economic problems resulting from WWII by maximizing the use of aid supplied through the Marshall Plan. It was superceded by the Organization of Economic Cooperation and Development in 1961 as a result of US pressure to broaden its objectives to incl. responsibilities to developing countries worldwide.

Organization of African Unity (OAU). The body of 48 African states established (1963) with HQ in Addis Ababa, Ethiopia. The founding membership was 31 nations but 17 more have since joined.

The OAU's objectives are the eradication of colonialism (now virtually accomplished); the promotion of solidarity and unity among the membership; the raising of living standards by increasing progress in the fields of education, health and social welfare; the expansion of cultural, economic, scientific and technical affairs; the promotion of international cooperation; and the defence of independence, sovereignty and territorial integrity.

Heads of state meet annually and the Council of Ministers bi-annually, but the Organization's purposes are at times frustrated by the different stages of development of its members, and by their cultural, economic, political and religious differences.

Organizations of American States (OAS). See O.A.S.

Organization of Petroleum-Exporting Countries (OPEC). See O.P.E.C.

Oscar. Name of 2 kings of Norway and Sweden. Oscar I (1799-1859), the son of Gen. Bernadotte, who afterwards become Charles XIV, become king in 1844 and estabd. the freedom of the Press. In 1848 he supported Denmark against Germany. Oscar II (1829-1907) a son of Oscar I, succeeded his brother, Charles XV, in 1872. His remarkable intelligence and great diplomacy resulted in Gt. Brit., Germany and the U.S.A. requesting him to appoint the chief justice of Samoa in 1889, and he became umpire in the Anglo-Amer. Arbitration Treaty of 1897. In 1905, Norway became indep. and Oscar abdicated from the Norwegian throne.

Ostpolitik. The term for West Germany's attempt to improve relations with the Warsaw Pact countries, instigated by Brandt when Foreign Minister, (1966-69) in Kiesinger's government and pursued later when he become Chancellor (1969-74). Agreements were reached on posts and telecommunications, traffic, and visits by relatives between East and West Berlin. West Germany recognized East Germany and the Oder-Neisse Line, and peace treaties were signed with Poland and the USSR (1972).

Oswald. (*c.* 605-42) King of Northumbria. He succeeded his brother as king of Bernicia in 635. He was successful as a soldier and united Bernicia and Deira into the kingdom of Northumbria. He was killed at Oswestry in a battle against Penda, king of Mercia, and was made a saint.

Othio. Marcus Salvius. (32-69) Rom. emperor. In 69 he supported Galba in a revolt against Nero. He next rose against Galba, who was slain, and proclaimed himself Emperor. When he had reigned only 3 months, Vitellius completely overthrew his forces, and he committed suicide.

Ottawa Conference (1932). The meeting convened to discuss economic problems affecting the UK and the dominions, India and Southern Rhodesia. It established an Imperial Preference system based on quotas and tariffs, following the introduction by the UK of Protective tariffs to combat the effects of the depression.

Otto. Four Holy Rom. Emperors. Otto I (912-73) called the Great, was the son of Henry I, and crowned German King in 936. His 1st wife was Edith, daughter of Edward the Elder; his 2nd wife, Adelaide, Queen of Lombardy. Otto II (955-83) son of Otto the Great was crowned German King in 961 and joint Emperor of Rome in 973. Otto III (980-1002) called 'The Wonder of the World', the son of Otto II, was chosen king as his father's successor and crowned in 983. His mother, Theophano, governed until her *d.* in 991, and he took over the government in 996. Otto IV (1174-1218), the son of Henry the Lion, was chosen German King, 1208, and crowned Emperor in Rome. 1209. He quarrelled with the Pope who excommunicated him, and in 1212 declared him deposed, upholding Frederick II in opposition to him.

Ottoman Empire. The former Turiksh empire in Africa, Asia and Europe, dating from *c.* 1300 to 1922 when the Sultanate was abolished in favour of the Republic of Turkey.

Oudh. A kingdom under the nawabs of Lucknow, a centre of Urdu culture. Dalhousie's annexation of Oudh in 1856 under the 'doctrine of lapse' helped precipitate the 1857 uprising.

P

Pacific. War in the. On Dec. 7, 1941, Pearl Harbor the Philippine Is. and Malaya were attacked without warning and war was declared on Japan by U.S.A., Gt. Britain., Holland, Australia, Canada, New Zealand and some Lat. Amer. nations, Burma was invaded from Siam on Dec. 14. Britain forces were pushed out by May 17, 1942, and the Burma road was cut. The Japanese occupied Java, then New Guinea, Gilbert Is., New Britain and the Solomon Is. The first setback suffered by the invaders was the battle of the Coral Sea when they wére prevented from moving farther S. towards Australia. In june 1942, the Japanese navy was decisively defeated at the battle of Midway Is. Lt.-Col. Doolittle made a daring bombing raid on Japan itself (April 18, 1942). In Aug. 1942 Guadalcanal was invaded by the Amers. under Gen. MacArthur. In Dec. 1942 Britain forces under Gen. Wavell thrust into Burma, and Gen. Wingate's 'Chindit' raiders had inflicted heavy losses behind the energy lines. Late in 1943 Gen. Jospeh W. Stilwell began his advance into N. Burma, while a Japanese counter-thrust to the S. moved into India and threatened Imphal and Kohima (Spring, 1944). The Japanese failed in their objective and Amer., Chinese and Brit. forces took the offensive from the N., E. the W. In Sept. 1944, the Allies had launched a 2-pronged attack towards Japan through the Pacific Is.: the 1st prong through New Guinea, New Brit. and the Philippine Is. (Oct. 1944) and the 2nd through the Gilbert Is. (Nov. 1943), the Marshall Is. (Jan. 1944), the Marianas (June 1944) and the Caroline Is. (Sept. 1944). The use of the atomic bomb on Hiroshima (Aug. 6, 1945) and Nagasaki (Aug. 9, 1945) and the entry of Russia (Aug. 9, 1945) into the Pacific war made the actual invasion of Japan unnecessary.

Pahlavi, Mohammed Reza (1919-80). Shah of Iran (1941-79). He was a popular monarch early in his reign when he instituted a liberal Westernized system of government, but lost favour when he imposed a series of autocratic reforms incl. the social emancipation of woman. Islamic susceptibilities were outraged and the most vociferous Moslem critic, Ayatollah Khomeini, was arrested and exiled.

For some time the Shah appeared to have quelled opposition but eventually high inflation, a series of repressive measures, displays of outrageous imperial grandeur, and lack of sympathy with Arab opposition to Israel, roused uncontrollable opposition from fundamentalist students and puritanical religious leaders, leading to massive street demonstrations and violence. The Shah left the country in 1979, and 2 months later he was deposed, dying in exile in Cairo.

Palaeolithic Age. In India, as elsewhere, the earliest inhabitants where what is technically called the palaeolithic men or men of old age. They were so called, because they used stone in making their tools and weapons. The stones chipped by them, were usually pieces of hard rock called quartzite and hence they are also called "*quartzite men*." These people were in the lowest stage of civilization, ignorant of the use of metal, pottery and art of the agriculture. Traces of the existence of palaeolithic men are to be found to the south of Narbada in Andhra Pradesh.

Palestine. An area on the E seaboard of the Mediterranean. It was part of the Ottoman Empire until after WWI, and is now occupied by the state of Israel. After the Turks had been expelled (1917-18) and following the Balfour Declaration, Palestine was a British mandated territory (1922-48), a period marked by mounting hostility between Arabs and Jews, with the British Army trying to maintain peace and stability.

As a result of the Arab-Israeli Wars, Israel has occupied the Palestinian lands allocated to the Arabs by the partition settlement, and it is this state of affairs that has been the cause of so much unrest in the Middle East since WWII.

Palestine Liberation Organization (PLO). The body formed (1964) in Jordan, uniting various Palestinian Arab factions and representing *c.* 1- ½ million Palestinian refugees who lived in Palestine until the creation of Israel. Formerly its intention was to destroy the state of Israel, but now it aims to secure a homeland for the Palestinian Arabs on the West Bank, occupied by Israel since 1967.

The principal unit is Al Fatah, led by Yasser Arafat, who in recent years has moderated the Organization from a terrorist-orientated body to one endeavouring to achieve its objectives by political means.

Pallas. A dynasty of north-east India rising in the 8th century A.D. that succeeded Harsa and a temporary revival of the Gupta Dynasty, reached its height in the 9th century and controlled parts of Bihar and Bengal until the 12th century A.D.

Pallavas of Kanchi. After the fall of the Andhras in the 3rd century A.D., Pallavas came into prominence. Their first great king was Sivaskandavarman. Pallavas were patrons of Sanskrit and Brahim culture. They were enemies of Tamil Kingdom. They were very prominent from the middle of the 6th century to the middle of the 8th century. They were at constant struggle with Chalukyas in the north and Cholas in the south. The dynasty of Great Pallavas was founded by the Simhavishnu, the father of Mahendra Varman I. Pallavas are remembered for rock cut raths (Seven Pagodas) at Mahabalipuram.

Mahendra Varman I (600 to 625 A.D.). He was one of the greatest Pallava Kings. He was defeated by Pulekesan II. He was converted to Saivism from Jainism. He is remembered for the rock-cut temples.

Narasimhavarman (625-645 A.D.). He was the most famous and powerful of the Pallava kings. He defeated and killed Pulekesan II and sent naval expedition to Ceylon. He built Mamallapuram.

Panch Sheel. 'Five Principles' of peaceful co-existence; foreign policy principles first drafted by India in 1945, promulgated at the 1955 Conference of Afro-Asian States at Bandung, Indonesia, and agreed to by various nations including China. The principles are: mutual respect for each other's territorial integrity, mutual non-aggression, mutual non-interference in each other's internal affairs, equality and mutual benefit, and peaceful co-existence.

Pandit (Mrs.) Vijayalakshmi. Indian politician. The daughter of Motilal Nehru and sister of Pandit Jawaharlal Nehru. Her public career began with service on the Allahabad City Council; thereafter she was elected to the Legislature of the United Provs. and held ministerial office. She was Pres. of U.N. 1953-54. Indian High Commissioner to Great Britain 1954-61.

Pandyas Dynasty. The Pandyas were subject to the Pallavas of Kanchi. Their capital was Madurai. In the 11th and 12th centuries, they were tributary to Cholas, but later became chief Tamil power in the south. Their kingdom declined after the Muslim invasion in 1310.

Panini. A Sanskrit grammarian and a scholar of Sanskrit in ancient India

Panipat. Situated near Delhi; a famous place for the three historic battles took place here; first battle of Panipat fought on April 21, 1526 between Delhi Emperor Ibrahim Lodi and Mughal invader Babur led to the establishment of Mughal rule; second battle fought between Akbar and Himu, Hindu general of Afghan King Adil Shah Sur enabled Akbar to recover throne of his ancestors; third battle of Panipat was fought between Afghan invader Ahmad Shah Abdali and Marathas who came as protectors of Mughal Emperor Shah Alam II; with the defeat of Marathas vanquished their dream of establishing their empire on the ruins of Mughal empire.

Panmunjom Armistice (1953). The peace agreement between North and South Korea ending the Korean War, signed at the village of Panmunjom in the demilitarized zone separating the 2 states. Talks had been in progress for over 2 years with political rather than military overtones, and it was Stalin's death that finally modified the previously inflexible Communist position, opening the way to agreement and a general relaxation of international tension.

Pan-Stavism. A movement of opinion in E Europe in the 19th cent. which sought to emphasize the brotherhood of Slavonic peoples and to integrate them culturally and linguistically. It was strong in Russia, sustaining and exploiting the country's historic purpose of gaining Constantinople (Istanbul) and freeing the southern Slavs from Austrian and Turkish domination. The movement was at its peak between the 1860s and 1880s, and it was revived during the Balkan Wars and WWI, albeit in a more moderate form.

Papen, Franz Von (1897-1969). German diplomat and politician. He was a Centre Party Deputy (1921-32) and Chancellor (1932). He tried to solve the country's political problems by making concessions to the Nazis, suppressing the Socialist government and calling fresh elections.

Paris Peace Conference (1919-20). The assembly held after WWI during which the League of Nations was established and the peace agreements between the Allied and Central Powers were evolved and ultimately concluded by the Treaties of Versailles, Saint Germain, Neuilly, Trianon and Sevres. Proceedings were dominated by Britain, France, Italy, Japan and the USA, although 32 nations participated.

Paris Peace Talks (1968-73). The series of meetings aimed at terminating the Vietnam War. These protracted negotiations between representatives of North and South Vietnam and the USA concerned political as well as military matters, and much time was wasted in procedural wrangling over such trivialities as the shape of the conference table. Within a fortnight of the cease-fire agreement being signed (1973) the first US troops left Vietnam, which remained partitioned until the North finally overran the South and unified the country (1975).

Paris Student Demonstrations (1968). The massive street disturbances caused by what many considered excessive defence expenditure, esp. on an independent unclear deterrent, at the expense of the educational and social services.

PARR, Catherine (1512-48). Sixth and last wife of Henry VIII of Eng. He was her third husband. After the *d.* of the King in 1547, she mar. Lord Thomas Seymour, but she *d.* the following year in childbed.

Partisan. The member of an armed resistance group within occupied territory. During WWII such guerrilla groups were Communist-led, Stalin having encouraged their formation. They operated successfully in parts of the USSR, Albania, Czechoslovakia, Greece, Italy and, in particular, Yugoslavia under the leadership of Tito. They lived off the land where possible, but also on supplies dropped by Allied air forces or captured from the enemy.

Patliputra (Modern Patna). The capital of Magadha and the Mauryan empire, site of the third council of Buddhism, convened by Asoka to deal with heresy and orthodoxy. Today Patna is the capital of the State of Bihar.

Patel, Vallabhabhai Jhaverbhai (1875-1950). Born in a peasant family of Nadiad (Gujarat); did his law studies and became a lawyer in his home town; shifted to Borsad when he became a brilliant defence lawyer taking up criminal cases of; wife, Zaveribai, died in 1909, bearing a son and a daughter; went to England in 1910 and joined the Middle Temple; stood first in Roman Law and was awarded a prize, was called to the bar in 2 years instead of the usual 3; on return to India in 1913, set up his practice at Ahmedabad and defended people who had fallen foul of the British Government (politically); meeting Gandhi in 1916 was greatly struck by his sincerity and integrity; elected municipal councillor at Ahmedabad (1917): elected secretary of the Gujarat Sabha, a political body which was of great help of Gandhi in his national work; joined the national struggle and did much meaningful social work and a great deal to relieve the distress of those who were the victims of the plague epidemic of 1917 and the famine of 1918; was the moving spirit in the Kheda satyagraha in that year, which was launched to seek the waiver of land revenue due to the failure of the harvest, the campaign meeting with official repression and much brutality before relief was obtained; gave up his practice for good and began his social and political work-addressing meeting, organising picketing of foreign cloth shops and liquor shops and touring the villages to educate the people about the non-cooperation movement and the struggle for freedom; was Gandhi's lieutenant of the Flag satyagraha (1923) at Nagpur; chairman of the municipal committee (1924-28); when government arbitrarily decided to increase the land revenue by 50 and 60 per cent in some areas of district Bardoli in 1928, he led the satyagraha there with great success in spite of ruthless repression and became famous as '*Sardar*' (leader); took a leading part in all the major campaigns of the non-cooperation movement such as the boycott of the Simon Commission, Salt Satyagraha (1930), etc.; was imprisoned from 1932 to 1934; as chairman of the Congress revolutionary sub-committee, guided the activities of the 7 Congress Governments which came into office in the wake of the Government of India Act of 1935; these governments resigned in 1939 on the issue of supporting the 2nd World War effort if India were assured of independence; when the Quit India Movement was launched (1942), he was imprisoned again; after 1945 was one of the chief national leaders to negotiate with the British Government, the terms, etc., of a free India. With the coming of Independence, became deputy prime minister and Minister for

Information and Broadcasting, Home Affairs and States and due to his powers of persuation and statesmanship and his administrative ability, he was the outstanding achievement of successfully integrating the 562 princely States (with 27 per cent of the country's population) into 26 administrative units in the Indian Union; he managed the problems imminent on the partition of the country (like the rehabilitation of refugees) with great administrative ability, reorganised the Services, restored law and order in the country and made the Congress an effective organisation. He was one of the chief builders of independent India. (Opted from India, Edited by Chopra).

Paul I (1754-1801). Tsar of Russia, 2nd son of Peter III and the Empress Catherine II, at whose d. in 1796 he succeeded to the throne. He rapidly became unpopular by reason of his violent temper. His nobles conspired to compel him to abdicate, and he was strangled.

Paul VI (1889-1978). (Giovanni Bettista Montini) Succeeded Pope John XXIII, 1963, like him having liberal sympathies. Sanctioned use of vernaculars in Mass, admitted women to debates of Ecumenical Council (1964); and went on pilgrimage to the Holy Land and to a conference in India. Made plea for world peace at U.N., 1965. He was succeeded by John Paul 1.

Peasants' War (1524-26). Rising of German peasants and poor artisans. Feudal lords were becoming autocratic and extortionate. The revolt began at Stuhlingen, and spread quickly, peasants demanding the abolition of serfdom, relief from lesser tithes, impartial courts, restoration of common lands, abolition of d. duties. It was ruthlessly suppressed. The preaching of Luther had helped to undermine respect for authority, but Luther was violently against the peasants in this war.

Pentagon. The main offices of the US Department of Defense and HQ of the US armed forces in Arlington, Virginia Hence the term is also used for the military leadership of the USA.

Perestroika. (Russ.) restructuring. The term is applied to the Soviet policy of economic liberalization embarked upon under Gorbachev since 1985.

Period of Religious Unrest. Growth of Buddhism and Jainism.

The period around 6th century B.C. was marked by religious unrest. The reasons were: (*i*) Vedic rites had become too elaborate and costly; (*ii*) Dominance of priestly class or Brahmins who had become unscrupulous and dishonest. (*iii*) Difficult and out-dated language used for religious ceremonies beyond commonman's under standing. Buddhism and Jainism grew out of this unrest.

Peron, Juan Domingo (1896-1974). Pres. of the Argentine Repub. 1946-55. Orig. a leader of the group of the pro-fascist army officers which seized power in 1943; elected Pres. June, 1946. After considerable unrest Peron was forced to resign and flee the country in 1955. His career had been favoured by the popular appeal of his second wife, Maria Eva Duarte (1922-52). He returned from exile in 1973 and was re-elected President. After his death, his third wife, Maria, Estela ('Isabel') Martinez became President, but she was deposed by a military junta in 1976.

Peshwas. They were also Marathas. They ruled from 1708 to 1818 A.D. Peshwa dynasty was founded by Baji Rao, who was their ablest ruler. They aspired for India's sovereignty. The Maratha rule came to an end after the battle with Ahmed Shah Abdali in Panipat in 1761. But neither side gained control of India. Thus, the scene was left free for the East India Company.

Peter I (1672-1725). Tsar of Russia, as the Great. He became tsar in 1682. He devoted himself to the reorganisation of his army and navy. In 1696 he went to war with Turkey, winning Azov, and in 1700 with Sweden acquiring the Baltic provs. and part of Finland after the victory at Poltava (1709). His wife eventually succeeded him as Catherine I. In 1703 he founded St Petersburg.

Philip. Name of 6 kings of Fr. Philip II (Philip Augustus, 1165-1223) estabd. a strong monarchy. He took from the Eng. kings the greater part of their lands in Fr. and secured his possession by victory over the combined forces of John and the Emperor Otto IV at Bouvines in 1214. Philip IV (1268-1314) was involved in a struggle with Pope Boniface VIII, in which he gained the victory, again strengthening the authority of the Crown. In the reign of Philip VI (1328-50) the Hundred Years' War with Eng. began.

Philip. Name of 5 kings of Spain, of whom the most important was Philip II (1527-98) who succeeded his father, the Emperor Charles V (*q.v.*) in 1556. His 2nd wife was Mary, Queen of Eng. An ardent Catholic, his aim was to restore the supremacy of the Ch., overthrown by the Reformation. He carried on a long struggle with Elizabeth of Eng.

Philip, Prince Duke of Edinburgh. B. Corfu. Great-great-grandson of Queen Victoria. Spent early life at home of his uncle, Earl Mountbatten, in Hants. Served with distinction in R.N. during World War II. Became Brit. citizen Feb. 1947. Married H.R.H. Princess Elizabeth, Nov. 20, 1947, being previously created Duke of Edinburgh. A son, Charles, Prince of Wales, Duke of Cornwall, was *b*. 1948, and a daughter, Princess Anne, in 1950. A 2nd son, Prince Andrew, was *b*. 1960 and a 3rd, Prince Edward, in 1964. In Feb. 1957, the Queen conferred the title of Prince on the Duke of Edinburgh.

Philip of Macedon (382-336 B.C.) King of Macedonia. He made himself ruler of the whole of Greece. Against his ambitious designs the Athenian orator, Demosthenes (*q.v.*), directed his famous *philippic* orations. He laid the foundations for the conquests of his son, Alexander.

Philistines. Ancient people occupying the Palestine coastlands S. of Joppa. Their confederacy came into conflict with Israel under Samson, Samuel and David.

Phoney War. The name given to the inactivity which prevailed between the start of WWII (1939) and the German onslaught in the West (1940). During these months little hostile action occurred, the period being used for the dissemination of propaganda and the mutual probing of enemy positions on land and in the air for strategic purposes. The most serious hostilities occurred at sea.

Pianoforte. A keyboard instrument in which the strings are struck by felt-covered hammers when the keys are depressed. The pianoforte has 2, sometimes 3, pedals. The right pedal raises all the dampers, so allowing the sound to continue after the key is released. The left pedal shifts the keyboard action so that the hammers now strike 2 instead of 3 strings tuned to each note and, in lower part of the instrument, 1 instead of 2; this is the case on the horizontal ('grand') piano; on an upright, the depression of this pedal brings the hammers closer to the strings.

Plassey. A village north of Calcutta, where in 1757 Clive defeated a large force of the Nawab of Bengal, primarily through a conspiracy with the Nawab's generals. Often said to mark the beginning of the British conquest of Bengal.

Plassey, Battle of. In the Battle of Plassey (1757), Clive led the Company's forces against Siraj-ud-Daula (the Nawab of Bengal) and defeated him with the help of a conspiracy with Mir Jafar. This proved the first step towards territorial supremacy. The Battle of Buxer (1764) finally, put the Company forces firmly in power. In this battle, Clive's forces defeated the conspiracy of Mir Kasim, Shah Alam II and the Nawab of Oudh. The main reason for the success of the British was their Naval Supremacy.

Plato (427-347 B.C.). Gk. philosopher. He came under the influence of Socrates and *e*. 387 founded an institute for the study of philosophy. His works have come down to us in the form of dramatic dialogues in which the chief speaker is Socrates, into whose mouth Plato put theories developed after the former's *d*. Of these dialogues, 35 remain, the most important being the *Gorgias*, the *Protagoras*, the *Phaedo*, the *Symposium*, the *Laws* and the *Republic*. His philosophy is social, and according to him, justice and the good can only be completely attained in the social sphere. It was the source of that great body of Platonism, and profoundly influenced Christian thought.

PLO. Palestine Liberation Organization.

Poincare, Raymond Nicolas Landry (1860-1934). French statement. He was PM of a coalition government (1912-13), and as President of the Third Republic (1913-20) he was an inspiring leader during WWI. When he again became PM (1922-24), he pursued a severe Reparations policy towards Germany.

Politburo. The abbreviation for 'political bureau of the central committee of the Communist party', the executive and policy making committee of a Communist party, esp. in the USSR, where the name was first used (1917). Stalin replaced the Politburo with the Presidium (1952), but the name was restored in 1966.

Polo, Marco (1256-1323). He was a famous Austrian traveller and explorer, who travelled through many countries and published the records of his journey to China.

Pompidou, Georges (1911-74). French Gaullist statesman. After WWII service with the French resistance he served De Gaulle as an administrator and advisor, and played an important part in achieving the Evian Agreements which ended the Algerian War (1962). He was PM (1962-68), and succeeded De Gaulle as President, (1969-74), following similar policies.

Popular Front. The name of various coalitions of centre and left-wing parties opposed to Fascism in the 1930s, esp. those that formed the governments in France, Spain and Chile. Social reforms and economic improvements for the working classes characterized these governments: In Spain, the violent reaction of the right resulted in increasing disturbances and ultimately the outbreak of the Spanish Civil War.

Potsdam Conference (1945). The meeting following Germany's defeat attended by the Allied leaders Stalin, Truman, Churchill and Attlee to decide the fate of postwar Germany and to implement the agreement reached at the Yalta Conference.

Prasad, Dr. Rajendra (1884-1963). Indian statesmen and first Pres. of the Republic of India 1950-62. He became a follower of Gandhi and was a prominent member of various committees working towards independent President of Congress, 1947-48.

Pre-Historic Races and Cultures in India. Sir Herbert Risley divided the races of India into seven groups: (1) Dravidian, (2) Indo-Aryan, (3) Turko-Iranian, (4) Scytho-Dravidian, (5) Aryo-Dravidian, (6) Mongolo-Dravidian.

Dravidian: The Dravidian type was found chiefly in south India. Their stature is short or below mean; their complexion very dark approaching black; hair plentiful with an occasional tendency to curl; eyes dark; head long; nose very broad, sometimes depressed at the root but not so as to make the face appear flat.

Indo-Aryan: The Indo-Aryan type was chiefly found in Kashmir, Punjab and Rajputana. Their stature is mostly tall; complexion fair; eyes dark; facial hair plentiful; head long; nose narrow and prominent but not specially long.

Turko-Iranian: The Turko-Iranian type was found in the North-Western Frontier Province, Baluchistan and those districts of Punjab and Sind which were to the west of the Indus. Their stature is above mean; complexion fair; eyes mostly dark but occasionally grey; facial hair plentiful; head broad; nose moderately narrow, prominent and very long.

Scytho-Dravidian: The Scytho-Dravidian type was found in east Sindh, Gujarat and Bombay. This type is clearly distinguished from the Turko-Iranian by a lower stature, a greater length of head, a higher nasal index, a shorter nose and a lower orbito-nasal index.

Aryo-Dravidian: The Aryo-Dravidian type was found in East Punjab, Bihar and Uttar Pradesh. The head form is long with a tendency to medium, the complexion varies from lightish brown to black, the nose ranges from medium to broad, being always broader than those of Indo-Aryans, the stature is lower than in the latter group and usually below average.

Mongoloid: The Mongoloid type was found in Burma, Assam and the sub-Himalayan tracts. The head is broad, complexion dark with yellowish tinge, hair on face scant, stature short or below average, nose broad, face characteristically flat; eyelids often oblique.

Mongolo-Dravidian: The Mongolo-Dravidian type was found in Bengal and Orissa. The head is broad, complexion dark, hair on face usually plentiful, stature medium, nose medium, and with a tendency to broadness.

The theory of Sir Herbert Risley was based on the assumption that the Dravidians were the earliest inhabitants of India. However, such a view has been given up on the ground that there were pre-Dravidian races and cultures in India. The latest view has been put forward by Dr. R.S. Guha, the director of the Anthropological Survey of India in his book *Racial Elements in the Population*. According to him, the six main races that came to India were the Negrito the proto-Australoid, the Mongoloid, the Mediterranean, the western Brachycephale and the Nordic.

The *Negritos* were the first human inhabitants of India. Originally, they came from Africa through Arabia, Iran and Baluchistan. They seem to have been either killed or absorbed by the races which came later. They are practically extinct on mainland India expect among the hill tribes of south India (Irulas, Kodars, Paniyans and Kurumbas). However, they are still found in the Andaman Island, Malaya and Indonesia.

The *Prota Australoids or Austrics* have contributed some base elements to the population of India. The Kol or Munda type in India and the Non Khmer type in Assam, Burma and Indo-China, have a proto-Australoid element. The Munda languages belong to the Austro-Asiatic family and are found at present in the eastern half of Central India, southern border of the Himalayas and Kashmir and the territory east of Nepal. According to one view the Kols at one time occupied the whole of North India and also the Deccan.

The *Dravidians* came to India from the eastern Mediterranean. They were long-headed. The Dravidian culture spread over northern India, central India, western India and possibly eastern India also. There is evidence to show that Dravidian speakers were found in the Punjab and the Upper Gangetic valley.

The Dravidians seem to have brought from their original homeland in the eastern Mediterranean, the idea of the Mother-Goddess and Father-God. The Mother-Goddess had for her symbol or vehicle the lion. The Father-God for his symbol or vehicle the bull. From these two concepts the Hindu cult of Uma and Shiva grew up.

Privatization. The policy of transferring industries and services from public to private ownership; the opposite of Nationalization.

Privy Purses of Former Rulers. Grant of Privy purses to former rulers of States *quid pro quo* for surrender by them of all their ruling powers and for dissolution of their States; besides also allowed to retain certain private properties and personal rights, privileges and dignities; amount of privy purse fixed in proportion to revenue of his State; for example a State with an annual revenue of 15 lakh would get 1,30,000; over 450 out of 554 States had an annual revenue of less than Rs. 15 lakh; ceiling of Rs. 10 lakh exceeded in case of Hyderabad (Rs. 43 lakh), Baroda (26.5 lakh), Maysore (26 lakh), Gwalior (25 lakh), Jaipur (18 lakh), Jodhpur (17.5 lakh), Bikaner (17 lakh), Patiala (17 lakh), Indore (15 lakh), Bhopal (11 lakh); however, increased amounts were to be paid only for life; after the Government's discretion on fix amount not more than 10 lakh may care; total amount of all privy purses Rs. 5.80 crore; privy purses were, however, abolished in 1971.

Proletariat. In Marxist philosophy, the class of wage-earners, esp.

Industrial workers, in a capitalist society, whose only possession of significant material value is their labour and who are exploited by the ruling class (the Bourgeousie).

Ptolemy. Name of a dynasty of Egyptian kings (305 B.C.-A.D. 40). The legitimate line ended in 80 B.C. when Ptolemy X was assassinated, the crown going to a natural son of Soter II (Ptolemy VIII). He was named Auletes' son, Philopator, succeeded in 51 B.C. reigning jointly with his sister, Cleopatra, as Ptolemy XII. On his *d.* in 47 B.C. his younger brother become Ptolemy XIII and reigned also with Cleopatra. The last kings of the dynasty were son and grandson of Cleopatra, Ptolemy XV dying in A.D. 40.

Protectionism. (*a*) Imposition of duties or quotas on imports, designed for the protection of domestic industries against foreign competition, (*b*) The policy, system or theory of such restrictions.

On occasion most industrialized countries have adopted such practices and since WWII the method has been used by trading blocs, such as the EEC, to protect their members' interests. The opposite of protectionism is free Trade.

Pulakesin II (609-642 A.D.). He was the most famous ruler of the line. His greatest achievement was his victory over Harsha Vardhan. He also defeated Pallava king Mahendra Varman I and established an empire extending from Narmada to the Kaveri. He was finally killed by Narasimhavarman who stormed Vatapi in 642 A.D.

Purge. The elimination of dissidents or opponents from a political party or state, esp. associated with events during Stalin's dictatorship the USSR. These purges (esp. in the period (1936-38) resulted in the execution, exile or imprisonment of millions of Russians after the charade of show trials, when the accused usually pleaded guilty to the 'crimes', frequently after a period of brainwashing or torture.

Putsch. German name for a sudden, violent political uprising. Hilter led an unsussful Nazi putch in Munich 1923, because of which he was imprisoned.

Q

Quebec Conferences (1943, 1944). WWII meetings between Churchill and Roosevelt and their respective Chiefs of Staff. The 1943 Conference discussed the implications of Mussolini's overthrow, the invasion of Europe, and operations in the Far East, particularly the Burma campaign. The 1944 Conference discussed the transfer of resources to the Far East after the ending of hostilities in Europe, the Philippines campaign, and the Lend-Lease Act, on the assumption it would continue after the War's ending. Henry Morgenthau (1891-1967), US Secretary of the Treasury, put forward a plan for the removal of Germany's means of industrial production. Churchill and Roosevelt agreed to the proposals but they were later rejected by their ministers as being too costly and impracticable.

Queen. The wife of a reigning monarch. She is crowned with solemnities similar to those used for a king.

Quisling, Vidkun (1887-1945). Norwegian fascist leader. He helped Germany to prepare the conquest of Norway (1940). He was made Premier (1942) by the invaders and remained in power till 1945. He was convicted of high treason and shot. From his name has come the word 'quisling', meaning traitor.

Quit India Resolution (August, 1942). The All India Congress Committee passed Quit India Resolution on 8th of August 1942. The Government arrested Mahatma Gandhi and all the members of the Congress Working Committee. The Congress organisation was banned and the police took possession of its offices. The people reacted violently and revolted. There was collapse of the machinery of the Government at several places. Jinnah was taken by surprise by the Quit India Movement and declared that the object of the movement was not only to turn out the British but also to subjugate the Muslims. He asked the Muslims to keep aloof. The Muslim League began to raise slogans for the division of India.

Qutab-ud-Din Aibek (1206-1210). He was the founded of the Slave Dynasty. He himself was a slave and a General of Mohd. Ghori. After Ghori's death, he became the ruler of his Indian possessions. During his reign he built the Great Mosque (Jama Masjid) at Delhi and started the celebrated Qutab Minar. This Minar is the highest tower in India. It is the first outstanding structure in the Islamic style.

The other important kings of the Dynasty were Altamash (1211-1236) *Razia Begum* (1236-1239), Ghia-din Balban (1266-1287).

The last king of the dynasty was *Kaliobad* (1287-90), who was killed by Jalal-ud-din Khilzi in 1290.

R

Racialism or Racism. (*a*) Belief that races possess distinctive cultural characteristics determined by hereditary factors and so endow some races with intrinsic superiority over others, (*b*) abusive or aggressive behaviour towards members of another race on the basis of such belief.

Racism was a tenet of Nazi philosophy and is still prevalent in many parts of the world, though rarely as government policy (a notable exception being Apartheid in South Africa).

Radhakrishnan, Sir Sarvepalli (1888-1975). Vice Pres. of the Republic of India 1952-62, Pres. 1062. He was Spalding Prof. of E. Religions and ethics at Oxford, 1936-52. From 1946-52 he was leader of the Indian Delegation to U.N.E.S.C.O. and Pres. of the General Conference, 1952-54. In 1949 he was apptd. Indian ambassador to the U.S.S.R., a post which he relinquished in 1952 to become Vice-Pres. of India. Knighted in 1931. O.M. 1963.

Rahman, Sheikh Mujibur (1920-75). Bangladeshi politician. He became leader of the Awami League (1954), the principal objective of which was to secure the independence from West Pakistan of East Pakistan as Bangladesh. After the war of independence (1971) and the establishment of the new state he declined the Presidency but became PM. His attempt to create parliamentary democracy based on socialist principles failed and he assumed dictatorial powers (1975) which resulted in his assassination when a military coup overthrew his government.

Rahman, Tunku Abdul. Malaysian statesman. He became PM of Malaya (1975) and of the Federation of malaysia (1963). Following the breakdown of the harmonious relationships between the country's different races which Rahman had worked hard to achieve, he retired from office (1970).

Rajaraja Chola (985-1016 A.D.). He established the supremacy of the

Chola power in the south. His capital was Tanjore. He built the *Brehadeshwara* temple.

Rajatarangini. 'River of Kings'; a Sanskrit poetic version of the history of Kashmir composed in the 12th century A.D. by the Kashmiri poet Kalhana.

Rajendra Chola (1016-1044 A.D.) He extended the dominions of Chola kingdom. His fleet crossed the Bay of Bengal with an army and conquered a number of states as Sumatra, Java and Malaysia. He built a new capital Gangaikonda Cholapuram to commemorate his victory in the north.

Rajendra Prasad (1884-1963). Born in district Saran (Bihar) in a rich Hindu zamindar family: father was scholar of Sanskrit and Persian and mother devoutly religious so childhood was spent in intellectual and religious atmosphere; brought up to live simply and mix with villages; schooling in village and then at Patna; married at 13 (a religious-minded girl, Rajbanshi Devi); in 1902 passed entrance examination of Calcutta University (which had its jurisdiction over extended area from Sadiya (on the extreme east) to a little beyond Peshawar), in first division, standing first; under his brother's influence became a follower of swadeshi trend; when in B.A. (Hons.) at Calcutta, joined Dawn Society run by Sister Nivedita, Surendranath Banerjea and Satish Chandra Mukarjee which was meeting place of many intellectuals, nationalists and liberal-minded persons under whose influence he came; under his auspices was started the Bihari Students' Conference in Calcutta (1908) which provided almost entire political leadership of nineteen twenties in Bihar; got a first class in both M.A. and Master of Law and became lawyer at Calcutta; joined Indian National Congress and was elected to All-India Congress Committee; shifted to Patna (1918) as lawyer where his incesiveness, wonderful memory, striking intellectual and forensic ability together with his integrity and honesty of purpose and mind made him a leading personality at court and outside; came to know Gandhi in 1917 when the latter went to stay at his house (in Patna) on his way to Champaran to fight the cause of the oppressed indigo cultivators; this meeting was the turning point in his life and after the Jalianwala Bagh atrocities and passing of the Rowlatt Act (but before Gandhi started his civil disobedience movement), he began resorting to civil disobedience, non-cooperation and anti-British governmental activities; gave up Senatorship of Patna University; started touring to educate the people about the political situation, exhort them to join the national movement and to introduce the khadi cult and spinning among them; became a close friend of Vallabhabhai Patel; went to Gandhi's *ashrama* (Sabarmati) and often toured India with him; though he suffered with asthma and had financial difficulties, never took monetary aid from Congress or other funds; imprisoned a number of times for his political activities, was in jail on January 15, 1934, when the catastrophic Bihar earthquake occurred; released on January 17, started organising relief measures and collected Rs. 38 lakhs for this purpose; in recognition of his dedicated services was elected President of the Bombay Session of INC; when the Congress ministries were formed in 1937, was on the Parliamentary Board (with Vallabhabhai Patel and Abul Kalam Azad) which provided Agriculture at the Centre and launched the 'grow more food' campaign; declined chairmanship of Planning Commission as he realised that industrialisation had to be shaped keeping in view the needs and patterns of the village community and had to be inspired by Gandhian values; became President of the Constituent Assembly which he guided with great patience, firmness and skill; became President of India (1950-62); an outstanding intellectual and a far-sighted man of the people, had a moderating influence and proffered effective guidance in an unobtrusive manner; his differences with other national leaders never alienated him from them; a great figure in national life and stalwart in the forefront of the battle for freedom.

Rajputs (650-1200 A.D.). The Rajputs dominated the Indian political scene for about 500 years. The well known Rajput rulers were: Prithviraj Chauhan who ruled over Delhi and Ajmar, and defeated Mohammad Ghori in 1191 in the First Battle of Tarain. But he was defeated and killed by Ghori in 1192, in the Second Battle of Tarain, Jai Chand Rathor was the last famous Rajput king, also to be defeated and killed by Mohammad Ghori in 1194. Palas ruled in Bihar and the Senas in Bengal. In Malwa the Parmars ruled the most famous of whom was King Bhoja. The Chandels ruled in Bundelkhand till Qutb-ud-din Aibak conquerred it in 1203. Mewar was the most important Rajput Kingdom. Rana Kumba was a famous ruler of this dynasty. He defeated Mahmud Khilji and erected a victory tower in Chittor. His son Rana Sangram Singh (Sanga) and Rana Pratap were other great rulers of this kingdom.

Salient features of Rajput rule: Country remained free of invasions, but lost foreign contact, and became insular. National character degenerated. Social life: Cast system was rigid. The Rajputs were proud, warlike but hospitable. But social vices such as *sati*, child marriage and infanticide of daughters was also prevalent. Culturally, many great fortresses and temples were built, such as the temples at Khajuraho (Madhya Pradesh) and Bhubaneswer (Orissa), the Sun Temple at Konarak and the Jagannath Temple at Puri, the Dilwara Jain Temples at Mt. Abu. Jayadev was a great poet of the period who wrote the *Gita Govinda*.

The downfall of the Rajputs is attributed to lack of unity and foresightedness, rigid caste system, geographical impediments, defective military organization, lack of a national leader, greed and fanaticism of the Muslim invaders.

Raman, C.V. (1888-1970). Famous Indian Scientist, got the Noble Prize for Physics in 1930, discovered the phenomenon, famous as Raman Effect.

Rameses. Gk. form of name of 11 kings of the 19th and 20th Egyptian dynasties. The most famous was Rameses II called the Great, who reigned 1558-1491 B.C. A prolific builder: he was responsible for the temple of Abu Simbel and the Ramesseum at Thebes.

Rampa Rebellion. Armed revolt organised by Alluri Sitarama Raju (or Andhra Pradesh) undertaken by tribal people several times against polices repressions; Raju was arrested and shot dead by police in May, 1924.

Ranjit Singh (Maharaja) (1780-1839). At 12 succeeded father as head of union of small Sikh estates which wielded limited military power against Afghan incursions into Punjab; from 1793 to 1798 Afghan leader, Zaman Shah, created great havoc; Ranjit took bold step to occupying Lahore (1798); expediency made Zaman Shah recognise him as Governor of Lahore and confer on him title of 'raja'; he gradually asserted his military might, threw off Afghan domination, occupied Amritsar and made Jammu his tributary State; Holkar and British (Lake) jointly tried miniatory tactics against him (1805); by his skilful manoeuvring, made a treaty with British by which Holkar was excluded from Punjab and British recognised his overlordship over Punjab north of the Sutlej; occupied Ludhiana (1807) which antagonised cis-Sutlej Sikh States and British; made permanent treaty of friendship (treaty of Amritsar) with latter (1809) by which he agreed to confine his military activity to north and west of Sutlej and not to interfere with cis-Sutlej States which British brought under their jurisdiction; conquered Kangra (1811), Attock (1813); gave refuge to Afghan king, Shah Shuja from whom he acquired famous diamond Koh-i-Noor (1814); continued to remain on non-aggressive terms with British who never attacked his territory; by time of his death, his strategy, diplomacy and determination and carved out a powerful Sikh State; not having set up a strong administration, it lacked cohesiveness and fell apart by (1850).

Rapallo, Treaty of (1922). The agreement between Germany and the USSR. Diplomatic relations were renewed after their severance during WWI, financial claims against each other (incurred during the War) were withdrawn, and economic cooperation pledged.

Rashtrakutas (753-973 A.D.). In 753, Dantidurge overthrew the Chalukya power and founded the kingdom of Rashtrakutas of Karnataka and Maharashtra. This kingdom extended from south Gujarat, Malwa Bundhelkhand in north to Tanjore in the south. They were considered to be greatest rulers of the time.

During the reign of Krishna I, the rock-cut temple of Kailash at Ellora and carved. Dhruva, another able king, defeated Dharmapala of Bengal and Mihira Bhoja, the Pratihara King. Govinda III was the most powerful king of the Rashtrakutas.

Rashtriya Swayam Sewak Sangh (RSS). Rounded in 1925 by Dr. K.B. Hedgewar at Nagpur, who was earlier connected with revolutionary activities and satyagraha to free India from British rule; M.S. Golwalkar succeeded Hedgewar; RSS believed in doctrine of Hindu superiority; they worked through *Shakhas* (branches), those who went to *Shakhas* were known as *Swayam Sewaks* or volunteers; they were further divided into sections according to age; these were *Shishu* (children). *Bal* (boys), *Tarun* (youth) and *Praudh* (adults); a *Shakha* had *Ghatnayak* (batch leader); *Shikshakas* (instructors) and one *Mukhya Shikshak* (chief instructor) the person incharge of *Shakha*; there were four organisers and district and provincial organisers; at the top was *Sarsanghachalak; Swayam Sewaks* put a uniform (khaki half pants, white shirt and black cap); they were given exercises in use of lathi, etc.; also taught fundamentals of Hindu religion; training camp held during vacations; money collected in form of *gurudakshina*; a disciple's tribute to his preceptor; organisation banned in 1948 after Gandhi's murder; ban was lifted in 1949; RSS accused by some having fascist tendencies and also working against non-Hindus. Now branches all over India.

Ratel. Genus of burrowing carnivores of the Weasel family (*Mellivora*), inhabiting India and Africa.

Reagan, Ronald Wilson. American Republican politician, President. He was Governor of California 1967-75. Before entering politics he was a film actor.

Rechabites. (1) Heb. religious community. They dwelt in tents, and avoided wine, vine-planting and grain-growing (2 Kings, 10). (2) Independent Order of Rechabites, a total abstinence Friendly Soc. Founded 1835.

Red Army. Armed land forces of the USSR established (1918) by the Bolshevik Government. The word 'Red' was dropped from the title in 1946.

Referendum or Plebiscite. The submission of an issue of national or public importance to the vote of the electorate of a state, region, etc. Referenda were held by Norway and the UK on the issue of EEC membership.

Reformation. The Reformation was another movement that the sixteenth century witnessed. It was started by Luther in Wittenburg (Germany) in 1517 by publicly protesting against the sale of *indulgences*. It was a revolt against the control of conscience by the priests. Thanks to the inborn spirit of revolt against the Catholic Church. Henry VIII could take the bold step of breaking away from the papacy on the issue of his first divorce in 1534.

With the breaking away from the Roman Catholic Church by such leaders as Luther and Calvin, Western Europe was split between Catholic and Protestant countries, a situation which developed enmities of the fiercest nature. The history of England during this period is throughout coloured with struggles between the supporters of the Church of England and the Englishmen who remained faithful to Rome as well as the power struggle between Protestant England and the Catholic forces in Ireland and on the Continent, especially Spain.

Reichstag Fire (1933). The conflagration which destroyed the German Reichstag (parliament building) in Berlin for which a Dutchman, Marinus van der Lubbe, was found guilty of arson and executed. The fire occurred a month after Hitler became Chancellor and he put the blame for it on the Communists, 3 of whom, Dmitrov, Popov and Tanev, all Bulgarians, were tried with van der Lubbe but acquitted.

Renaissance. The sixteenth century is commonly designated as the Age of Renaissance also called the Revival of learning. It is said to have started from the capture of Constantinople by the Turks in 1453 and the dispersal of the scholars throughout Europe, who sought asylum in Italy. Constantinople, then the capital of the East Roman Empire, was the centre of art and culture in Europe. Italy practically became the home of the Renaissance—and it meant the revival of the study of the literature of classical antiquity. It resulted in the emancipation of the mind of man from the shackles of *effete* dogmatism, and in the creation of fresh intellectual atmosphere and ideals of life. The movement spread to other countries of Europe also, especially to France and Germany, and at last it reached the shores of England. The Renaissance movement was enormously, helped by the invention of the printing press with the help of which old and classical books were multiplied leading to a great increase in knowledge and in the spirit of enquiry and experiment.

Reparations. Payments made in money and kind, esp. by Germany as compensation for the damage done by her troops during World War I. The principle was laid down in the Treaty of Versailles. In 1921, at a conference held in London, the amount was fixed at £ 6,600,000,000.

Republic. A country in which the head of state is an elected or nominated president, as opposed to a monarch, and in which the people of their elected representatives possess (at least nominally) supreme power. Examples incl. India, France, Italy and the USA. The USSR and Yugoslavia are both federations of semi-autonomous republics.

Republican Party. Refers to one of the two main political parties in the

USA. Founded in 1854, its strength is drawn from the higher-educated, higher-income, business and professional classes based in small towns and suburbs across the country, and the rural areas of the NE and Middle West.

Resistance Movements. The underground organizations engaging in sabotage and secret operations against collaborators and enemy occupying forces, esp. in France, Norway, etc., during WWII. See also partisan Maquis.

Restoration (1660). Charles II, the son of Charles I, ascended the throne of England in 1660. This event is popularly known as "Restoration." Monarchy in England was re-established, though the king now enjoyed much less powers.

In 1679 came the *Habeas Corpus Act*. This Act was passed during the reign of Charles II. According to this Act: (*i*) Judges were obliged on application to issue to any prisoner a write of *habeas corpus*, directing the jailor to produce the body of the prisoner, and show cause for his imprisonment; (*ii*) prisoners should be indicated in the first term of their commitment and tried not later than the second; and (*iii*) no person once set free by order of the court could be again imprisoned for the same offence. The Act gave facilities to a prisoner for obtaining either speedy trial or release on bail and safeguarded the personal liberties of the people against arbitrary imprisonment.

Revisionism. Marxist movement developed in Germany about 1900, favouring evolutionary rather than revolutionary transition to socialism; considered by Marxist-Leninist ideologists as a dangerous departure from Marx's precepts.

Revolt of 1857. The Mutiny was *mainly a rebellion of the army* which took place at a time when there was a great deal of social and political unrest in the public mind owing to the policy of Lord Dalhousie. Some of his reforms had created panic in the minds of Indians. Fortunately for the British, the Mutiny was not widespread.

Some historians regard this Mutiny as the *First War of Indian Independence* because although its leaders joined the movement for different reasons, *their one common aim was to turn out the English and win independence for the country.*

Queen Victoria's Proclamation, 1st November 1858. It is called the *Magna Carta of Indian liberties*. It transferred the Government to the British Crown. It granted right of adoption, put an end to the policy of annexation, assured religious freedom, promised equality of treatment, gave general amnesty and held out a promise of material and moral progress.

Revolution. (*a*) The fundamental political change, esp. activity supporting the overthrow or repudiation of a government, ruler or system, and the substitution of another by the governed. (*b*) In Marxist theory, historically necessary, violent transition from one system of production in a society to another, as from feudalism to capitalism, and from capitalism to socialism.

Reynaud, Paul (1878-1966). French Radical Party politician. He held several ministerial offices during the 1930s before becoming PM (1940). He was in power only 3 months during WWII before having to resign when the Assembly decided to sue for peace and dissolve the Third Republic. He was subsequently imprisoned by the Vichy Government and later sent to concentration camps by the Germans. After the War he became Finance Minister (1948) and Deputy PM (1953-54), campaigning for European integration.

Rhineland. The area of West Germany on both banks of the Rhine bordering France and the Low Countries.

Rhodesia and Nyasaland, Federation of. The union (1953-63) of Northern and Southern Rhodesia (now Zambia and Zimbabwe) and Nyasaland (now Malawi), championed by Sir Godfrey Huggins and Sir Roy Welensky. They considered that the copperbelt industries of Northern Rhodesia, the sophisticated economy of Southern Rhodesia and the agriculture of Nyasaland could be profitably integrated within a single political entity.

The union failed largely because African nationalists saw it is hindering moves towards independence, and because right-wing whites in Southern Rhodesia objected to the Federation's policies of improving the status of black Africans.

Richard I. (1157-99) King of Eng. 3rd son of Henry II. Succeeded Henry as king in 1189. He reigned for 10 years, but passed only a few months in Eng. He took a leading part in the Crusades. In 1192 he was taken prisoner in Germany and ransomed in 1194. Known as

Coeur de Lion (Lionheart) he was killed in battle at Chaluz. He mar. Berengaria, daughter of the King of Navarre, but left no legitimate children. His successor was his brother John.

Richard II. (1366-1400) King of Eng. Son of the Black Prince, he succeeded his grandfather Edward III, in 1377. His reign was full of trouble. Taxation was heavy, and risings took place in many parts of the country, the most serious being that of Wat Tyler (1381). The preaching of the Lollards (*q.v.*) helped to increase discontent. Henry of Lancaster forced him to abdicate in 1399.

Richard III. (1452-85) King of Eng. Throughout the reign of his brother, Edward IV, he gave him loyal assistance, but on his *d.* he usurped the crown from his nephew, Edward V, whom he is believed to have had murdered in the Tower. He *d.* fighting Henry of Richmond at Bosworth.

Rigvedic India. The Rigveda points to a highly organised society. Monogamy was the general rule but, among the princes, polygamy was also practised. Dowry was usual at the time of marriage. The marriage of girls was not considered essential.

The father had complete control over his children and marriages were arranged by parents. The right of adoption was recognised. The people were active, joyful and warlike. The joint family system was in vogue. People wore garments of various colours. Women wore ornaments like necklaces, ear-rings, bracelets and anklets. They wore their hair plaited. Men grew beards but shaving was also known. Their food included wheat, barley, milk products, porridge, meat of goat and sheep. The cow was a sacred animal. The amusements of the people were chariot racing, horse racing, music, dancing and dicing. The people of the Rigvedic India lived a settled life and built cottages of wood.

They were essentially agriculturists. They also resorted to hunting. The carpenter played an important part in the Rigvedic society. It was his duty to make chariots for sport and fighting.

There was the system of barter. The people worshipped a large number of gods in the form of the phenomena of nature.

Rio Treaty (1947). Formally known as the Inter-American Treaty of Reciprocal assistance, signed at Rio de Janeiro, Brazil, by 21

American states, the only non-participating nations being Canada, Ecuador and Nicaragua. The Treaty, entirely military in character and operative only in the America's security zone, provides for aid to be given by all member states to any of their number subjected to aggression, an armed attack against any being considered an attack against all.

Robert. Name of 2 dukes of Normandy. Robert I (*d.* 1035), called the Devil, was the father of William the Conqueror. Robert II (*c.* 1055-1135) the eldest son of William, succeeded him as Duke of Normandy (in 1087) but not as King of Eng.

Robert. Name of 3 kings of Scot. The first is more generally known as Robert the Bruce (*q.v.*). Robert II (1316-90) was a son of Walter the Steward and a grandson of Robert Bruce. He was the first of the Stewart Kings.

Roman Civilisation. Italy is the peninsula that projects into the Mediterranean Sea in the west of Greece. The river Tiber on which the city of Rome is located runs through the central part of the peninsula. The Alps protect the peninsula from cold winds, but are not an effective barrier to the north-south movement of people.

The city of Rome was founded about 1000 B.C., in the district of Latium, south of the Tiber river. The language of the ancient Romans, Latin, gets its name from Latium. The early Romans had a king, an Assembly and a Senate. Towards the end of the sixth century B.C., the king was overthrown and a republic was established. By 265 B.C., the Romans controlled Italy. The political system of the Roman republic consisted of two Consuls, the Senate and the Assembly. The Senate was a powerful body and could veto the acts of the Assembly.

The Roman society was divided into two classes—*patricians* and *plebeians*. The particians were the upper class and considered of the aristocracy and big landlords who controlled the Senate. The plebeians were the workers, small farmers, artisans and small traders and soldiers. The plebeians had few rights, were forced to pay heavy taxes and were often unjustly punished. In the beginning of the fifth century B.C., they revolted and the particians were forced to grant them concessions. They won the right to elect *tribunes* who could veto the acts of the Consuls and the Senate that concerned the plebeians. Another victory of the plebeians was the codification of laws in 454 B.C. The laws were written on tablets of wood and were known as the *Laws of Twelve Tablets*.

The Romans were involved in a series of wars with Carth-age, a city on the north coast of Africa. By the beginning of the first century B.C., they had conquered Greece and Asia Minor and established a protectorate over Egypt. Wars increased the political power of the army generals. Rivalry for power grew between two generals, Pompey and Julius Caesar. War between Pompey and Caesar followed and Pompey was murdered by his enemies in Egypt. Caesar remained in Egypt for some time, attracted by the captivating beauty of the Egyptian queen, Cleopatra. On his return to Rome, in 46 B.C., he made himself dictator but was assassinated in 44 B.C., in a Senate meeting. Power passed into the hands of Mark Antony and Lepidus, Caesar's friends, and Octavian, Caesar's grand nephew. The leaders of the conspiracy, Brutus and Cassius, fled and organised a large army, but they were captured and slain.

In 37 B.C., Octavian became the most powerful man in the Roman empire. He ruled for 44 years under the titles of *Augustus*, which meant 'holy', and *Imperator*, meaning 'Victorious general'. He also called himself *Princeps*, 'first citizen of the State'. The period of roman history beginning with his rule up to 284 A.D., is called the Principate. His rule and the period following it were peaceful and known in history as *Pax Romana*, which means, 'Roman Peace'. Most of the successors of Augustus were tyrants. Finally in A.D. 284, when Diocletian became ruler, he destroyed even the semblance of republican government; the Senate lost all authority and the *imperator* or emperor became absolute. From this time on, Roman civilisation declined rapidly.

One of Diocletian's successors Constantine built a new capital called Constantinople on the site of ancient Byzantium. Not long after the Roman empire was divided into two empires—Eastern and Western. The eastern part was called the Byzantine empire. The western part soon broke into many pieces. By A.D. 476, the once powerful Roman empire was no more.

The early Romans were known for their patriotism. They lived mostly by agriculture and raised sheep and cattle. They attached great importance to marriage and family life. Women were respected; they took part freely in politics and the business of their husbands. Parents and ancestors were revered. The Romans worshipped as many gods and goddesses as the Greeks. Jupiter sent rain for the crops; Mars helped them in War; Juno protected their women; Mercury carried their messages. Every object of nature was 'inhabited' by some unseen power.

The Roman society was divided into four main classes—the aristocracy, wealthy merchants and bankers, the plebeians and slaves. The roman developed their own alphabet after the Greeks, and the Latin language became the language of all educated people in western Europe. They adopted Greek philosophies. Epicureanism and Stoicism were popular in Rome. Lucretius, author of the poem *On the Nature of Things*, was an Epicurean philosopher. Cicero was their famous orator. The Roman civilisation developed its literature and is noted for many achievements in poetry. Horace and Virgil were the famous poets. Virgil is known for his *Aeneid*, which was written in the style of *Iliad* and *Odyssey*. The *Aeneid* describes the wanderings and adventures of Aeneas, a legendary hero of Troy. Tacitus was the most famous Roman historian.

Roman law and principles of governance are Rome's greatest contribution to the world. Their achievements in architecture and engineering were second only to their work in law and administration.

Romany. Language of the Gipsies, belonging to N.W. (Dardic) group of Indo-Aryan languages. 3 main dialects: *(a) Asiatic, (b) Armenian, (c) European. Parlyaree* (language of showmen,tinkers, etc.), has a Romany base.

Rome, Treaties of (1957). The agreements establishing the European Economic Community and the European Atomic energy Community, effective from 1958. They were signed by Belgium, France, West Germany, Italy, Luxembourg and the Netherlands.

Romulus. Founder of Rome and its first king. Legend says that in infancy, Romulus and his twin brother, Remus, were thrown into the Tiber by their uncle, but the trough in which they were placed went aground. The children were suckled by a wolf and brought up by a shepherd. While they were building walls a quarrel arose and Remus was killed. Romulus became king of Rome.

Roosevelt, Franklin Delano. (1882-1945) 32nd Amer. Pres. In 1932, as a Democratic candidate for the Presidency, he defeated Herbert

Hoover and during his term of office the gold standard was abandoned and the dollar devalued. He introduced the Utilities Act and the Social Securities Act in 1935. He defeated Alfred Landon in 1936. Soon after the outbreak of war he launched a vast rearmament programme and introduced conscription. He was re-elected in 1940 and introduced his 'lease-lend' plan for the supply of war materials to the Allies. In 1941 he drew up the Atlantic Charter with Mr. Churchill. From the time of the attack on Pearl Harbour he concerned himself solely with the conduct of the war. He was re-elected in 1944 but *d.* suddenly on April 12, 1945, having fought a continual battle against polio since 1921. His wife (Anna) Eleanor Roosevelt (1884-1962) actively helped in his polit. life and did much social welfare work. She was U.S. representative to the U.N. General Assembly 1945-52.

Roosevelt, Theodore. (1858-1919) 26th Pres. of the U.S.A. Gov. of New York State in 1898, he was elected as Republican Vice Pres., 1900. On McKinley's assassination in 1901 he became Pres. and was re-elected in 1904. A split in the Republican vote between Roosevelt and Taft caused his defeat by the Democrat Wilson in 1902.

Roses, Wars of the. (1455-85) Civil war in Eng. Richard, Duke of York, claimed the throne when Henry VI became insane. Henry's supporters, the Lancastrians, took a red rose as their symbol, and the Yorkists a white. At the Battle of Northampton, 1460, Henry was made prisoner and in 1461, York was killed at the Battle of Wakefield. The Lancastrians were defeated at Towton and their cause was hopeless until the Earl of Warwick changed sides in 1470. Henry was then released from prison and restored to the throne. At Barnet and Tewkesbury in 1471, the Lancastrian armies were crushed and the war was virtually over, although it is usually regarded as ending with the Battle of Bosworth, 1485, where Henry Tudor, defeating his enemies became King Henry VII.

Round Table. Legendary table used by King Arthur and his knights. It was made round so that there should be no jealousies about precedence.

Round Table Conference. A series of there conferences called by the Labour Party Prime Minister Ramsay MacDonald in London 1930-1932 to discuss with representatives of India's different interests the subject of reforms in the Constitution of India. The 1933 White

Paper published as a result of these conferences served as a basis for the 1935 Government of India Act.

Rowlatt Act, 1919. In 1918, the Government appointed a Sedition Committee with Mr. Justice Rowlatt as its chairman. Its object was to report on the nature and extend of revolutionary movement in the country and to suggest how to deal with it. On its recommendations the Rowlatt Act was passed in March 1919. This Act gave extraordinary powers to the Government in dealing with the terrorists. *The administration could detain people in prison for an indefinite period without trial.*

Ruhr. The principal manufacturing and mining area of NW West Germany. It was occupied by the French (1923-25) because Germany did not pay her reparation dues imposed by the Treaty of Versailles. During WWII the region suffered severely from Allied bombing raids.

Rupar. A minor site of the Harappa culture in eastern Punjab.

Russia. Union of Soviet Socialist Republics.

Russian Revolution. Many years. of revolutionary propaganda culminated an open rebellion on Mar. 12, 1917. The army refused to deal with food rioters in Petrograd and the navy joined the strikes. The Duma elected a provisional government and on Mar. 15 the Tsar abdicated. Lenin returned from exile, and the struggle for mastery was won by the Bolshevists. On Nov. 7 they seized Petrograd, deposed the Kerensky government and obtained complete power. On Mar. 3, 1918, they concluded the Peace of Brest-Litovsk with the C. Powers, the Tsar and his family were assassinated, the Ch. repressed and the Nat. debt repudiated. Lenin was Dictator and Trotsky Foreign Secretary. By the end of 1921 all opposition had been suppressed. Lenin *d.* in 1924 and was succeeded by Stalin. That there was dissension within the Communist party was evident from the exile of Trotsky to Siberia in 1927, and from purges and mass trials of 'counter revolutionaries'. Meanwhile, educational, industrial and scientific development went on in the U.S.S.R., and the Red army and air force became ever more powerful. The avowed object of the Russ. rulers is world Communism.

Russo-Japanese War. War (1904-5) caused by the clash of Jap. and Russ. interests in the Pacific. It was begun by Japan, with a successful attack on the Russ. fleets at Chemulpo and Port Arthur. The Russ. resistance was finally broken in May, when her fleet under Rozhdestvensky was routed by Admiral Togo in the battle of Tsushima. Peace was signed, Sept. 5, 1905, at Portsmouth, U.S.A.

Russo-Turkish Wars. Several wars between Turkey and Russia, mainly caused by the treatment of Christian subject peoples by the Sultan, and the desire of Russia for domination of the Black Sea and for an outlet to the Medit. The first in 1696 gave Russia Azov. The war of 1827-29 rose out of Mahmud II's cruel treatment of rebel Gks., which united Brit, Fr. and Russia against him. The Turkish fleet was destroyed at Navarino, 1827, and the Treaty of Adrianople, 1829, gave indep. to the Gks. The Crimean War (1854-56) lost Russia her Danube possessions and naval power in the Black Sea. Treaty of Berlin, 1878, practically ended the Turkish Emp. in Europe but alienated Russia from Austria and Germany.

Ryotwari. A British system of land assessment originally employed in South India beginning early in the 19th century, but later spreading to western and central India. Land tax assessments were made directly upon the individual cultivators (ryots) rather than upon the landlords or tax farmers and were temporary (usually for 30 years) rather than permanent.

S

SA (Sturmabteilung). The German organization which was founded in 1921, andalso known as the Brown Shirts, Storm Division of Storm Troopers. It was a Paramilitary organization, eventually becoming a political arm of the Nazi Party. Under Ernst Rohm's leadership (1931-34) it came more and more into conflict with the SS and the army, including Hitler to put an end to its activities and have it absorbed by the SS. He did this by liquidating Rohn and the rest of the SA leadership in what came to be known as 'The Night of the Long Knives'(1934).

Saarland. The area of West Germany bordering France and Luxembourg with important mining and iron and steel industries. It was placed under League of Nations Control (1919), France being granted permission to exploit the coalmines for 15 years as part of its reparation claim against Germany. As the result of a plebiscite it was returned to Germany (1935). After WWII it was in the French occupation zone until being integrated with West Germany (1957).

Sadat, Anwar El (1918-81). Egyptian statesman. He succeeded Nasser as President (1970-81), and continued Egypt's confrontation with Israel, culminating in the 1973 Arab-Israeli war. After the failure to overcome the Israelis, Sadat began a policy of rapprochment with the West and ended the country's military dependence on the USSR. The Suez Canal, blocked during the War, was reopened (1975), and then Sadat, in a bold initiative, went to Jerusalem (1977) for talks with Israeli ministers and to address the Knesset (Parliament). This remarkably courageous act led to the Camp David Agreement and a peace treaty with Israel (1979), which ultimately restored to Egypt territory previously occupied by Israel. However, scorn and vilification was heaped on Sadat by redical Arab states and the PLO, and he was assassinated in 1981. He was awarded the 1978 Nobel Peace Prize jointly with begin.

Saint Germain, Treaty of (1919). WWI peace settlement between the

Allies and Austria. It limited the Austrian Army to 30,000 men, forbade Austria to unite with Germany, dismembered the Austro-Hungarian Navy, and provided for the payment of reparations. Austria's territorial and population losses were enormous : Bohemia and Moravia were transferred to Czechoslovakia; the Trentino and South Tyrol to Italy; Galicia to Poland; Bukovina to Romania; and Bosnia-Herzegovina, Dalmatia and Slovenia to Yugoslavia.

Sakas and Parthians. These foreigners of Central Asia, who came to India in search of conquest, settled in India. Nahapona, the greatest of Kshaaratha Satraps, is credited to have commenced the Saka era in 78 A.D.

Salazar, Antonio de Oliveria (1889-1970). Portuguese dictator, PM (1932-68). Although Fascist in character, his administration carried out many beneficial reforms, incl. improvements in education, industrial development, living conditions and public works. However, independence movements in the Portuguese colonies and political opposition at home were suppressed, the only permitted party being Salazar's own, the Portuguese National Union.

Salt. Strategic Arms Limitation Talks.

Sanctions. The coercive measures (usually in the form of trade bans) taken by one or more states against another guilty of violating international law. As there are always methods of circumventing such measures, sanctions have proved ineffective when they have been attempted, notably by the League of nations on Italy when it invaded Ethiopia (1935), and by the UN on Rhodesia to counter its policy of unilateral independence and white-minority rule (1966-80).

Sardar Vallahbhbhai Patel (1857-1950). He is known as Bismarck of India. He was the Deputy Prime Minister of India 1947-50. He is famous for Integration of Indian States.

Satavahanas. Sometimes called Andhras, the dynasty probably established in the first century B.C. It lasted for about 3 centuries. Its main areas were Deccan and western India with *Pratisthana* as capital.

Satellite State. A country economically, militarily and politically controlled or dominated by another more powerful state. The Warsaw Pact countries are often regarded as satellite of the USSR.

Saturation Bombing. The heavy and sustained air attack with the objective of obliterating the target in a single decisive operation; frequently practised during WWII by the Luftwaffe, RAF and USAAF.

Satyagraha. (literary holding on to or insistence on truth)—Method adopted by Gandhi (based on Tolstoy's concept) of non-violent passive resistance against government in struggle for freedom; first practised by him in South Africa to improve condition of indentured (Indian) labour there; non-cooperation movement carried out by him and followers in India by offering satyagraha against governmental repression, etc. throughout national struggle.

Scapa Flow. The large natural anchorage in the Orkney Islands, used as a British naval base in both World Wars. A large part of the German fleet was impounded there at the end of WWI and scuttled (1919) on the orders of Admiral von Reuter. During WWII The battleship HMS *Royal Oak* was torpedoed and sunk there by a German U-boat (1939). The base was closed in 1956.

Schlieffen Plan. The detailed scheme prepared by General Count Alfred von Schlieffen (1833-1913) who was German Chief of General Staff (1891-1905).

Schmidt, Helmut. West German Social Democratic statesman. He was Federal Defence Minister (1969-72), Finance Minister (1972-74) and Chancellor (1974-82). Schmidt followed the policy of Ostpolitik initiated by his predecessor, Brandt, and coupled it with full commitment to the EEC and NATO. He was succeeded by Kohl.

Schuman Plan (1950). The proposal submitted by the French Foreign Minister, Robert Schuman (1886-1963), for pooling the coal and steel resources of Western Europe. It got implemented when the European Coal and Steel Community got established.

Schuschnigg, Kurt Von (1897-1977). Austrian Christian Socialist Chancellor (1934-38). He followed a moderate middle of the road policy based on an external reliance on Italy against German threats of Anschluss.

SDI. Strategic Defence Initiative.

SDLP. Social Democratic and Labour Party.

SDP. Social Democratic Party.

SEATO. Southeast Asia Treaty Organization.

Second Round Table Conference, 1931. Second Round Table Conference began in London in September 1931 and lasted for three months. Mahatma Gandhi participated in it as the sole representative of the Congress. The British Government made an offer of partly responsible government at the Centre. But this conference could not solve the communal problem. It could not arrive at a decision whether the electorates should be joint or separate; nor could it agree on the number of seats to be allotted to the various communities in the central and provincial legislatures, nor on the reserved seats for the depressed classes. At last the solution of this problem was left to the discretion of Mr. Ramsay MacDonald, the then Prime Minister of England.

Self-determination. The right of a nation or territorial unit to determine the form of government or political status it desires without external coercion or influence.

Separation of Powers. The constitutional principle (effective in most democracies) that the 3 branches of government legislative, executive and judicial should be independent of each other.

Sevagram. As preservation and protection of various places associated with Gandhiji's work and life, is one of the aims of Gandhi Smarak Nidhi, Sevagram, the *ashram-home* of Gandhiji's later years, naturally features prominently in this programme. The original *ashram* area of *Sevagram* comprises cottages occupied by Gandhiji and Kasturba at one time or the other, as also those of his closest followers, Mahadev Desai and Kishorilal Mashruwala. This *Ashram* campus, as indeed the whole of Sevagram, now constitutes a charge on *Sarva Seva Sangh* of which Vinobaji was the head, the Sangh has decided that the campus should be preserved intact as a relics of national importance, and preferably as it had been during Gandhiji's times.

Sevres, Treaty of (1920). The post-WWI settlement following the Paris Peace Conference. Turkey was to give Greece extensive rights on the E side of the Dardanelles, and to cede most of European Turkey and most of the Aegean Islands to Greece. The waterway connecting the Aegean and Black seas was to be demilitarized and internationalized under a 10-power League of Nations commission, and to be opened to merchant vessels and warships of all nations in times of peace and war. Armenia was granted independence, Kurdistan was permitted autonomy, and the Arabian peninsula achieved independence as the Kingdom of Hejaz. Mesopotamia and Palestine were to become mandates of Britain, and Syria a mandate of France. Turkish finances were placed under British, French and Italian supervision.

These arrangements got rejected by the Turkish republican movement and ultimately led to the Chanak Crisis, the rebellions against the Sultan by Mustapha Kemal (Ataturk), and the downfall of Lloyd George's coalition government in the UK. The settlement was later revised by the Treaty of Lausanne.

Seyss-Inquart, Artur Von (1892-1946). Austrian politician. His friendship with Chancellor Schuschnigg enabled him to keep Hilter informed of the Chancellor's every move to retain the country's independence. Seyss-Inquart hoping that he would be appointed Chancellor after the Anschluss.

Shahjanan (1627-1659 A.D.). He came to the throne after a war of succession in 1627. His reign is known for promotion of art, culture, and architecture. Red Fort, Jama Masjid, Taj-mahal etc., were built by him. In the last years of his life, he was imprisoned by his son Aurangzeb and died a captive in 1666.

Shastri, Lal Bahadur (1904-66). Indian Congress Party politician, PM (1964-66). He was responsible for the introduction of the law against caste and separatism, and language and religious discrimination, and refused to commit the country to the development of nuclear weapons.

After the outbreak of hostilities between India and Pakistan over Kashmir (1965), Shastri attended the Taskent Conference (1966). Agreement was reached on a truce but at the end of the conference Shastri died of a heart attack.

Shevardnadze, Eduard. Soviet statesman. As foreign minister under Gorbachev he has been involved in the thawing of East-West relations.

Sher Khan Sur (Sher Shah Suri) (1472-1545 A.D.). An Afgan chief who captured much of North India from the Mughals and forced

Humayun, the Mughal emperor, to leave India for 15 years.

Siegfried Line. The series of German fortifications built (1936-44) from N of the Ruhr, up the Rhine to the Swiss frontier and named after the mythical German hero. It seriously delayed the Allied advance into Germany from the W in 1944.

Sikhs. Sikhism was started as a religious sect but became a military community. Guru Nanak Dev (*b.* 1496) founded the Sikh faith which lays emphasis on unity of God, rejection of casteism and rituals, and brotherhood of man. Guru Govind Singh (1666-1702) transformed the religious sect to a military brotherhood. It was the martyrdom of Guru Arjan Dev in Jehangir's reign which was a turning point in Sikh history, making them enemies of the Mughals. After Banada Bairagi, the Sikhs laked effective leadership and they took refuge in the Himalayan hills. They formed *misls*, or groups which established independent kingdoms in the Punjab in the 18th century.

Simmon Commission (1927). Consisted 7 members of British Parliament with (Sir) John Simon as chairman to suggest measures of political reform for India as all members were non-Indian; among other things recommended abolition of dyarchy, establishment of provincial autonomy and some sort of federal government of India.

Sino-Japanese War (1937-45). The conflict developing from Japan's seizure of Mukden (1931) and its annexation of Manchuria (1932).

Sino-Soviet Split. The schism which developed between Communist China and the USSR (1956) and which he still causing friction between them.

Six-Day War. Arab-Israeli Wars.

Sivaji (1627-1680). Founder of Maratha empire, last of great Hindu empires; son of Shabji Bhonsle (of Kumbu caste) which claimed descent from Maharajas of Karnataka. He rose to distinguished heights.

Slave Dynasty. The period or 1206-1290 A.D. in India. See Quatab-ud-Din Aibek.

Smith, Jan. Rhodesian politician. With the breakup of the Federation of Rhodesia and Nyasaland he became a founder of the Rhodesia Front Party (1962) and PM (1964-78). Dedicated to immediate independence without African majority rule in Southern Rhodesia, his government made a unilateral declaration of independence (UDI) in 1965 in defiance of the UK decision to forestall independence until there was black majority rule.

Social Democracy. The beliefs, practices, principles or programme of social democrats or a social democratic party, based on the transformation of captalism into socialism by gradual reform within a parliamentary system.

Socialism. (*a*) An economic and political theory advocating collective or government control over the means of distribution, exchage and production, distinguished by equality of wealth, the absence of competitive economic activity, production for use rather than profit, and frequently by government determination of investment, prices and production norms; (*b*) In Marxist theory, a transitional period in society's development from capitalism to communism, based on income distribution according to work done as opposed to need.

Solidarity. An independent Polish trade union founded in 1980. Led by Lech Walesa, Solidarity received widespread popular support for its demand for wage increases and political liberalization. It was banned following the imposition of material law in 1981, but was continued its activities underground. Walesa was awarded the 1983 Nobel Peace Prize. In 1989 solidarity gets his PM in Poland.

Somme, Battle of the (1916). A 20-week engagement of WWI fought along a 32 km front N of the River. Somme in N France. Well over a million men perished, and the Allied territorial gain was a mere 16 km.

Southeast Asia Treaty Organization (SEATO). The defensive alliance established (1954) in Pakistan, the Philipines, Thailand, the UK and USA. Pakistan withdrew (1973) and France (1974) and the remaining members resolved (1975) to phase out the Organization due to changing circumstances in the area.

Soviet. The elected administrative or governmental council in the USSR at either local, regional or national level, culminating in the Supreme Soviet.

Soviet Security Service. The organization which incl. the secret police.

Soweto. Black township in the Transvaal, South Africa, were rioting occurred (1976) after he had been announced that Afrikans would be the compulsory language of instruction in schools. The trouble lasted 3 days and a further 3 days elsewhere in the Transvaal, 236 blacks being killed and over 1,100 wounded when he polish opened fire. The proposed compulsory teaching of Afrikans was abandoned a few weeks later.

Spanish Civil War (1936-39). The conflict between the Republican Spanish Government and rebel forces. Alarmed by the land reforms anti-clerical and left-wing tendencies of the Popular Front Government of the Republic, a group of high-ranking army officers started a rebellion, launched from Spanish Morocco and the Canary Islands. The rebels were supported by the land-owning aristocracy, big industrialists, the RC Church, nationalists, monarchists and the Falange (fascist party), while the Republican Government drew support from socialists, communists, anarchists, and those seeking regional autonomy, esp. in the Basque country, Catalonia and Galicia.

Spartacist Rising (1919). The name given to a week of street violence in Berlin organized by radical socialists of the Spartacus League, which was named after the leader of a slave revolt against Rome (73-71 B.C.). The movement was founded in 1916 and was reconstituted as the German Communist Party in 1918. All its leaders were either arrested or killed in the rioting, incl. the founders Karl Liebknecht and Rosa Luxemburg. The Spartacists' objective was the overthrow of capitalism, and they believed this could only be achieved by a revolutionary rising of German workers throughout the country. In the same year, Soviets of revolutionary workers, soldiers and sailors were established in several major German cities, but these were similarly suppressed.

Sri Lanka. Annexed from the Dutch by the British (1815), the country became independent in 1948. In recent years the main problem has been increasingly violent civil strife between the majority Sinhalese and the minority Tamils, many of whom want to set up a separate state in the N and E of the Island. India which has a large Tamil population in the SE, has tried to play a mediating role, but with little success.

SS (Schutzstaffel). German organization (literally meaning 'protection squad') founded in 1925 as Hilter's bodyguard, but when Himmler took command (1929) he transformed the black-uniformed troopers into a militarily trained and ideologically indoctrinuated Nazi elite. It was used to supperss the larger rival SA (1934), absorbed the police force (1936) and became the most feared and powerful movement in the country. It embodied racialism at its worst, and carried out the Nazi policy of exterminating all opposition, esp. in the concentration camps which it controlled.

Stalin, Josef. Orig. Dzhugahsvili (1879-1953), Soviet Communist statesman and dictator. He spent some years in the exile before the Revolution, and formed close ties with Lenin and the Bolsheviks. From 1919 he contrived to gain control over the principal levers of power in party and state, culminating in his election as First Secretary of the Communist Party (1922), a post he held until his death.

During the War Stalin directed the campaigns against the invaders and wielded immense political power over the Allied leaders, which resulted in far from satisfactory outcomes to postwar problems as far as the West was concerned. These incl. the dropping of the Iron Curtain and the opening of the Cold War. One of history's greatest tyrants, Stalin was denounced publicity by Khrushchev at the 20th Party Congress (1956).

Stalingrad. The city of the USSR, renamed Volograd in 1961. It was the scene or a massive soviet victory after the Germans besieged the city (1942-43). The battle was the decisive turning point on the Eastern Front in WWII.

Stern Gang. Zionist underground movement, founded (1940), by Abraham Stern (1907-42) When he left Irgun Zvai Leumi due to decision to suspend anti-British activities in Palestine during WWII. The Gang had been responsible for various acts of terrorism incl. the assassination of the UN mediator in the first Arab-Israeli War, Count Folk Bernadottee (1948). The movement got dissolved in 1948.

Strategic Defense Initiative (SDI). (popularly known as 'Star Wars'). A proposed US system of artificial statelites armed with lasers to destroy enemy missiles in space. The USSR is conducting research into a similar system.

Stresemann, Gustav (1878-1929). German statesman. He became leader of the National Liberal Party (1917), which was re-formed as the German People's Party (1919).

Subhash Chandra Bose (1896-1945). He was an active Congress worker. On account of his difference with Mahatama Gandhi, he started Forward Block. He was a determined fighter or national freedom. He had organised I.N.A. at Singapore.

Sungas. About 185 B.C. *Pushyamitra*, who was the Commander-in-Chief of the last Maurya King Bridratha, killed his master and became the king of Magadha. He was an orthodox Hindu, who started revival of Brahmanical movement. He was founder of Sunga dynasty.

Surat Split 1907. In 1907, at the Surat Session of the Congress, there was a row over the election of the President. The split was now complete and the Congress was divided. The Moderates being in a majority captured the Congress and carried on the work for about ten years. The split weakened the Congress. Now the object of the Congress was to obtain *Dominion Status* for India by peaceful means.

Surenderandth Banerjee (1848-1925). He was a great Bengali patriot, who took prominent part in anti-partition movement in Bengal. He evolved national conscious as a formal concept.

Suri Dynasty (1540-1555 A.D.). The Suri dynasty is particularly noted for the administration and reforms brought about by Sher Shah Suri in the fields of central and provincial administration, land revenue, police, military and judicial spheres. Roads were to encourage trade—the most important one being the Grand Trunk Road. *Sarais* were made Economic conditions improved. Currency was reformed with pure gold and silver coins being struck. Postal department was very advanced. Education was encouraged, through state aid. As far as religious policy, he did not force Hindus to embrace Islam and his treatment of Hindus was tolerant though he too destroyed some temples. Sher Shah before Akbar attempted to build an Indian Nation by reconciling the followers of divergent racial creeds.

Suharto. Indonesian army officers and politician. He played a leading part in the independence war against the Dutch. After the army seized effective power from Sukarno (1967), Suharto became Acting President. As full President from 1968 he has concentrated on economic development, suppression of the Communist Party (*c.* 80,000 members were killed in the coup), encouragement of foreign investment, and a non-aligned foreign policy.

Sukarno, Achmed (1902-70). Indonesian politician. He founded the Indonesian National Party (PNI) in 1927, and was imprisoned and subsequently exiled by the Dutch for independence and revolutionary activities (1929-42). During WWII he led the nationalists in cooperating with Japan (1942-45) and proclaimed an independent republic with himself as President (1945), fighting off all attempts by the Dutch to reassert their authority. His authoritarianism coupled with economic stagnation and a readiness to follow a pro-Chinese Communist policy eventually alarmed the army and other right-wing circles which seized power in 1967 and finally removed him from office in 1968. He was succeeded by Suharto.

Sun Yat-sen (1866-1925). Chinese politican. He was educated in the West and became a Christian. Because of Revolutionary activities against the Manchu Dynasty he had to flee the country in the 19th cent. The early years of the 20th cent. were spent in organizing revolution from outside China. His growing support as leader of the Kuomintang within the country eventually led to the uprisings which overthrew the Dynasty (1911).

Sun Yat-sen was briefly President (1912), but handed over to a military regime, with Yuan Shihkai as president (1912-16), which was later opposed by Sun Yat-sen. After Yuan's death the country collapsed into civil strife between rival warlords. Sun Yat-sen attempted to unify the country by establishing a military government in 1923, but this goal was not achieved until after his death.

Swadeshi Movement (1905). The agitation spread throughout India and a movement for 'Swadeshi' *i.e.*, the use of homemade goods, and the "*boycott of British goods*" especially cotton goods was started in 1905. Sir Surendranath Bannerji, an eminent Bengali patriot and statesman, organized this movement. Other leaders of this movement were Shri Aurobindo Ghosh and Bipin Chandra Pal. Gandhiji later adopted this movement.

Swarajist Party. It dominated the scene from 1923 to 1925. They believed in attaining swaraj by putting obstacles in the way of Government. Its leaders were C.R. Dass, Pt. Moti Lal Nehru, etc. Its members frequently walked out of the legislatures.

T

Tacitus, Publius Cornelius. (58-120) Rom. historian. His extant writings are the *Life of Agricola*, a biography of his father-in-law; the *Germania*; the *Annales*, the hist. of the Rom. emp. from Tiberius to Nero (14-68), and the *Historiae* (69-97).

Taft, William Howard (1875-1930). US Republican President (1909-13). Although an able administrator he was a conservative and cautious politician, having uneasy relations with congress even though both Houses had Republican majorities. This led to a Party split result in Taft's overwhelming defeat by the Democratic candidate, Woodrow Wilson, in the 1912 Presidential election. Taft became Chief Justice of the Supreme Court (1921), an office he held until his death.

Taj Mahal. Mausoleum at Agra, India, built in 1632 by the Epm. Shah Jahan for his favourite wife.

Tamerlane. (1336-1405) Mongol conqueror. In 1358 he began a series of conquests which took him from his kingdom in Turkistan as far as the Caspian Sea, the Urals, the Volga, through Persia, to Egypt and India. Samarkand was his chief city.

Tannenburg, Battle of (1914). The engagement between German and Russian armies in East Prussia during WWI when a Russian force was routed to such an extent that a second Russian army was easily defeated a fortnight later near the Masurian Lakes. The Russians retreated in good order from the Masurian lakes and the pursuing German forces were in their turn thrown back by the Russians so that on balance the two encounters resulted in stalemate, although Russian forces never again entered Germany in WWI.

Taoism. Chinese philosophical system which was developed into a popular religion. Its origins are obscure but Lao-tzu (6th cent. B.C.) wrote the *Tao-Teh-King* which provides the basis of the system.

Tara Singh, Master. Born at Harial in Pothohar district near Rawalpindi; educated at Amritsar; started career as teacher, joined Gurudwara Reform Movement in 1921; suffered imprisonment several times; President Akali Dal in 1930; participated in Non-Cooperation Movement; arrested while leading a *jatha* of 100 Sikhs to Frontier after massacre there; elected President S.G.P.C.; rejected Cripps Proposals; approved division of country; after independence led agitation for a separate Sikh State and observed fast unto death; re-elected President of Akali Dal in 1954; a well known writer in Punjabi; Tara Singh edited *Sant Sepahi*, a monthly magazine; died 1967.

Tarquinius, Lucius. Surnamed Superbus (the Proud) seventh and last of the traditional kings of Rome. He greatly extended the Rom power. He completed the Capitol, built the temple of Jupiter, and acquired the Sibylline books (see Sibyl). He was driven from Rome, following the outrage perpetrated by his son Sextus on Lucretia.

Tashkent Conference (1966). The meeting between President Ayub Khan of Pakistan and PM Shastri of India, convened by the Soviet PM Kosygin following the 1965 Indo-Pakistan War. The War had arisen over the false claim of Pakistan over Kashmir, where border incidents and disturbances led to full-scale conflict. At the Conference both countries renounced the use of force in the settlement of the Kashmir dispute, and agreed to withdraw their respective armed forces to the original frontier.

Teheran Conference (1943). The first meeting during WWI between Churchill, Roosevelt and Stalin. Agreement was reached to coordinate a Russian offensive with the opening of a second front in W Europe; on a declaration of war at a convenient time by the USSR frontier to the Curzon Line, with a compensatory acquisition of German territory by Poland along the Oder-Neisse Line; and on the establishment of a postwar peace keeping organization.

Terrorism. The systematic use of terror manifesting itself in violence and intimidation. Terrorism has been used by groups wishing to coerce a government in order to achieve political or other objectives, and also by dictatorships or other autocratic governments in order to overcome opposition to their policies.

Thant, U (1909-74), Burmese diplomat, Secretary-General of the UN

(1961-71). He played a leading role in resolving the Cuban Missiles Crisis; formulated a plan for the ending of the Congolese civil war (1962); initiated the establishment of a peace keeping force in Cyprus (1964) and the cease-fire arrangements after the 1967 Arab-Israeli War; and obtained the acceptance of Communist China as a member of the UN with a seat in the Security Council.

Thatcher, Margaret. British Conservative stateswoman, former PM of England (U.K.). She was Secretary of State for Education and Science (1970-74), and was elected Leader of the Conservative Party in 1975. She is the first woman in the UK to lead a political party and to hold the post of PM.

Her government's economic policies have generally favoured unfettered free enterprise, which has involved cutting taxes and public expenditure, extensive privatization, and legislation to reduce the power of the trade unions. Her government has also had to deal with high levels of uncmployment. She has favoured a hard line in relations with the Soviet Bloc, and a strengthening of the UK's nuclear forces. She was re-elected in 1983 and 1987; her 1983 success has been partially attributed to the UK victory in the Falkland's War.

Theodosius I (The Great) (*c.* A.D.346-395). Rom. Emperor. After the *d.* of Gratian and Valentinian II he became (the last) sole ruler. Soon after his *d.* began the barbarian invasions which eventually led to the overthrow of the empire.

Third Reich. The name given by the Nazis to their regime in Germany (1933-45), which Hitler boasted would last for a thousand years. According to the Nazis the First Reich was the Holy Roman Empire (1962-1806) and the Second Reich the German Empire (1871-1918).

Third Round Table Conference, 1932. The Third Round Table Conference was summoned in November 1932 and lasted for about five weeks. In it, deliberations were held on the Indian constitution. It proposed among other things that there should be an All India Federation consisting of British India and the Indian States. The proposals of this conference were published in a white paper.

Third World. The term which became current in the 1960s to distinguish the rest of the world from the 2 blocs of the USA and USSR. It is now loosely applied to the developing countries, esp. those of Africa, Asia and Latin America, which are largely non-industrialized and therefore poor.

Thirty Years' War. (1618-48) A general European war, mainly fought in Germany. The offer of the Bohemian crown to the Lutheran prince, Frederick, Elector Palatine, son-in-law of James I of Gt. Brit. was followed by the defeat of Frederick and the seizure of his lands by the Emperor Ferdinand. The german Protestant princes and Gustavus Adolphus of Sweden then carried on the struggle for protestantism against Catholicism but after the *d.* of Gustavus the war became a polit. Struggle between the Habsburgs and Spain on the one side, and Fr. on the other. It ended in 1648 with the signing of the Treaty of Westphalia (*q.v.*).

Thucydides. Athenian historian (*c.* 471-399 B.C.). *His History of the Peloponnesian War* (423-403 B.C.) is remarkably impartial and scholarly.

Tiberius. (42 B.C.-A.D.37) Rom. Emperor. Son of Tiberius Claudius Nero and Livia. By Livia's influence. Tiberius succeeded in A.D.14. His reign was prosperous for the Empire.

Tibet. On suspicion that Russia was gaining a foothold in the country, and that such a presence would be a danger to India, a British expeditionary force under the command of Colonel Francis Young husband was despatched to Lhasa (1904). Many of the inhabitants were killed by the invading force and no evidence was found of Russian penetration. However, a trade treaty was negotiated providing a commercial relationship between India and Tibet.

China occupied the country (1910-13), forcing Tibet's spiritual ruler, the Dalai Lama, to seek refuge in India. He returned when the Chinese left and the country practically vanished behind a screen of self-imposed isolation from the rest of the world.

China reoccupied Tibet (1951) and for 8 years held the country in subjection. Then in 1959 a serious rebellion occurred, involving heavy fighting and the flight of the new Dalai Lama to India, accompanied by many thousands of his subjects. At first Chinese rule was harsh and illiberal but in recent years there has been considerable relaxation of oppression, hospitals and schools have been opened, highways constructed, air links inaugurated with

China, frontiers opened for trade, agriculture expanded and reformed, irrigation, mining, forestry and industrial projects instituted, and closed monasteries reopened.

Tipu Sultan (1750-1799 A.D.). Son of Hyder Ali and ruler of Mysore 1782-1799; he continued his father's fight against the British but was killed in the last of a score of wars. His dominions were divided among the British and their Indian allies.

Tito Josip Broz. Marshal (1892-1980). Pres. of Yugoslavia after 1953. A Communist agitator, he spent some time in Russia and fought on the Repub. side in Sp. After the German invasion of Yugoslavia he organised the Partisan Nat. Army of Liberation, which fought a guerrilla war against the occupying forces. After the liberation he became Min. of Nat. Defence and virtual dictator. He governed on Communist lires, in close assoc. with Russia, until in 1948 he was expelled from the *Cominform* for 'nationalist deviation'.

Titus.(A.D.40-81) Rom. Emperor. T. Flavius Sabinus Vespasianus, son of Vespasian (*q.v.*). The terrible eruption of Vesuvius occurred during the first year of his reign. He completed the Colosseum.

Toja, Hideki (1884-1948). Japanese general and politician. He was leader of the militarist party from 1931 and Chief of Staff of the Kwantung Army (1938-40). His appointment as Minister of War (1940-41) and PM (1941-44) marked the final control of the military over the country's political affairs and transformed the state into a dictatorship. US successes in WWII eventually persuaded Emperor Hirohito that Tojo was leading Japan to disaster and Tojo ultimately resigned. He was executed as a war criminal by Americans.

Totalitarianism. Centralized control by an authoritarian, autocratic, single-party regime. Examples incl. the USSR, Nazi Germany and Fascist Italy.

Total Warfare. The waging of comprehensive and unrestricted hostilities against an enemy, incl. the civilian non-combatant population. Such warfare was not conducted on a large scale until WWII, when *c.* 14 million civilians are thought to have died.

Trianon, Treaty of (1920). Allied peace settlement with Hungary after WWI which resulted in the transfer of two-thirds of Hungary's prewar population and territory to Austria, Czechoslovakia, Italy,

Poland, Romania and Yugoslavia. The Treaty also provided for reparations to be made and the army to be limited to 35,000 men.

Triple Entente (1914-17). The alliance in WWI between Britain, France and Russia arising from 3 separate understandings developed in the period 1894-1907 to counterbalance the Triple Alliance. These were the Franco-Russian Alliance (1894), the Entente Cordiale between the UK and France (1904), and the Anglo-Russian Entente (1907).

Truce. Word used for a cessation of war for a definite time. It differs from an armistice, which is a cessation of war preparatory to the negotiation of a peace treaty.

Trudeau, Pierre. Canadian Liberal statesman. He was Minister of Justice and Attorney-General (1967-68) and PM (1968-79,and 1980-84).

Truman, Harry S. (1884-1972) 33rd Pres. of the U.S.A. A Senator from 1934, Truman was elected as Roosevelt's Vice-Pres. in 1944, and on the latter's *d.* in 1945 became Pres. following his policy of participation in world affairs and support for the European democracies. In 1948 he was re-elected. During his 2nd term of office Truman dealt vigorously with the war in Korea. Pres. Truman continued to support Aid for Europe. In 1952 he nominated Adlai Stevenson as his successor. The latter was defeated by Gen. Dwight D. Eisenhower (*q.v.*)

Truman Doctrine. The policy expounded by President Truman in a message to Congress in 1947 stating that the USA should be committed 'to support free peoples who are resisting attempted subjugation by armed minorities or by outside pressures'. The message was in support of his request for economic and military aid to Greece and Turkey to help them withstand Communist subversive pressures, and signalled a change to all-out anti-Communism by the Truman administration with the onset of the Cold War. The Marshall Plan (proposed in 1947) put into practice the Doctrine's objectives.

Tsar. Title of the pre-1917 rulers of Russia.

Tughlaq. A Muslim dynasty ruling 1320-1413 A.D. when the Delhi Sultanate reached its height, containing most of present-day India and Pakistan. By 1947 most of the Deccan had become independent of the Tughluqs. Timur's invasion 1398-1399 dealt the dynasty its death blow.

Tughlaq Dynasty. The period of 1320-1414 A.D. in India. See Mohd. Tughlaq.

Tut-Ankh-Amen. Egyptian king of 18th dynasty who reigned from 1595-86 B.C. His tomb was found at Luxor by the Earl of Carnarvon in 1923. It was virtually intact and contained his mummified body and magnificent treasures.

Twenty-Sixth January. On midnight of 31 December 1929, the Indian National Congress under the presidentship of Jawahar Lal Nehru adopted attainment of complete independence Purna Swaraja as its goal. It was decided to celebrate 26th January, 1930 as the Independence Day when the country took the pledge not to rest till the independence was achieved. The day marked the beginning of a new spirit. To commemorate the day, our Republican Constitution was promulgate on 26th January 1950.

U

U-2 Incident (1960). The name given to the shooting down by the Russians of a US Lockheed U-2 high altitude photographic reconnaissance aircraft over the Soviet city of Sverdlovsk. The pilot, Francis Gary Powers, was captured and confessed to being on an espionage operation. Similar missions had been going on for several years without Soviet protest, but this time Khrushchev demanded an apology from President Eisenhower at the Paris summit conference a fortnight later, and when it was not forthcoming withdrew from the meeting. Thereafter such flights ceased and Powers was exchanged for a Soviet spy (1962).

U-boats. German submarines, which were used effectively in WWI and WWII to put economic pressure on Britain by sinking large numbers of merchant ships carrying vital food and other supplies.

Ulbricht, Walter. (1893-1973), East German Communist politician. He went into exile (1933-45) on Hitler's rise to power, spending most of it in the USSR. On returning to Germany he had by 1950 become deputy PM of the GDR and Party Secretary-General. He was chairman of the Council of State (1960-71) and the country's virtual dictator, believing in Stalinist repressive measures without resorting to the drastic enforcement practices of the USSR. He was responsible for the building of the Berlin Wall (1961), and influential in urging the Warsaw Pact invasion of Czechoslovakia (1968).

Ulster Loyalists. Those Protestants who desire to maintain Northern Ireland's link with the British Isles. Many Loyalists are members of the Orange Order and the majority are represented by the Ulster Unionist Party, the largest political entity in the province.

UNO. United Nations Organisations.

UNCTAD. United Nations Commission for Trade and Development.

UNESCO. United Nations Educational, Scientific and Cultural

Organization.

UNHCR. United Nations High Commissioner for Refugees.

UNICEF. United Nations International Children's Emergency Fund.

Unification. Refers to the process of uniting or joining together by states or parts of divided nations, usually for mutual defence, economic or political benefit, and arising out of nationalist sentiments.

United Nations Conference on Trade Development (UNCTAD). The organization with HQ in Geneva, established (1964) and comprising the Trade and Development Board and 4 committees responsible for matters relative to their titles. The board meets biannually and its committees on Commodities, Manufacturing, Shipping, and Invisibles and Finances Related to Trade meet annually. The Conference convenes every 4 years to consider and pass judgement on the Board's activities.

United Nations Educational, Scientific and Cultural Organization (UNESCO). The agency with HQ in Paris, established (1945) to promote collaboration in the spheres of communications, culture, education and science, and to develop universal respect for justice, the rule of law and human rights without distinction of language, race, religion or sex.

United Nations High Commissioner for Refugees (UNHCR). The agency with HQ in Geneva, established (1951) to provide international protection for refugees, and to seek permanent solutions to their problems through voluntary repatriation, resettlement in other countries or integration into the country of present residence. It was awarded the Nobel Peace Prize (1955).

United Nations International Children's Emergency Fund (UNICEF). The organization with HQ in New York established (1946) to aid child health and welfare projects in countries afflicted by the ravages of WWII. Since 1950 its functions have been extended to assist the expansion of maternal and child health services and educational and vocational training schemes in developing countries. The Fund relies for financial assistance on voluntary contributions from individuals and UN member governments. It was awarded the Nobel Peace Prize (1965).

United Nations Organisation. The successor to the League of Nations, set up at the San Francisco Conference in 1945, comprising 110 States. The essential organs of U.N.O. are the *General Assembly, Security Council, Economic and Social Council, Trusteeship Council,* and the *International Court of Justice*; of these the Security Council is the most important, as it concentrates upon the peaceful settlement of disputes and the prevention of aggression. The Assembly has wide powers of discussion and recommendation, but cannot intervene in a dispute already being handled by the Security Council. The sessions of the Assembly and Security Council have not revealed a high degree of unity, and the use of the veto has created much disharmony. An 'internat. police force' made up of small detachments of troops from some member states was set up by UNO for the first time in 1956, following milit. intervention by Brit. and Fr. to separate the armies of Israel and Egypt. Similar forces have since been sent to various troublespots. UNO works through its Specialised Agencies such as the United Nations Educ., Scientific and Cultural Organisation (UNESCO): Food and Agriculture Organisation (FAO): Internat. Labour Organisation (ILO) etc.

United Nations Relief and Works Agency (UNRWA). The organization with HQ in Vienna, established (1950) for the resettlement of Palestinian Arab refugees and the provision of relief services and work opportunities for them. The refugees mostly live in camps in the Gaza Strip, Jordan, Lebanon and Syria and funds are primarily provided by Canada, Sweden, West Germany, the UK and the USA.

V

Valentinian. Rom. Emperor (364-75) who succeeded jovian in 364. He was intolerant in religious matters, but made useful laws. He divided the empire into E and W. and ruled the W. division.

Vardhana Dynasty. The period of 560-647 A.D. in India. See Harsh Vardhana.

Vedic Age. The Aryans Coming of the Aryans into India. The European scholars place the period of their coming between 2000 B.C. and 1500 B.C. They occupied North India, pushing the Dravidians to the South.

(*a*) *Political life of the Aryans.* In the early Vedic age, the Aryans used to live in villages or *grams.* The head of a village was called *gramani*. The affairs of the village were managed by an elected Panchayat. Every tribe or *jana* had one chief, who was called *Rajan*. He was mostly hereditary but he was sometimes elected. The chief duty of the king was the protection of the territory and welfare of his subject. The *Rajan* was helped by several officers like the Royal Priest: (*Purohit*). Commander-in-chief (*Senani*) and the Head of the village (*Gramani*).

The priest was the distinguished officer. He was a sort of Chief Minister. The king had two elected assemblies called the *Samiti* and the *Sabha*. These bodies exercised a check on the power of the king.

(*b*) *Social life of the Aryans.* (*i*) Their culture was pastoral (*ii*) Aryans had a joint family system. The father was known as *Grihapat*. (*iii*) In Vedic society women were held in great respect. There was no *purdah*. Their education was pertaining to language, literature, fine arts like dancing and music, and military science. Child marriage and *sati* of women were not known. (*iv*) Food and clothing of the Aryans were very simple. (*v*) There was no rigid caste system among the early Aryans. (*vi*) Their dress was simple. (*vii*) Education stressed on character building. (*viii*) The Aryans were fond of dancing, wrestling, boxing, dicing, listening to the bards and chariot racing.

(*c*) *Economic life of the Aryans* : (*i*) The main occupation of the Aryans was agriculture. They used to plough the land and grow crops. (*ii*) Cattle-rearing was another occupation. The cow was considered very sacred and could not be killed. (*iii*) They were very good at weaving cloth, tanning leather, and making ornaments. There were carpenters, black-smiths, goldsmiths, tanners, potters and weavers. (*iv*) The barter system was popular in trade.

(*d*) *Religion of the Aryans:* The Aryans of the Vedic times were lovers of nature. They were influenced by the powers of Nature, *e.g.* the sun, and water and fire. In the Aryan period there was no idol worship. Yajna or havan was an essential part of the Aryan religion. *The Aryans, as far as historians know at present, were the originators of the Hindu civilization.*

(*e*) Various religious books of the Aryans are : (i) The *Vedas*, the most sacred books of the Hindus. The Vedas are four in number: The *Rig Veda*, The *Yajur Veda*, The *Sama Veda*, The *Atharva Veda*.

(*ii*) The *Upanishads* deal with Aryan philosophy and theology. They elaborate the main problem of man: What is God ? What is Soul What is Matter ? How are they related ?

(*iii*) *Manu Smriti*. Manu was the great law giver in the Aryan period. His book, *Smriti* deals with law of inheritance, duties of kings and subjects of the four estates and the four ashramas.

(*iv*) The *Puranas* are eighteen in number. The most important were the *Bhagawata* and *Vishnu Purana*. The former describes the life story of Shri Krishna.

Verdun, Battle of (1916). WWI engagement which raged for most of the year around the fortress town of Verdun in NE France. Enormous casualties were suffered by both sides but after initial German gains, the French under Petan recaptured most of the lost ground, assisted by diversionary attacks launched by the British on the Somme and the Russians on the Eastern Front.

Versailles, Treaty of (1919). The settlement concluded at the end of WWI between the Allied powers and Germany at the Paris Peace

Conference.

Vespasian. (A.D.9-79) Rom. emperor. Served in Brit. under Aulus Plautius. In 69 he was declared emperor and seized Rome from Vitellius.

Viceroys of India. Lord Canning was the First Viceroy of India (1858-1862). He introduced many reforms. *Bengal Tenancy Act* improved the position of tenants. The *Indian Penal Code* came into force. High Courts were established. The *Indian Council Act, 1861, was the first step towards constitutional government*. Universities were opened in Calcutta, Madras and Bombay.

During Lord Elgin's rule (1862-63) the *Wahabis*, sect of Muslims, revolted on the North-Western frontier, but were suppressed.

Sir John Lawrence's rule (1864-69) saw the war with Bhutan famine in Orissa, and friendly contacts with Afghanistan.

Lord Mayo's (1869-72) achievement was decentralization of the government. In 1871, first cencus took place.

Lord Northbrook (1872-76) suppressed the Kuka movement removed the ruler of Baroda, lowered import duties and abolished export duties.

Lord Lytton (1876-80) held a magnificent darbar at Delhi where Queen Victoria was proclaimed Empress of India. The Darbar aroused great discontent because of the money wasted instead of being spent for relief in the Deccan famine. A famine Commission was appointed which suggested a famine fund and construction of railways and irrigation works. In 1878 *Vernacular Press Act* restricted the independence of the press. The *Indian Arms Act* was another repressive measure.

The *Second Afghan War* aroused discontent because of the high cost involved.

Lord Ripon (1880-84) was a liberal statesman who favoured giving a greater share of administration to Indians. The *Factory Act* (1881) tried to improve the position of factory workers, prohibited children below twelve from working more than nine hours a day. In 1881, the *second Census* took place. The Venacular Press Act was repealed. Education was extended. Policy of free trade was followed. The most constructive work was the enactment of Acts regarding local self-government. The *Ilbert Bill* was passed, which sought to remove judicial disqualifications on race distinction.

Lord Dufferin's rule (1884-1888) saw the formation of the Indian National Congress in 1885.

Lord Lansdowne's Viceroyalty (1888-1894) saw the passing of the Second Indian Councils Act, 1892 by which the functions of the Legislative Councils were enlarged, the number of members in the Imperial and Provincial Legislative Councils was increased.

Lord Curzon (1899-1905) was a very able Vicerocy and introduced many reforms. He laid strategic railway lines. N.W.F.P. was formed. Financial reforms included reduction of salt-tax. Police reforms saw salaries raised, training schools and C.I.D. established. Agricultural reform included the *Punjab Land Alienation Act,* (1905) which was useful to the cultivators, establishment of co-operative credit societies. Agricultural Research Institute. Agricultural Department, and improvement in irrigation. The ancient *Monuments Preservation Act* and the founding of the Archaeological Department has helped to save ancient historical buildings. The famine and plague of (1899-1900) led to the recommendation of more railways, agricultural banks and greater irrigation facilities. In 1905, Bengal was partitioned on administrative grounds and it evoked strong criticism of the people.

Lord Minto II (1905-1910) came at a time when the country was full of discontent. In 1906, *Muslim League* was formed. Anglo-Russian Convention (1907) was achieved to counter the common danger from Germany. The *Minto Morley Reforms* (also called Indian Councils Act, (1909) increased the number of elected members of the Central and Provincial Legislative Councils. System of communal electorates was introduced. The reforms were bitterly criticised.

Lord Hardinge II (1910-1916) held a magnificent durbar at Delhi to celebrate the accession of King George V in 1911, Delhi was the new Capital. When Lord Hardinge made his state entry, a revolutionary threw a bomb. However, Lord Hardinge remained sympathetic towards Indians. During his viceroyalty the First

World War broke out. India gave whole hearted cooperation to the Allies.

Lord Chelmsford's viceroyalty (1916-21) saw the *August Declaration* in 1971 that control over the Indian Government would be gradually transferred to the Indian people. The *Government of India Act* (1919), also called the Montague-Chelmsford Reforms, introduced the system of *dyarchy in* the provinces *i.e.* a few subjects, which the provinces were empowered to administer were transferred to the Ministers responsible to the provincial Legislature Councils *i.e.* Education, Public Health etc. The rest of the subjects were left in the charge of Members of Executive Councils, who were not responsible to provincial legislatures. A High *Compression* for India was appointed. The *Rowlatt Act* of 1919 created great anger among the Indians and was instrumental in leading to Mahatma Gandhi's *Satyagraha* and other protests. On 13th April 1919, the Jalliawala Bagh massacre took place under the direction of General Dyer. The *Khilafat Movement* began as a protest against the Allies' shabby treatment of Turkey.

During the rule of Lord Reading (1921-26), the visit of the Prince of Wales was boycotted. Non-cooperation Movement was at its height but was abruptly suspended following the violent Chauri Chaura incident.

The Viceroyalty of Lord Irwin (1926-31) sawthe appointment of the *Simon Commission* and its boycott by the Indians. The congress passed its *Independence Resolution* in 1929. Mahatma Gandhi began the *Civil Disobedience Movement* with the Dandi March to break the salt law. In 1930 the *First Round Table Conference* took place, unattended by Congress representatives. Then came the *Gandhi-Irwin Pact* (1931) and political prisoners were released.

The Viceroyalty of Lord Willingdon (1931-36) saw the *Second Round Table Conference* attended by Mahatma Gandhi, but it was useless. Gandhi was arrested . *The Communal Award* of August 1932 assigned seats to different religious communities, and gave separate electorates to the Scheduled Castes. To protest Gandhi went on a fast unto death. The *Poona Pact* between caste Hindus and the Depressed Classes agreed upon a practically joint etectorate. The *Third Round Table Conference* was again useless.

The Government of India Act. 1935 was passed. Bihar and Quetta suffered severe earth-quakes.

In Lord Linlithgow's viceroyalty (1936-43) provincial autonomy was established. Congress ministries were established. Then there was a split in the Congress. When India joined the Second World War without consulting the Central Legislative, the Congress ministries resigned as a protest. The day was observed as Day of Deliverance by the Muslim League leader Jinnah. He also made a demand for Pakistan. The *Cripps Mission* in 1942 was failure. The *Quit India Revolution* was passed by the Congress. Its leaders were thrown into prison.

Lord Wavell's viceroyalty (1944-47) saw the end of the Second World War (1945). The *Wavell Plan* put forward in June 1945 at the Simla conference was rejected by the Muslim League. The *Cabinet Mission Plan* (1946) provided for an interim government and laid down the procedure for framing the Constitution of India. The period is also known for the *Naval Mutiny* observation of *Direct Action Day* by Muslim League in Calcutta leading to riots and bloodshed. On 20th February, 1947, the Prime Minister of England, Clement Atlee announced that transfer of power would take place before June 1948. Riots and disturbances led to a vigorous demand for partition of India.

Lord Mountbatten (March 1947-August 1947) decided that *Partition of India* was the only way to resolve the political deadlock. *June 3rd Plan* partitioned the country. *Indian Independence Act* made India and Pakistan Dominions, India on 15th August 1947 and Pakistan on 14th August 1947. Bloodshed marked the exodus of refugees. The state of Kashmir acceded to the Indian Union after the raids which were helped by Pakistan.

Vichy Government (1940-44). The French semi-Fascist administration set up after the fall of France in WWII. It took its name from the town in the unoccupied centre of the country where it was established by Petain, its other prominent leaders being Darlan and Laval. After the armistice with Germany, it terminated the Third Republic, introduced anti-Semitic legislation, banned strikes, dissolved trade unions and introduced regimented organization of agricultural and industrial workers.

Victor Emmanuel II. (1820-78) Kings of Sardinia, afterwards King of Italy. With the help of his army and Garibaldi, and by diplomacy with the help of his min., Cavour, he was the real creator of a united Italy. Victor Emmanuel III (1869-1947) King of Italy, son of Umberto I, he came to the throne in 1900. He refused to oppose Fascist occupation of Rome and became Mussolini's tool. He abdicated in 1944, in favour of his son, Umberto.

Victor Emmanuel III. (1869-1947), King of Italy (1900-46). In defiance of the wishes of Parliament he took Italy into WWI on the Allied side (1915), and appointed Mussolini as PM (1922). Mussolini made him Emperor of Abyssinia (1936) and King of Albania (1939), but during the Fascist regime he was little more than a constitutional puppet, although he was assertive enough to dismiss Mussolini when the Allied victory in WWII became obvious (1943). He abdicated in 1946 and died in exile in Egypt.

Victoria. (1819-1901) Queen of the U.K. of Gt. Brit. and Ireland and Empress of India, only child of Edward, Duke of Kent, 4th son of George III. She succeeded William IV in 1837, and mar. her cousin, Prince Albert of Saxe-Coburg-Gotha, in 1840. Her long reign saw more changes than any other in Brit. hist. The Emp. was considerably enlarged; the greater colonies achieved self-government; successive reform bills extended the franchise; the Corn Laws were repealed, and Free Trade was adopted. Educ. was made compulsory; rlys., the telegraph and telephone came into being; penny postage was inaugurated; and many measures for improvement in working class conditions were passed. Gt. Brit.'s interests abroad involved her in several wars. In the E. she waged war in China and Afghanistan ; her rule in India involved her in the Indian Mutiny, 2 Sikh wars and 2 Burmese wars, and in Africa the Zulu and Boer Wars. In Europe she took part in the Crimean War. Among the Queen's P.M.s were Melbourne, Peel, Palmerston, Disraeli, Gladstone and Salisbury. She followed the policy indicated by them, but made her influence felt. She celebrated her Diamond Jubilee in 1897.

Viet Cong. The name given in the 1960s and 1970s to the Communist-led armed forces of the Front for the Liberation of South Vietnam. In the Vietnam War they waged a guerrilla campaign against the South Vietnamese regime and US forces, and were supported and increasingly controlled by the Communist regime in North Vietnam.

Viet Minh. The Revolutionary League for the Independence of Vietnam, a political movement founded (1941) by the Indo-Chinese Communist Party in North Vietnam to resist the Japanese attack on Indo-China in WWII. It operated with the Workers' Party and the army in expelling the French from the country and its authority N of the 17th parallel of longitude (*i.e.* in North Vietnam) was recognized by the 1954 Geneva Agreements. The movement's leading members were Ho Chi Minh, Pham Van Dong and Vo Nguyen Giap.

Vietnam War. Hostilities in S.E. Asia initiated following the 1954 partition of Vietnam into N. Vietnam and S. Vietnam. Communist Viet Cong guerrillas had the support of N. Vietnam and Soviet equipment, while the S. Vietnamese government was supported by the U.S.A. American forces became increasingly involved, and there was much opposition to this involvement amongst the American public. The American forces withdrew in 1973, but guerrilla activity in the S. continued, and the S. Vietnamese government forces fell in 1975, leading to the unification of the two parts of Vietnam in a Socialist Republic in 1976.

Vikramaditya. A title, 'son of prowess', assumed by some early kings; tradition says that Vikramaditya was an (unidentified) king of Ujjain (? 95 B.C. to A.D.78) who defeated the Sakas, captured Ujjain and part of the western sea board from them, conquered the whole of India and brought peace and prosperity to he people; he is said to have set in use the *Vikram Samvat* (era)-commencing from 58 B.C. which was named after him; other kings who used the title were Kanishka (*d.* A.D.144), Samudra Gupta (*d.*380), Chandragupta II (*d.*412) and his grandson, Skanda Gupta (*d.* 468), Yasodharma of Malwa (*d.* 528), Harsha (*d.* 648), Bhoja of Dhara (*d.* 1060), and the Chalukya kings; many romantic stories have been told about Vikramaditya of Ujjain; 9 luminaries—brilliant men—are said to have been the gems of his court—Varahamihira (astronomer), Brahmagupta (mathematician), Kshampanka (astrologer), Sankhu (architect), Vararuchi (grammarian), Vaitalika (magician), Dhanvantri (physician), Amarsinha (lexicographer)and Kalidasa (foremost Sanskrit dramatist and poet of India) but as these men lived over span of two centuries, all of them could not have lived within the lifetime of any one person; nor does history know of any such great king ruling in western India during the latter half of the first century B.C. Vikramaditya is generally identified with Chandra Gupta II (3rd emperor of the Gupta dynasty of Magadha) who made Ujjain his capital at the end of the 4th century and till his death in 413.

W

Waldheim, Kurt. Austrial diplommat. He was Foreign Minister (1968-70), and UN Secretary-General (1972-82). He was elected to the Austrian presidency (1986).

Wall Street Crash (1929) The financial collapse of the US economy, which experienced an artificial Boom in the 1920s caused by wild speculation on the stock market. Doubt about the security of certain major business enterprise caused panic selling to develop on the New York Stock Exchange (sited in Wall Street), and millions of shares changed hands in 4 days. Banks and businesses failed, unemployment rose rapidly to *c.* 17 million, and there was commercial recession throughout the country which eventually spread to Europe, causing the Depression of the early 1930s. This in turn contributed to the rise of Fascism, and eventually to WWII.

War Crimes. The idea that the defeated side in was could be held criminally responsible for their actions during the war was first embodied at the U.N. War Crimes Commission in 1943. War Criminals included many generals, etc. whose connection with 'atrocities' was indirect. At Nuremberg, 21 Nazi major war criminals were tried, 18 found guilty, 11 condemned to *d.* and 9 executed. Major Japanese criminals were tried in Tokyo.

War of 1812. War between Gt. Brit. and the U.S.A. The war, declared by Congress, was caused by the rigorous exercise on the part of Brit. of her rights of search over neutral (in this case Amer.) vessels. In 1814 a Brit. force under Ross captured Washington and burnt the White House, but a 2nd contingent under Pakenham was repulsed at New Orleans in 1815, by Andrew Jackson, with great loss.

Warsaw Pact. Technically the Eastern European Mutual Assistance Treaty (1955), signed in Warsaw by Albania, Bulgaria, Czechoslovakia, East Germany, Hungary, Poland, Romania and the USSR. The Pact was signed following West Germany's entry into NATO. It established a unified military command with each country undertaking to refrain from using, or threatening to use, force in its international relationships, and to give immediate assistance by all means it might consider necessary to any member subject to attack in Europe.

Washington Conference (1921-22). The international assembly held with the objective of arranging re-educations in naval armaments and the relaxation of tension in the Far East. The participating countries were Belgium, China, France, Italy, Japan, the Netherlands, Portugal, the UK and the USA.

Washington, George (1732-99). Amer. soldier and statesman. B. Virginia, he became a tobacco planter. Elected a member of the House of Burgesses in 1758; he came to the front as a champion of colonial liberties, 1770. He did not favour Amer. Indep. but in 1775 he was chosen to command the colonial forces. In 1776 he succeeded in occupying Boston. Defeated in 1777 at Brandywine Creek, he wintered at Valley Forge, fought an indecisive battle at Monmouth in 1778, and in 1781 received the surrender of Cornwallis at Yorktown. In 1787 as representative of Virginia he presided at the Federal Convention in Philadelphia and in 1788 was chosen first Pres. of the U.S.A.

Watergate Affair. The incident during the US 1972 presidential election campaign when agents employed by President Nixon's re-election organization were caught breaking into the Democratic Party's HQ in the Watergate Building, Washington, DC. The subsequent scandal was exacerbated by attempts to conceal the fact that senior White House officials had approved the burglary. Eventually the President was implicated in the cover-up and was forced to resign (1974).

Welfare State. A system by which a government undertakes prime responsibility for the economic and social well-being of the population by such means as unemployment insurance, pensions of various kinds, health services, and housing.

West Bank. Refers to that part of Jordan to the W of the River Jordan occupied by Israel since the 1967 Arab-Israeli War. The provision of the Camp David Agreement (1978) that Israel should gant a degree of Palestinian autonomy in the West bank has not been carried out, and instead the area has been increasingly settled by Israelis, who have also developed agricultural and industrial enterprises. This has led to acts of civil disobedience, rioting and guerrilla activities by the PLO and the indigenous Arab population.

Western European Union WEU. The organization established (1955) to supercede the Brussels Treaty Organization, a military alliance formed in 1948 with the same membership as the WEU apart from Italy and West Germany. Its members are belgium, France, Italy, Luxembourg, the Netherlands, the UK and West Germany. The foreign ministers form a Council, and there is an Assembly of representatives of the WEU in the Consultative Assembly of the Council of Europe, and an Armaments Control Agency which operates in conjunction with NATO. The Union's objectives are cooperation on cultural, economic, military and social matters.

White House. The official Washington residence of the US President. The term is also used for the President and his executive.

White Supremacy. The theory based on the supposition that white races are inherently superior to other races, esp. negroes, a view inherent in the Apartheid policies of South Africa.

Wilhem II (1859-1941). Emperor (*Kaiser*) of Germany (1884-1918). An arrogant and self-opinionated man, he had visions of German world domination and set out to strengthen the country's military and naval forces at the expense of trying to achieve harmonious relationships with Britain France and Russia.

William I (1027-87). King of Eng. surnamed the conqueror, the natural son of Robert II, Duke of Normandy, he succeeded to the dukedom in 1035. He invaded Eng. in 1066, landing at Pevensey and defeating the Eng. army under King Harold at Senlac, near Hastings, on Oct. 14. He had to quell insurrections in Eng. and later in Normandy. He carried out a complete survey of his Eng. realm, the results of which are preserved in the Domesday Book. William II, Rufus (*c*. 1058-1100) King of Eng. 3rd son of William I. He gained milit. successes in Normandy and Scot. but his cruelty and profligacy earned the hatred of his subjects. He was found in the New Forest slain by an arrow.

William III (1650-1702). King of Gt. Brit., posthumous son of William

II, Prince of Orange and Mary, daughter of Charles I. As Capt.-Gen. of the Dutch forces, he carried on the struggle of the Dutch against Louis XIV. In 1677 he mar. Mary, daughter of James II. In 1689 after the deposition of James II (*q.v.*) he and Mary became joint rulers of Brit. His last years were occupied with negotiations concering the Sp. Succession (see Spain), and war had just been declared when he *d.*

William IV (1765-1837). Brit. King, 3rd son of George III. After a term of service in the navy, he was created Duke of Clarence in 1789. His 20 years' assoc. with Mrs. Jordan was broken when he mar. Adelaide of Saxe-Meiningen, but he had no issue. He succeeded George IV in 1830. The Reform Act of 1832 was the outstanding measure of his reign.

William I (1797-1888). King of Prussia and German Emperor. He took part in the final campaigns of the Napoleonic Wars. He supported repression of the revolutionary movement of 1848. In 1861 on the *d.* of his brother, he became king. He worked in harmony with Bismarck (*q.v.*) in carrying out the policy which led to the formation of the German Emp. During the Franco-Pruss. War he was in command of the Pruss. forces. He was proclaimed German Emperor at Versailles, 1871.

William II (1851-1941). German Emperor and King of Prussia. B. Berlin, the eldest son of the Crown Prince Frederick (afterwards Frederick III), and of Victoria (eldest daughter of Queen Victoria). Within 2 years of his accession (1888) Bismarck was dismissed, and the Emperor went ahead with his policy of expanding Germany's power. At the beginning of World War I he directed operations in person. On Oct. 9, 1918, he abdicated and crossed the Dutch frontier to reside at Doorn Castle where he *d.* in exile.

Wilson, Sir Harold, Lord Wilson of Rievaulx and Emley. British Labour statesmen, PM (1964-70 and 1974-76). In 1963 he was elected Leader of the Labour Party, and became PM in 1964, increasing Labour's majority in the 1966 election.

Wilson, Woodrow (1866-1924). US Democratic President (1913-21). He kept the US out of WWI until 1917 when the revelations of the Zimmermann Telegram and the unrestricted Uboat campaign (see Lusitania), coupled with aroused public indignation, forced him to realize he could no longer keep the country out of hostilities.

Windsor, House of. Name of the Brit. royal family. King. George V is regarded as the founder of the House of Windsor, having, in 1917, abandoned for himself and his family all German titles. In 1960 H.M. the Queen declared that all her descendants would use the name Mountbatten—Windsor except those males bearing royal style and title.

Women's Suffrage. The right of women to the franchise, *i.e.*, to vote in public elections.

Wood, Edward Frederick Lindley, Baron Irwin and Earl of Halifax (1881-1959). British conservative politician. He was appointed Viceroy of India (1926-31) at a time of unrest on the North-West Frontier. As Foreign Secretary (1938-40), he at first supported Appeasement, but he played an important part in inducing Chamberlain to take a stronger line with the Germans after 1939. He was Ambassador to the USA (1941-46).

World War I (1914-18). *Causes.* The causes of the First World War are as under:

(1) *Militarism.* This means the dangerous and burdensome mechanism of great standing armies and large navies along with an espionage system.

(2) *Narrow nationalism or competitive partriotism.* The love of one's country demanded the hatred of the other. Love of Germany demanded the hatred of France and vice versa.

(3) *Economic imperialism which let to international rivalries.* Every country tried to capture markets in every nook and corner of the world. This led to bitterness and heart-burning.

(4) The charter of William II, Emperor of Germany. He was arrogant, haughty and ambitious. He wanted Germany to be the strongest power in the world. He believed in the policy of "world power or downfall."

(5) The desire of the people of France to get back Alsace-Lorraine which had been snatched away from them in 1871 by Germany.

(6) Lack of machinery to control international relations.

(7) The permeation of Germany by the Prussian spirit. According to that: "He who succeeds is never in the wrong." Victory was identified with morality.

(8) The immediate causes of the war was the murder of Archduke Ferdinand who was the heir to the Austrian throne. He and his wife were killed at Serajevo by a Serbian. The Austrians held the Government of Serbia responsible for the murder and ultimately attacked Serbia. There was strong rivalry already between Austria-Hungary and Serbia in the Balkans

Course of War. To begin with, Austria was in favour of a local war but as time passed, the situation became more grave. Other countries jumped into the fray. Germany, Austria, Hungary, Turkey, and Bulgaria were on one side; they were called Central Powers. On the other side were England, France, Serbia, Belgium, Japan and Russia; they were called the Allies. The Allies were joined by Italy in 1915 and USA in 1917. The war started on 4 August 1914 and ended on 11 November 1918.

Peace Settlement (1919-20). After prolonged discussion, the *Treaty of Versailles* was signed between the Allies and Germany on 28 June 1919. This Treaty Rearranged the boundaries of Europe, and many new states—Poland, Czechoslovakia, Yugoslavia, Estonia, Lithuania, etc., were formed. William II, the German Emperor, abdicated and took asylum in the Netherlands. The Treaty of Versailles was followed by the Treaty of St. Germaine (1919), the Treaty of Neuilly (1919), the Treaty of Trianon (1920) and the Sevres (1920).

The peace settlement of 1919-20 has been severely criticised. The terms of the Treaty of Versailles were harsh and humiliating for Germany. The peace settlement was based on the principle : "To the victors belong the spoils and Allies are the victors."

During the war many suggestions were made from time to time for the creation of an international organisation which could check wars in the future. At the instance of Woodrow Wilson, the President of America, the League of Nations officially came into existence of 10 January 1920. Its head-quarters were fixed at Geneva in Switzerland.

World War II. (1939-45)*Causes*. (1) The Treaty of Versailles had in itself the germs of the war of 1939. Germany was very badly treated. She was forced to sign the Treaty at the point of a bayonet, in a spirit of revenge.

(2) The rise to the Nationalist Movement in Germany and Italy added fuel to the fire. Although Hitler tried to assure the world that he meant peace, he could not conceal his ambition for long. He embarked on a career of aggression which ultimately led to war. The same was the case with Mussolini who had established his dictatorship in Italy in 1922.

(3) There was a conflict of ideologies between dictatorship on the one hand and democracy on the other. Countries like Germany, Italy and Japan represented one kind of ideology and Great Britain, France and United States represented another. Mussolini described the conflict between the two ideologies thus ; "The struggle between the two worlds can permit no compromise. Either we or they."

(4) Unfortunately, when hostility was growing between the two camps there was no effective international organisation which could bring the leaders of the two camps on a common platform and bring about a reconciliation between them. The League of Nations was practically dead.

(5) The colonial and commercial rivalry between England and France on one side, and Germany and Italy on the other brought them in conflict with each other.

(6) Germany had became very aggressive. She annexed the Saar Valley, occupied Rhineland and Austria, captured Czechoslovakia, etc.

Course of the War. World War I was in a sense the last major traditional war. But World War II was a new kind of war in which armoured cars, tanks and aircraft were used. Only six European countries remained neutral, *viz.*, Ireland, Portugal, Spain, Sweden, Switzerland and Turkey. Britain escaped invasion in 1940 by a hair's breadth.

The immediate cause of the war was the refusal of Poland to surrender. Germany gave an ultimatum to Poland to surrender the port of Danzig, and to grant the right of establishing a rail link between Germany and East Prussia through the Polish corridor.

These two demands were rejected by Poland. So Germany invaded Poland on 1 September 1939. Britain and France as they were under treaty obligations to aid Poland declared war against Germany on 3 September 1939. On one side were Germany, Italy and Japan, called the Axis Powers, and on the other were United Kingdom, Russia, France, USA, etc., called the Allies.

Germany had to face defeat once again. Hitler, Goebbels and Himmler committed suicide and their successors surrendered unconditionally on 7 May 1945. After the fall of Germany, the United States and Great Britain concentrated their forces against Japan. On 6 August 1945, an atom bomb was dropped on the city of Hiroshima and it is estimated that more than one lakh persons were killed. Japan was asked to surrender and when she refuses another bomb was exploded on 9 August on the city of Nagasaki. On 14 August Japan surrendered unconditionally, and the war came to an end.

Peace Settlement. After about 15 months of preparatory work, the peace treaties were given a final shape by the 21 participation countries and they were signed on 10 February 1947 in Paris by the representatives of the five enemy states and the allied Powers. As regards Germany she was occupied by the Big Four. After its fall in May 1945, it was divided into four zones, each of which was administered separately by one of the occupying powers. Berlin came under joint occupation. Ultimately out of one Germany came two countries—West Germany and East Germany. As regards Japan, a peace treaty was signed with her at San Francisco in 1951.

X

Xerxes. King of Persia (485-465 B.C.). Son of Darius I, he led the 2nd Persian expedition against Greece in 480 B.C. The Persians defeated the Gks. at Thermopylae, and were then defeated on sea at Salamis. A further defeat at Plataea in 479 led X, to abandon his attempt to conquer the Gks. He was assassinated.

Y

Yahya Khan, Agha Mohammed (1917-80), Pakistani soldier and statesman. He was commanding general of the Army (1966) and replaced Ayub Khan as president (1969-71), imposing martial law. He resolved to settle political problems by allowing the first 'one man, one vote' elections in the country (1970-71). Civil war broke out as a result of his refusal to accept the verdict in favour of the Awami League independence movement in East Pakistan (Bangladesh). India's military intervention on behalf of Bangladeshi independence (1971) led to Pakistan's defeat and Yahya Khan's enforced resignation. He was replaced by Bhutto.

Yalta Conference. Conference held at Yalta in Crimea, Feb. 4-11, 1945, attended by Mr. Churchill, Pres. Roosevelt and Marshal Stalin, with their foreign mins-and Chiefs of Staff. Complete agreement was reached on milit. operations. It was also decided to call a conference at San Francisco on April 25, to prepare charter of U.N. Organisation.

Yaounde Agreements. (1963 and 1969), conventions signed in the Cameroons Capital between the EEC and former Belgian, Dutch, French and Italian colonies which wanted to continue their association with EEC after independence.

Provision was made for duty-free entry into the EEC of certain exports from the former colonies, with a similar arrangement for exports from the EEC into most of the countries. A European Development Fund was also established to assist the associated countries.

Following the enlargement of the EEC (1973), former British colonies entered the Agreements, which were superseded by the Lome Convention in 1975.

Yasovarman of Kanauj. He was a vigorous ruler in Kanauj after Harsha in the 8th century. He was the patron of the great dramatist, *Bhababhuti*.

Young Plan (1929). The scheme for the settlement of Germany's WWI reparations proposed by a committee chaired by a US businessman, Owen D. Young (1874-1962).

Young Turks. Turkish reform movement (1903-09) in the Ottoman Empire instrumental in masterminding a rebellion by liberal army officers in Salonika (1908), followed by the founding of a committee of Union and Progress in Constantinople (now Istanbul).

Ypres, Battles of. 4 conflicts of WWI centred around the Belgian town of Ypres, which was completely destroyed but never captured by the Germans. The first battle (1914), resulted in the Germans capturing the Messines Ridge. The second battle (1915) was the first occasion when gas was used in warfare. The third battle (1917) involved a combined Australian, British and Canadian offensive against the Messines Ridge and the village of Passchendaele. The fourth battle (1918), also known as the Battle of the River Lys, occurred when the Germans attempted to encircle Ypres. In total the Germans suffered some quarter of a million casualties while the Allied losses amounted to about twice that figure.

Z

Zahiruddin Babar (1483-1530 A.D.). He laid the foundation of Mughal rule in India. After several unsuccessful invasions of India, he at last defeated Ibrahim Lodhi in the battle of Panipat, in 1526. Thus the Lodhi rule ended: there was a development in Indian civilization and culture. In 1527, Babar defeated Rana Sanga at Kanwaha near Fatehpur Sikri. In 1529, in the battle of Gogra he defeated the Afghans under Mahmud Lodhi. He thus became master of nearly the whole of Northern India.

Zain-ul-abidin (P). (1420-1470 A.D.). Muslim rule of Kashmir who abolished the *jizyah*, encouraged translations of the *Mahabharata* and *Rajatarangini* from Sanskrit into Persian, and fostered the study of Hindu literature and philosophy.

Zenobia. Queen of Palmyra. On the *d.* of her husband she took the name Augusta and claimed to be Queen of the E. Her subjugation of Egypt caused the Emperor Aurelian to lead an exped. against her in A.D. 271.

Zhou Enlai or Chou En-lai (1898-1976). Chinese Communist statesman. He was a founder member of the French Communist Party when he lived in Paris (1920-24). On returning to China he organized revolts against the war lords in Shanghai, Nanjing and Canton, spent 2 years in the USSR, and then became Mao Zedong's urban revolutionary affairs adviser. During WWII he was the Communists' liaison officer in the capital, Chongquing. He was PM (1949-76) from the time of the Republic's establishment, also holding the office of Foreign Minister until 1958. Pragmatic and urbane, he became the best known of China's leaders on the international scene, travelling widely on diplomatic missions, and as leader of detente with the USA (1972-73).

Zhukov, Georgi (1896-1976). Soviet marshal and politician. The outstanding commander of WWII, he was prominent in the siege of

Leningrad, the defence of Moscow (1941), the victory at Stalingrad (1943), the capture of Berlin (1945). He was Minister of Defence (1955-57). Shortly after achieving membership of the Presidium (1957) he was dismissed from government and party posts on the grounds of encouraging his own personality cult, and of undermining the Party's position within the armed forces.

Zia Ul, Gen. Mohammed. (1924-1981) Pakistani politician and General, President of Pakistan after the overthrow in a military coup in 1977 of Bhutto, who was subsequently executed. Zia was assassinated in 1981 in a military insurrection.

Zionism. A political movement (founded 1897) for the establishment and maintenance of a national homeland for Jews in what was Palestine, and now concerned with the development and prosperity of Israel.

Zogu, Achmet (or Zog) (1895-1961). Ex-king of Albania. After serving in the Aust. Army during World War I, he became PM 1922 He was elected Pres. of the Albanian Repub. 1925 and proclaimed king, 1928. Defeated by Mussolini in 1939.